Interdisciplinary Research Journeys
Practical Strategies for Capturing Creativity

Catherine Lyall, Ann Bruce, Joyce Tait
ESRC Innogen Centre, University of Edinburgh

Laura Meagher
Technology Development Group

Bloomsbury Academic
An imprint of Bloomsbury Publishing Plc

B L O O M S B U R Y
LONDON · OXFORD · NEW YORK · NEW DELHI · SYDNEY

Bloomsbury Academic
An imprint of Bloomsbury Publishing Plc

50 Bedford Square	1385 Broadway
London	New York
WC1B 3DP	NY 10018
UK	USA

www.bloomsbury.com

BLOOMSBURY and the Diana logo are trademarks of Bloomsbury Publishing Plc

First published in 2011 by Bloomsbury Academic
Paperback edition first published 2015

British Library Cataloguing-in-Publication Data
A catalogue record for this book is available from the British Library.

ISBN: HB: 978-1-8496-6013-6
PB: 978-1-4742-6301-6
ePub: 978-1-8496-6014-3
ePDF: 978-1-8496-6447-9

Library of Congress Cataloging-in-Publication Data
A catalog record for this book is available from the Library of Congress

Cover designer: Sharon Cluett
Cover image: © Modomatic, photograph licensed under a Creative Commons licence

Printed and bound in Great Britain

Contents

Figures

Tables

Boxes

Case Study Boxes

Key Advice Boxes

Illustrations

Acknowledgements

M any people, including research participants and research funders, have contributed to the studies that underpin this book. We would also like to acknowledge helpful discussions with colleagues at the University of Edinburgh and their contributions to Interdisciplinary Masterclasses and other workshops. The participants at these events have encouraged us to develop our work further and have provided valuable insights into the interdisciplinary research process. This work has been supported by the UK Economic and Social Research Council (grants to the ESRC Innogen Centre RES-145-28-1004 and RES-145-28-0002 and under the ESRC Researcher Development Initiative RES-035-25-0001).

We would like to acknowledge the work of other authors who have contributed to the case studies used throughout. Full citations to all of this work are included in the Bibliography at the end of the book. This book would not have happened without the support of Emily Salz and her colleagues at Bloomsbury Academic whose innovative approach to twenty-first-century book production will, we hope, ensure wide dissemination and uptake of this work. It was our intention that this book – whilst making a serious contribution to the study of interdisciplinarity – would also convey our avowed belief that interdisciplinary research is fun. So we are delighted that our colleague Shawn Harmon has contributed original cartoon illustrations, which we hope will help to convey this message, at the same time as making some serious points. Finally, a good index is essential for navigating a book of this type and we are indebted to our colleague Moyra Forrest for her professional input.

Acronyms

AHRC	Arts and Humanities Research Council
BBSRC	Biotechnology and Biological Sciences Research Council
CASE	Collaborative Awards in Science and Engineering studentships
CCSP	Climate Change Science Program
COSEPUP	Committee on Science, Engineering and Public Policy
CRÊPE	Co-operative Research on Environmental Problems in Europe
CSO	civil society organization
Defra	Department for Environment, Food and Rural Affairs
ECR	early career researcher
EPSRC	Engineering and Physical Sciences Research Council
ESRC	Economic and Social Research Council
I2S	Integration and Implementation Sciences
ICT	information and communication technologies
IDR	interdisciplinary research
IGERT	Integrative Graduate Education and Research Traineeship
II-FP5	interdisciplinary integration in the Fifth Framework Programme
Innogen	The ESRC Centre for Social and Economic Research on Innovation in Genomics
IP	intellectual property
IPR	intellectual property rights
IRGC	International Risk Governance Council
LWEC	Living with Environmental Change
MISTRA	Swedish Foundation for Strategic Environmental Research
MRC	Medical Research Council
NASA	National Aeronautics and Space Administration
NERC	Natural Environment Research Council
NIH	National Institutes of Health
NSF	National Science Foundation
OECD	Organisation for Economic Co-operation and Development
PACCIT	People at the Centre of Computers and Information Technology
RAE	Research Assessment Exercise
RCUK	Research Councils UK
RDG	Research Development Grant
REF	Research Excellence Framework

Relu	Rural Economy and Land Use
SEPA	Scottish Environment Protection Agency
SFC	Scottish Funding Council
SMEs	small and medium-sized enterprises
SNIFFER	Scotland and Northern Ireland Forum for Environmental Research
SPIRIT	Strategic Priority Investment in Research and Innovation Translation
STFC	Science and Technology Facilities Council
STS	science and technology studies
SUPRA	Scottish Universities Policy Research and Advice
TDG	Technology Development Group
td-net	Network for Transdisciplinary Research

1

Signposts for Interdisciplinary Travellers

Introduction and some tips for reading this book

Introduction

We live in increasingly interdisciplinary times. Creative researchers find scope for adventurous work at the interface of disciplines and funding organizations recognize that many problems facing society demand research that crosses disciplinary boundaries. After decades of increasing specialization in the academic enterprise, more recent funding programmes have attempted to promote interdisciplinary research as a means to encourage scientific and technological advance and to foster its more effective use in society so that we can harness research outputs for economic development and improved quality of life. Internationally, the research funding trend is towards ever more focus on interdisciplinarity and impacts beyond academia.

But interdisciplinary research does not occur automatically, even when money is available. It is not a simple case of aggregating several disciplines into one research project. Extra effort is needed to achieve the promise of synergy and to form a genuinely cohesive team that combines expertise from several specialisms. Yet, the sustained development of strategies to help researchers understand *how* to collaborate effectively and integrate soundly across different domains remains a key research gap. Disciplinary and interdisciplinary research approaches are both essential to produce knowledge and solve problems but much of the existing literature focuses primarily on discussions of the relative merits of these respective forms of research and there is still a dearth of guidance on interdisciplinarity as a way of doing research. So at the heart of this book is a practical guide for researchers and research managers – in academia but also in industry and public sector research – who want to create interdisciplinary research strategies, programmes or projects at a personal, institutional, multi-institutional or international level. This book is neither a discursive text on the theory of interdisciplinarity nor a research methods manual on how to approach a particular interdisciplinary project. Instead, the focus of the book is on developing and delivering strategies for building interdisciplinary research capacity. We therefore say quite a lot about the challenges faced by interdisciplinary research teams but also discuss what this might mean for individual researchers who adopt an interdisciplinary approach.

Illustration 1.1 Interdisciplinary research doesn't occur automatically

We see disciplines and interdisciplinarity as complementary. Discipline-based research provides an essential set of standards, an established way of framing problems, key theories and methods, but the model of the lone scholar working in one narrow discipline is changing. So far we have made some great strides forward among the foothills of interdisciplinary research but there are still challenging peaks to scale. There is still much to learn and this requires capacity-building for those working in, and leading, interdisciplinary teams. Hence the book is targeted not just at interdisciplinary researchers themselves but also at those who lead, manage or indeed fund such research initiatives at all levels. To generate this sort of multi-dimensional guidance, the book draws on wide-ranging literature, deep analyses of efforts to promote interdisciplinarity and the experiences of the authors and others.

How to read this book

While we hope that all of the book will be useful to some degree to all types of reader, we have structured it so that readers at different stages of their interdisciplinary 'journey' can dip into it and find some guidance without necessarily reading the book from cover to cover. The numbered list of chapters in this section may help with the navigation depending on readers' interests.

We have described the key steps involved in individuals' journeys towards effective interdisciplinarity, and have devoted a chapter to each step. We do see the sum total of individual journeys as generating ever more robust interdisciplinarity and thus having an impact on the shape of the research landscape of the future. But our immediate focus is our readers; we use journey metaphors throughout to remind our readers that they are travelling an adventurous road, with some bumps along the way but still leading to some fascinating and rewarding vistas.

Chapter 2 'Departure Point' sets the stage for the book by discussing why people do interdisciplinary research, what sorts of motivation and levers may lead to different types and quality of interdisciplinary efforts, and what sorts of challenges and rewards they may encounter.

Chapter 3 'Planning the Expedition' (designing an interdisciplinary research project) provides research leaders with guidance on that too often overlooked critical early stage of design, identifying a team and coming up with a research plan.

Chapter 4 'Making the Expedition a Success' (managing interdisciplinary projects and teams) addresses the good news/bad news challenge of what happens when funding is secured and the real work has to begin.

Chapter 5 'Permit to Travel' (supporting the next generation of interdisciplinary researchers) provides guidance for those who find themselves playing the key role of supervisor (or mentor) for those embarking upon an interdisciplinary career. Funders of interdisciplinary training schemes and institutional research leaders may want to review this chapter; graduate students and postdoctoral fellows may also want to read this chapter to learn what support they should be encouraging their supervisors and mentors to provide.

Chapter 6 'Charting a Course for an Interdisciplinary Career' encourages self-reflection by discussing what it can mean to have an interdisciplinary career, at various professional stages, what incentives exist and what challenges might need to be addressed.

Chapter 7 'Assessing the Route' (evaluating interdisciplinary proposals, programmes and publications) discusses underlying challenges of assessment of quality and puts forward suggestions for those involved in key points at which evaluation can make a difference as to whether or not sound interdisciplinarity thrives: proposal review, examination of students, assessment of work for publication, post-programme review and internal institutional judgements.

Chapter 8 'Knowledge Travels' (getting interdisciplinary research into policy and practice) considers the motivating destination for many researchers, although it may seem to some to be an optional extra leg of the journey: benefiting the world beyond academia through the fusion of different disciplines' approaches and evidence.

Chapter 9 'Navigating the Interdisciplinary Landscape' brings together the discussions and guidance of the preceding chapters into a big-picture view of how the promotion, facilitation, implementation and utilization of interdisciplinary research might take place in order to shape the future research landscape.

We are self-confessed enthusiasts for interdisciplinarity; we want readers to have a fair chance of success in their interdisciplinary research. We have therefore tried to make each chapter as useful and accessible as possible. Grounding in the academic literature is provided and, throughout the book, academic studies of interdisciplinarity have been referenced. We hope that readers playing a variety of roles in a wide range of 'disciplinary combinations' will find useful guidance within the following chapters, where straightforward discussion is illustrated by a series of short case studies and key advice boxes.

For those of a reflective nature, we have provided a set of thought-provoking questions at the end of each chapter. Because interdisciplinarity can take so many forms, and mean so many things to different people, we are not attempting to provide all the answers but proceeding through these questions should help readers to reflect critically on their own situation and adapt the guidance most useful to them individually. For ease of reference, these questions are also collated at the end of the book in Appendix 2, which acts as a further signposting for readers interested in specific aspects. The extensive Bibliography of academic literature and relevant policy documents provided at the end should allow the keen reader to travel well beyond the pages of this book.

Our approach

This book is written by a team with extensive experience of advising on and doing interdisciplinary research in the UK, the European Union and the United States, in both academic and consultancy contexts. Each of us has academic training in both natural and social sciences. Individually and collectively we have a long track record in the analysis of interdisciplinary research, as well as in the facilitation of interdisciplinarity, the evaluation of complex processes of change, and the distillation and dissemination of good practice.

Catherine Lyall, Ann Bruce and Joyce Tait have had a long association at the University of Edinburgh. Examples of previous research collaborations include their work for the European Commission on interdisciplinary integration within the Fifth Framework Programme (Bruce *et al.* 2004) and their assessment for the Scottish Executive of the end user engagement undertaken by the Scottish Agricultural and Biological Research Institutes (Lyall *et al.* 2004). Bruce, Tait and Lyall have coordinated and contributed to a number of other interdisciplinary studies, notably for the European Commission (e.g. Braun *et al.* 2005; Tait *et al.* 2006a).

Laura Meagher and Catherine Lyall have worked together on many projects, including their evaluation of interdisciplinary schemes designed to support early career researchers, which made recommendations to the Research Councils UK as to the broader context of long-term career pathways for inter-disciplinary researchers, as well as the capacity-building needs of postgraduate students (Meagher and Lyall 2005a; Meagher and Lyall 2009). We have also collaborated on the review of seed-corn funding mechanisms employed by the cross-council programme Rural Economy and Land Use (Relu) to foster inter-disciplinarity (Meagher and Lyall 2007a) and the evaluation of the Scottish Higher Education Funding Council's Research Development Grant (RDG) Scheme, which promoted new interdisciplinary centres of excellence in emerging areas (Meagher and Lyall 2005b; Meagher and Lyall 2005c). We draw on all of these experiences in what follows.

The team's recent work together focuses on interdisciplinary capacity-building and we have collaborated on the delivery of a series of Interdisciplinary Masterclasses for early and mid-career researchers, funded by a UK ESRC Researcher Development Initiative grant. These Masterclasses acted as a catalyst for a range of other activities and outputs of which this book is one.

Across this extended programme of work, team members have focused upon capturing and disseminating guidance as to good practice in interdisciplinarity, knowledge exchange and multi-institutional collaborations. Thus contributions have been, and are being, made to the research community's capacity to take integrated approaches to key issues relating to the environment, society and economy.

The ESRC Centre for Social and Economic Research on Innovation in Genomics (Innogen), where Lyall, Bruce and Tait are based, provides a focus for interdisciplinary collaborations with the University of Edinburgh's world-class research strengths in both the social and natural sciences, including the life sciences. Technology Development Group (TDG), led by Meagher (who is a Visiting Fellow at Innogen), has a long track record in strategic change related to research, knowledge exchange and higher education. TDG has worked with individuals ranging across the natural and medical sciences, social sciences and the arts. In the United States, Meagher guided the growth of a variety of interdisciplinary initiatives (e.g. an EcoComplex, an EcoPolicy Centre, a Nutraceuticals Institute and the North Carolina Biotechnology Center). In the UK and in the United States, Meagher has catalysed the formation of novel initiatives (usually involving collaboration across disciplines, institutions and sectors) and evaluated schemes intended to encourage such initiatives.

Our own personal interdisciplinary journeys are described at the end of the book but it is fair to say that among our team we have experienced:

- good interdisciplinary proposals that have been rejected 'because they did not contribute to advancement of specific disciplines';

- bad interdisciplinary projects that have been funded because they follow current fashions;

- good projects that have had difficulty in delivering expected outcomes, either through lack of competent interdisciplinary management or through a poorly structured team;

- and, above all, good projects that were funded and delivered important outcomes according to plan.

We write mainly from a UK perspective because that is the situation we know best but much of the literature we draw on is from the United States. While acknowledging the contextual and institutional differences, in particular in terms of research funding and university structures, we believe that most of the fundamentals of interdisciplinary research, its conduct and management, are universal.

There are at least two possible approaches to addressing the challenges posed by interdisciplinary research capacity-building: either to build from and across the different disciplinary/substantive bases or to adopt a more generic approach that recognizes that many of the research design, development and management issues are also universal and largely independent of the particular research topic being addressed. While we attempt to blend both, our focus is more on the latter.

Finally, we should also acknowledge some of the editorial choices that we have made, including the fact that many of the examples we discuss in what follows are drawn from interdisciplinary research between the social and natural sciences (and indeed often from social studies of the life sciences) because, again, these are areas we know best, arising from recent research within the ESRC Innogen Centre and our previous work with the Scottish Universities Policy Research and Advice (SUPRA) network. But our experience in additional areas (involving, for example, computer sciences, language sciences, earth system sciences, creative disciplines and the arts) leads us to contend that the lessons we draw are equally applicable in other situations.

2

Departure Point

Our approach to interdisciplinarity

Introduction

Interdisciplinary research is challenging and difficult but most of all it is fun. People do research because they want to find out something new – to create knowledge that did not previously exist, or to refine existing knowledge, so that further insights or practical applications can emerge. At its best, this process can generate intense intellectual excitement, the 'eureka' moment that may enable whole new fields of enquiry to emerge or that may require numerous researcher lifetimes before the full implications of the discovery can be worked out.

This has been the authors' experience of conducting interdisciplinary research, but it has to be admitted that many of the books on the subject tend to emphasize the difficulties likely to be encountered. This may be because, in an attempt to gain academic respectability, they constrain their subject matter within the language of current academic discourse, rather than celebrating its difference and its undoubted power to arrive at otherwise unreachable outcomes.

To pick just one example of exciting interdisciplinary research in the last 60 years, the elucidation of the structure of DNA by Watson, Crick, Franklin and Wilkins (Watson 1970; Crick 1989) radically changed the potential for new discoveries and shifted the direction of many fields in the biological sciences. Two members of this group (they could not be described as a team), Franklin and Wilkins, were discipline-based researchers whose approach to their work was to move forward carefully at the frontier of their discipline, perfecting the methodology and avoiding distractions that did not seem relevant to their final goal. On the other hand, Watson (with a background in microbiology) and Crick (with a background in agricultural research), both working in a physics laboratory, were more like intellectual butterflies, seeking relevant information wherever they could find it, building models to test and reject ideas. Two crucial insights provided by chemists Erwin Chargaff and Jerry Donohue, passing through Cambridge University where the group was working, enabled them to understand the relationships among the four bases that form the backbone of the double helix molecule: adenine always linking to thymine and guanine to cytosine. Based on these insights, along with data from Franklin and Wilkins's research, they devised the now-accepted structure for DNA (Watson and Crick 1953).

The accounts of Watson and Crick do not mention any difficulty in working across disciplinary boundaries, but Crick does refer to the 'plodding and somewhat cautious attitude' of biologists. He refers to interdisciplinary collaboration as helping to jolt one out of mistaken assumptions and to his early career as having enabled him to avoid the usual fate of scientists who are trapped by their expertise by the time they are 30.

Waves of new disciplinary development emerged from this early interdisciplinary research: first the 'moleculars' (molecular biology, molecular biochemistry, molecular medicine); then the '-omics' (genomics, proteomics, metabolomics, pharmacogenomics); and more recently synthetic biology and systems biology. Interesting points on this research from the perspective of this book are:

1 the new knowledge (the structure of DNA) would not have been established at all without contributions from leading experts in several different disciplines;

2 the structure of DNA would have been elucidated eventually, if more slowly, without the interdisciplinary approach adopted by Watson and Crick;

3 this interdisciplinary approach effectively prepared the ground for a new collaborative model of research in the life sciences.

A parallel strand of development that goes well beyond the academic context, but that is very relevant to interdisciplinarity, aims to deal with complex problems related to the management of systems – organizations, companies, large installations such as electricity grids, ecosystems and transport systems. The complexity and interconnectedness of issues in such areas mean that they cannot be addressed through the lens of a single discipline.

Ross Ashby, one of the founders of cybernetics and systems theory, proposed the Law of Requisite Variety (Ashby 1956) which, put simply, implies that in responding to a complex variety of external and internal challenges, any organization or system needs to have a comparable variety and flexibility of response in order to survive and prosper. In the foreseeable future, the organizations (political, commercial and public) that survive will be those that best manage to cope with this complexity. Without going into the mathematical details behind these ideas, Ashby was pursuing the concept that he called 'ultrastability' – the ability of a system to resume a steady state after it has been disturbed *in a way not envisaged by its designer* (Beer 1966: 278, authors' emphasis), a capacity that is clearly important for the complex systems that support most of our daily routines.

Pressures for more interdisciplinary research are thus coming from two main directions: from the funders of basic research who expect more breakthroughs and better value for money from their investment, whether from public or commercial sources; and from the owners of complex, practical, real-world problems who expect to see better, more resilient and robust solutions to these problems from an interdisciplinary approach.

The moments of intense intellectual excitement that sustain researchers through the more routine periods of their research can come from either discipline-based or interdisciplinary research. For discipline-based research, it will come from pushing forward the boundaries of the discipline through new knowledge and understanding. For interdisciplinary research, it could come from spotting a very important connection between two previously unconnected disciplines or areas of enquiry. Both are necessary and complementary parts of the overall research process but only in the case of discipline-based research is there a clear academic support structure involving teaching and research departments in universities, well-defined theoretical foundations and methodology, and a set of publications and journals associated with each discipline.

New research journeys

As soon as you stray from the academically well-defined disciplinary path you are in unknown territory with few maps to guide you and perhaps not even a very clear idea of where you are going and how you will get there. Nobody explained to Watson and Crick how they should do interdisciplinary research. They were strong-minded individuals who followed their instincts and developed a way of working that suited their personalities despite admonitions from supervisors to follow a more conventional research path. The same has been true of most ground-breaking interdisciplinary researchers since then. Very few have been taught how to do it, or have read books about how to do it until after they have become fairly expert themselves, often through a process of trial and error or by reading widely in a range of disciplinary literatures.

So why is there a need for a book on the subject? The most pressing reason is that, in our experience, interdisciplinary research is becoming more mainstream, linking disciplines and subject areas within and across the natural and social sciences. Research funders are giving increasing amounts of money to interdisciplinary initiatives and programmes so that many researchers, who would previously have opted for conventional discipline-based academic careers, are finding themselves part of interdisciplinary teams working on major national or international projects, or are finding that the orientation of sources of funding for PhD research projects and beyond is increasingly interdisciplinary. And, of course, research careers in industry and public service have always been much more interdisciplinary than those in academia.

This book will use examples from a wide range of interdisciplinary projects and programmes, covering natural and social sciences, to provide guidance on doing interdisciplinary research, in a variety of roles and at different career stages, from postgraduate researcher to principal investigator to senior manager. Examples and case studies will be based on our own experience of interdisciplinary research and insights from others who have made similar journeys.

For example, the University of Sussex (Case Study 2.1) is one of the few universities in the UK to have had an explicitly interdisciplinary ethos since its foundation in 1961. However, across most universities, research institutes and research funding organizations, despite advocacy and funding for interdisciplinary research, the processes of funding, management, support and evaluation are still conducted mainly by people with strong disciplinary backgrounds who may have little practical understanding of how to promote interdisciplinary research or how to evaluate interdisciplinary research proposals and reports, an issue that we explore further in chapter 7.

Much of the knowledge that surrounds interdisciplinary research capacity-building is tacit, with practitioners often 'learning by doing' through a process of apprenticeship. This book should help to formalize this craft knowledge. 'Interdisciplinarity' encompasses different approaches suited to specific circumstances and we will describe why, when and how researchers can best pursue interdisciplinary research, and also how to overcome some of the barriers.

Case Study 2.1 Functions and benefits of interdisciplinary research

Vice-Chancellor Professor Gordon Conway described the University of Sussex's interdisciplinary traditions in an address to the University Court in 1995 in the following way:

> First, many of the practical challenges of the future are inherently interdisciplinary, and we will fail if they are tackled piecemeal. They range from manufacturing systems in engineering ... to the tackling of poverty and the problems of the environment that require insights drawn from across the social and natural sciences.
>
> Second, because so much is unpredictable, we need greater flexibility among individuals and institutions ... [S]tudents, while benefiting from the rigour of disciplinary study, also need to develop 'transferable intellectual skills' defined ... as 'a knowledge of underlying intellectual principles that are capable of being applied outside their original point of encounter, an ability to analyse complex issues involving both facts and values, and the capacity to draw on disparate sources of information to solve practical problems'.
>
> And third, in an increasingly multicultural word, we need insights derived from across the humanities and social sciences that will enable us to live productively and harmoniously in a society where different religions and cultural practices and beliefs are constantly impinging on one another.

Source: Cited in Scottish Universities Policy Research Consortium 1997.

There are dangers and inefficiencies in promoting interdisciplinary research without a good understanding of how to manage and evaluate projects and institutions, and also in the uncritical advocacy of interdisciplinarity or its ill-informed application. There is much to learn in order to avoid 'naïve borrowings' of terms and methods (Lowe *et al.* 2009) and this requires better training for those working in interdisciplinary teams, a theme that we explore further in chapter 5. We will also examine the intellectual challenges of interdisciplinary research beyond the 'instrumental rationale' often stressed by sponsors and users and also point to cases where concepts developed in one discipline are uncritically applied to another with consequences that are often meaningless or worse, for example, taking the metaphor of ecology and applying it in the context of innovation (Papaioannou *et al.* 2009).

Disciplines and subject areas

Before describing what we mean by interdisciplinary research, we need to consider the disciplines and subject areas that make up the bulk of the academic community.

Disciplines can be described as stable communities within which researchers concentrate their experience into a particular worldview. This puts limits on the kinds of questions they can ask about their material, the methods and concepts they use, the answers they believe and their criteria for truth and validity (Klein 1990). Disciplines thus provide a relatively clear map for research journeys, dictating not just the overall goal but also the route taken, the mode of transport and a clear indication of how you will know when you have arrived.

Tony Becher, in his book *Academic Tribes and Territories* (Becher 1989: 23–4), describes how academic subcultures form around disciplines which, as they grow more specialized, have fewer things in common, in their background and in their daily problems. Distinctions emerge particularly through the medium of language and the use of symbolic artefacts: 'a chemist's desk is prone to display three dimensional models of complex molecular structures, an anthropologist's walls are commonly adorned with colourful tapestries...while a mathematician may boast no more than a chalkboard scribbled over with algebraic symbols' (Becher, 1989).

For Becher, an important part of establishing the cultural identity of a discipline is this symbolism and the specialist terms that place it beyond the reach of an uninitiated audience: 'the tribes of academe define their own identities and defend their own patches of intellectual ground by employing a variety of devices geared to the exclusion of illegal immigrants ... To be admitted to membership of a particular sector of the academic profession involves ... a proper measure of loyalty to one's collegial group and of adherence to its norms.'

We discuss the impact that interdisciplinarity can have on academic careers in chapter 6.

Illustration 2.1 Overcome disciplinary boundaries to make the connections

Beyond the disciplines themselves, the rest of academic space is largely occupied by subject areas such as medicine, engineering or agriculture, designed to train people for careers in the relevant professions. Expertise in a range of disciplines is needed to practise any of these professions, requiring similarly diverse academic staff. However, these academics may often associate with people in their parent discipline in another part of the university rather than with their neighbours in the same department. Thus, an agricultural economist might associate with fellow-economists rather than with the soil scientist down the corridor.

As Donald Schön observed (Schön 1983), based on his experience in the 1980s, young graduates in such interdisciplinary subject areas were generally unprepared to apply their discipline-based learning to the real-world problems they would meet throughout their careers and thus had to undertake an apprenticeship before they were competent to practise their chosen profession.

Beyond disciplines

Pressures to cross disciplinary boundaries in conducting research can arise for a variety of reasons. The resulting models and approaches have been variously described as 'interdisciplinary', 'transdisciplinary', 'multidisciplinary' and 'cross-disciplinary'. Such an approach is not new: looking back to Darwin's integrative theory of evolution, the European Enlightenment or further back to the Renaissance would suggest that previous eras were much less constrained by disciplinary boundaries than our own, although for some time now there has been a separation between natural sciences and 'people' as a subject for scientific study. And indeed Klein warns that focusing on interdisciplinarity as 'new' opens it up to being dismissed as a 'fad' (Klein 2010: 153). Modern interdisciplinary scholars tend to ascribe the first use of the expression to the US Social Science Research Council in the 1920s (e.g. Abbott 2001: 131) although the Organisation for Economic Co-operation and Development (OECD/CERI 1972) is generally attributed with formalizing the term. There is, however, often a lack of consistency in, or agreement on, basic definitions. Is interdisciplinarity what happens in the gaps between disciplines or in the overlaps between them (Lattuca 2001: 82)? Terms like 'transdisciplinarity' and 'interdisciplinarity' are used differently by different research groups and/or in different national cultures.

Rather than an extended discussion of such questions, we have developed the following relatively simple and easily applied set of definitions, used first for our EC Fifth Framework Project on interdisciplinary research (Tait *et al.* 2002). They have proved useful on many occasions since then, covering all the varieties of research project with which we have been involved. These are the definitions we will use here, with no claims that they are in any sense superior to others also in current use.

Multidisciplinary research

Multidisciplinary research tackles a research project from the perspectives of a range of disciplines, but researchers from each discipline work in a self-contained manner with little cross-fertilization among disciplines, or synergy in the outcomes. Researchers may each contribute a few pieces to the jigsaw puzzle, but there is no improved understanding of the nature of the picture as a whole, and no fundamental change in perception, understanding or quality of knowledge-based outcomes. The final report from a multidisciplinary project is likely to consist of sections, each written from the perspective of a particular discipline, with a conclusions section that merely summarizes these contributions without attempting to integrate outcomes across disciplines.

Thus, multidisciplinary research involves low levels of collaboration, does not challenge the structure or functioning of academic communities or hierarchies and does not lead to any changes in the worldviews of the researchers themselves.

Interdisciplinary research

Interdisciplinary research, on the other hand, with its potential to effect important changes in worldviews of participants and academic structures, as well as to generate synergistic project outcomes is, in our view, a more important and rewarding category than multidisciplinary research but also more difficult to achieve. It approaches an issue from a range of disciplinary perspectives, and the contributions of the various disciplines are acknowledged and integrated to provide a holistic or systemic outcome: good interdisciplinary research is much more than the sum of its parts.

Transdisciplinary research

The greatest departure from a discipline base arises in a transdisciplinary approach which may focus on processes of knowledge production, rather than the disciplines and subjects into which knowledge is currently organized in academic settings (Nowotny *et al.* 2001), thus 'transcending' the academic disciplinary structure. As we discuss in chapter 8, definitions vary in different countries, ranging in meaning from 'deep' interdisciplinarity to interdisciplinary research that extends to co-production of research with non-academic stakeholders. In the context of problem solving, soft systems analysis has many parallels with transdisciplinary research, attempting to devise approaches which are tailored specifically to the problem context and do not rely on any predetermined disciplinary foundation (Checkland and Scholes 1990). On the other hand, multidisciplinary and interdisciplinary research explicitly build on the knowledge foundations that arise from academic disciplines. Chapter 8 picks up this discussion of transdisciplinarity within the explicit context of knowledge exchange.

We describe below two distinct types of interdisciplinary research: (i) academically oriented, and (ii) problem-focused. Most descriptions of interdisciplinary research process do not make this distinction, even although the two approaches have very different aims, methods and outcomes.

Academically oriented interdisciplinary research

The research on the structure of DNA described at the beginning of this chapter is a classic example of academically oriented interdisciplinary research, targeted to the solution of academic questions, for example where disciplines have reached the limits of their methodological capacity and need to bring in insights from new disciplines to overcome a blockage to their progress.

This is thus one of the primary engines of the evolution of disciplines. While it may create some short-term turbulence in academic institutions, in the longer run it supports, rather than challenges, their discipline-based structure. Researchers working on such projects are engaged in forging new disciplines or sub-disciplines and, if they are successful, they are in effect building themselves a new academic home. Thus, there are fewer academic barriers to this type of interdisciplinary research and, although difficulties of evaluating and administering projects may arise in the short run, in the long term they can be accommodated within traditional academic structures. In the short term, entrepreneurial universities and funding bodies may establish centres or institutes manifestly outside of normal departmental structures; if successful, such trial structures may become permanent although chapter 9 discusses some of the challenges that this may entail.

The observation that academic disciplines become stale, less innovative and less productive over time is not new, as the example in Case Study 2.2 demonstrates.

Abbott describes 'a structure of flexibly stable disciplines, surrounded by a hazy buzz of interdisciplinarity' (Abbott 2001: 136): disciplines in a constant state of flux but ultimately little radical change. While this may be true from Abbott's social science perspective, interdisciplinary interactions are transforming the natural sciences and the social scientists who work with them. As Weingart and Stehr note, 'disciplines do not keep up with rapid developments

---

Case Study 2.2 John Barclay on the history of anatomical research

The following description of a discipline in decline comes from an exhibit titled 'Barclay's Geese' in the Sir Jules Thorn Exhibition of the History of Surgery in the Royal College of Surgeons in Edinburgh. John Barclay MD was a lecturer in Anatomy and Surgery in the University of Edinburgh, around the 1820s. He worked in comparative anatomy and was remembered as a youth for 'aye skinning puddocks' (frogs). He described the history of anatomical research up to that point in these graphic terms:

> Anatomy may be likened to a harvest field. First came the reapers who, entering upon the untrodden ground, cut down great store of corn from all sides of them. These are the early anatomists of modern Europe, such as Vesalius, Fallopius, Malpighi and Harvey. Then come the gleaners who gather up ears enough from the bare ridges to make a few loaves of bread. Such were the anatomists of last century, Valsalva, Cotunnius, Haller, Winslow, Vicq d'Azyr, Camper, Hunter and the two Monros. Last come the geese who still contrive to pick up a few grains scattered here and there among the stubble and waddle home in the evening, poor things, cackling with joy because of their success. Gentlemen, we are the geese.

Source: 'Barclay's Geese' exhibit, Sir Jules Thorn Exhibition of the History of Surgery, Royal College of Surgeons, Edinburgh.

in modern societies' so that the 'map of knowledge ... is always outdated' (Weingart and Stehr 2000: 29).

Elucidation of the structure of DNA was an example of *academically oriented interdisciplinary research* that transformed the basic research environment, stimulated a host of major new insights into living organisms and processes, and inspired innovative applications from agriculture to health care. From that point on, in Europe, the United States and most other countries with major research budgets, 'life science' became the focus for major interdisciplinary programmes of research with money targeted to promoting collaboration across disciplines, with specific, applicable research outcomes in mind. Indeed, given the increasing pace and scope of change in interdisciplinary collaborations in life sciences, one could claim that some disciplines are being purposively engineered and re-engineered in response to pressures from research funders rather than being allowed to evolve more 'naturally' as would have been the case in the past (Tait 2009).

This re-engineering of academic disciplines in the life sciences, involving teams of researchers with a wide range of disciplinary skills, has been quite successful but other disciplinary combinations – in particular those required to address research questions that span the social and natural sciences – can be much more challenging. Individual scientists who want to pursue fundamental research on a single discipline-based idea (particularly in the life sciences) might also be concerned that purposive funding strategies go too far in favour of large interdisciplinary teams, potentially undermining the single-discipline progress on which interdisciplinary research often depends.

Turning to other disciplinary combinations, some social scientists believe that working with cognate disciplines in the social sciences may be more difficult than working with natural sciences (Greaves and Grant 2010). The social sciences often have a stronger focus on method and this may give the impression that they are more discipline-bound than the natural sciences: different methods can either open up or close down the possibility to ask different sorts of questions. One of the explanatory factors may be that the social sciences often emphasize a certain body of knowledge that reinforces disciplinary differences: there may be particular problems among the social sciences where competing methodologies are brought to bear on the same research topic (Greaves and Grant 2010). Natural scientists may be more oriented around the fluidity of experimental activities and the sharing of techniques. Among the natural sciences there may be more experience of the benefits to disciplines from interdisciplinary collaboration, for example in terms of the evolution of new disciplines such as materials science in the 1980s and synthetic biology in the current decade. There can be real challenges in forging synergies across seemingly distant disciplines. Genuinely integrating teams, research and findings across natural and social science disciplines, for example, has typically been viewed as problematic but, as Case Study 2.3 illustrates, this too is starting to change.

Case Study 2.3 The role of social scientists in synthetic biology

Social scientists can adopt many different roles and responsibilities in relation to natural science research; they can be advocates, intermediaries, translators, connoisseurs, critics, activists or reformers. They can reflect on the implications of a finished piece of research, or become involved at a much earlier stage. In newly emerging areas of scientific endeavour such as synthetic biology, we are seeing novel arrangements forming between natural and social scientists, whereby social scientists are becoming a required component of research programmes and are even involved in the creation of new fields. Social scientists can be cast as 'contributors' (entering the scene after the scientific knowledge has been produced) or 'collaborators' (immersing themselves in authentic interdisciplinary work that does not just follow the scientific research, but interacts with it). Although there has been much quality research on the social and ethical impacts of new biology, the majority of social scientists have in the past tended to perform the former role with little systematic attempt to develop a more integrative approach.

Source: Calvert and Martin 2009.

Problem-focused interdisciplinary research

The second key type of interdisciplinary research, *problem-focused interdisciplinary research*, addresses issues of social, technical and/or policy relevance where discipline-related outputs are less central to the project design. Stimuli for problem-focused interdisciplinary research can arise anywhere from individual researchers to national and international research programmes. There are cases where an individual researcher, anywhere from PhD level upwards, sees a gap in understanding or analysis of a practical question and sets out to bridge this gap by bringing together insights from more than one discipline. If the researcher lacks external support this can be a difficult task, but if successful it can also be very rewarding.

More often, the problems on which interdisciplinary research is focused are perceived as important by those with research funds at their disposal. The US National Science Foundation (NSF) has linked its funding priorities to those of the US Congress and of President Obama, 'to ... tackle pressing societal problems, and foster collaboration across disciplines'. The interdisciplinary areas mentioned include: environmental biology; electrical, communications and cyber systems; geosciences; earth sciences; climate research; Antarctic and Arctic sciences (Anon 2009: 1128).

Risk analysis is a rich source of examples of problem-focused interdisciplinary research, or of the multiple ways in which things can go wrong if such research is not undertaken. A recent report from the International Risk Governance Council (IRGC) describes one important risk governance deficit as 'a lack of appreciation or understanding of the potentially multiple dimensions of a risk and of how interconnected risk systems can entail complex and sometimes unforeseeable interactions' (IRGC 2009). The report lists 23 deficits, many of which are related to issues of interdisciplinarity, and explains their background in a number of case studies, for example on mobile phones and power lines, hurricane Katrina, fisheries depletion, genetically modified crops, bovine spongiform encephalopathy and the sub-prime mortgage crisis.

Decisions on which disciplines to include within a problem-focused interdisciplinary analysis will depend on the nature of the project, rather than arising from the constraints being experienced in specific disciplines (as would be the case for academically oriented interdisciplinary research). Researchers working in this area are likely to find themselves working with different sets of disciplines from one project to the next. They thus build up expertise on the integration of disciplines and the management of, or collaboration with, researchers from different disciplines working together. Yet, these skills are not highly valued in an academic context.

Some argue that, despite being a relatively constant preoccupation, interdisciplinarity has not changed the US academic system (Abbott 2001: 134). Abbott attributes this to the fact that interdisciplinary research is problem driven and problems have a limited lifespan: 'problem-based knowledge is insufficiently abstract to survive in competition with problem-portable knowledge' (Abbott 2001: 135). Problem-focused interdisciplinary research is thus sometimes seen as undermining academic research, taking its evolution in a direction with which many academics are uncomfortable. Pursuit of multifaceted problems beyond the scope of any one discipline is often seen by discipline-based researchers as at best irrelevant and at worst threatening so that the barriers to this type of interdisciplinary research are correspondingly greater, as are the difficulties of evaluating and managing it.

The value of disciplinary and interdisciplinary research

Well-conceived and conducted interdisciplinary research can lead to new academic disciplines or sub-disciplines, new insights, shortcuts and solutions to intractable problems and better decision-making.

Perhaps counter-intuitively, a biosciences researcher at a British university who was being interviewed about interdisciplinary research described it as 'the best way I know to promote reductionism', in reference to its value in resolving blockages to the development of disciplines in academically oriented interdisciplinary research.

This draws attention to an overly simplistic dichotomy that is often put forward in the context of interdisciplinary research, the notion that holism, and by implication interdisciplinary research, is always a good thing, to be contrasted against 'inevitably' limited and limiting insights that can be obtained from reductionist, discipline-based research. This is, of course, not the case. While a holistic, interdisciplinary approach can lead to outcomes that are greater than the sum of the parts, it can also lead to poor quality research. It is always important to justify fully the adoption of an interdisciplinary approach and to be clear about the likely benefits, rather than automatically favouring interdisciplinarity over other approaches.

Some interdisciplinary fields clearly 'congeal' to the point that they are recognized as disciplines in their own right with a shared epistemological base and associated professional markers such as journals and learned societies (Vickers 1997, quoted in Klein 2010: 27). Science and technology studies would be one example of such an 'interdiscipline'. Simons *et al.* use the metaphors of 'bridge building' (between complete and firm disciplines) and 'restructuring' (where parts of several disciplines are detached to form a new coherent whole) (Simons *et al.* 1975: 42–5). Whichever approach we use, interdisciplinarity, by definition, builds on discipline-based research, be it academically oriented or problem-focused, and progress in knowledge generation requires both types of research to be supported and pursued enthusiastically in the appropriate contexts.

Integrative approaches

Disciplines dictate what you can know and what you can do with that knowledge. While disciplines can limit what we are required to know, they can also limit the questions we are expected to ask: shaping problems to fit disciplines is not a very rewarding or creative approach. If you need to know more to understand a problem or to effect change, you need to bring in knowledge from a wider range of disciplines and also probably knowledge that is not codified in terms of disciplines at all. How can a researcher cope constructively with this degree of complexity?

As we have already observed, the culture of an academic discipline is intimately linked to the methods employed in that discipline. For example, economists tend to be most comfortable with multiple regression analysis and social psychologists with factor analysis. From the earliest stage of conception of a new discipline-based project, the researcher will have a pretty good idea of the methods to be employed and hence of the range of questions that can be asked. Indeed, one of the most frequent criticisms of discipline-based research, in

contrast to problem-focused interdisciplinary research, arises from this methodologically constrained focus which may bear little relationship to real-world
problems. Extending the methodological reach of a discipline is often, on the
other hand, the primary motivation for academically oriented interdisciplinary
research. For organizers of interdisciplinary research projects and programmes,
when bringing together a team of people from different disciplines, one of the
most common challenges is to help researchers to envisage how their methods
can be adapted to accommodate insights from other disciplines, as we discuss
in chapters 3 and 4.

One of the most important skills in interdisciplinary research is the setting of a constructive but manageable boundary around the research area: this
boundary is not determined by a discipline or disciplines but enables a feasible
and creative approach to the research. This question of boundary definition is
most difficult for problem-focused interdisciplinary research where the very
earliest stage usually requires significant time to be spent on first opening up
discussion on the full range of factors relevant to the issue under consideration,
followed by a structuring stage that focuses on the relationships among the
various components identified as relevant, and deciding on a finite set of the
appropriate disciplines, knowledge, methods and evidence to be incorporated
on the basis of that early analysis.

In the current stage of development of interdisciplinary research there are
a few guidelines that can help in this process, but it is still very much a craft
skill, best learned as an apprenticeship with an experienced interdisciplinary
researcher. Once a decision has been made on the relevance of various components and disciplines, the quality of the available disciplinary evidence bases
that are able to contribute to the interdisciplinary research will be very important. Researchers should be aware of:

1 the temptation to select the evidence used to suit some desired outcome
   from the interdisciplinary research;

2 the possible accidental introduction of bias.

Unexpected bias can also be introduced in combining evidence from more
than one discipline. As in every area of scientific endeavour, researchers should
be aware of their own motivations and how these might affect the outcomes of
the research. However, unlike discipline-based research, procedures to guard
against bias in research methods and outcomes are much less developed for
interdisciplinary research.

Some authors claim that notions of objectivity, neutrality and rationality are
deeply flawed, that disciplines are power structures which need to be challenged,
and that interdisciplinary research can lead to more genuine understanding and
equality (Lattuca 2001). We would not subscribe to this view. Objectivity, rationality and neutrality are the only bases for progress in the sense of contributing

to an evolving knowledge base. The alternative is likely to be 'perennial debates that produce proliferating lineages with peculiar properties of self-similarity, self-replication and rootlessness ... [and] the processes of drift and rediscovery that the unfolding of such debates produces' (Abbott 2001: 121).

One of the most useful attributes of disciplines is their function in setting standards for the quality of the knowledge base that emerges from research. Although it is still very much 'work in progress', interdisciplinary research also needs to develop such firm foundations, as illustrated in Figure 2.1.

The central, positive feedback loop in this diagram could be either a virtuous or a vicious circle, illustrating the important factors that either support or constrain the development of an academically accepted interdisciplinary research system. Taking the negative interpretation, and starting at the right-hand side of the vicious circle, institutional support structures for interdisciplinary research are currently not well developed, leading to a lack of incentives to undertake interdisciplinary research and a low level of participation by the most able researchers, along with poor continuity of participation. All these factors mitigate against the development of strong intellectual foundations for interdisciplinary research and hence a relative lack of ability to assess the quality of interdisciplinary projects and their outcomes, completing the loop by further undermining the development of institutional support structures.

Considering what levers could be activated to convert this vicious circle into a virtuous one, the diagram includes the two most important potential incentives: availability of finance (currently increasing and therefore with a positive sign on the arrow) and appropriate research evaluation approaches (still

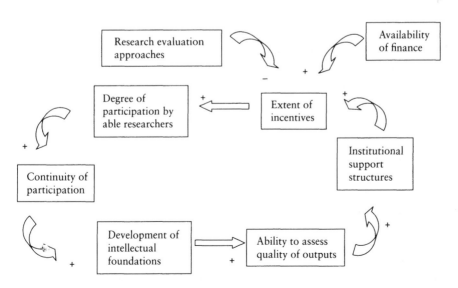

Figure 2.1 The interdisciplinary academic research system: A vicious or a virtuous circle?

not well addressed and therefore with a negative sign on the arrow). Recent increases in the amount of funding available for interdisciplinary research have had a positive effect, stimulating the participation of able researchers, providing for greater continuity of participation in some cases, particularly through support for major interdisciplinary research centres with long-term funding of up to ten years or more. However, this potential positive impact is often counteracted by the negative impact of most research evaluation approaches, such as the UK Research Assessment Exercise and the evaluation systems adopted by most research funders throughout the developed world, contributing to maintaining the vicious circle. Evaluations are almost always conducted by panels that consist mainly of discipline-based experts (perhaps with a token interdisciplinary presence) who tend to evaluate research proposals or outcomes on the basis of their contributions to academic disciplines and who fail to see or to value the alternative benefits of interdisciplinary research. This factor therefore acts first as a disincentive to participation in interdisciplinary research feeding through the other factors leading to continuing lack of ability to judge the quality of interdisciplinary research and hence to continuing poor institutional support structures.

Within this interdisciplinary research system, the increases in funding referred to above strongly influence the structure of, and relationship between, the disciplines (Lowe and Phillipson 2006; Lowe and Phillipson 2009). Not only do these institutional relationships recreate disciplinary divides, they also form the rules, priorities and reward mechanisms that set the scope for both mainstream research and boundary-transgressing endeavours (Lowe and Phillipson 2009). Viewed from this perspective, understanding the nature of interdisciplinarity can illuminate allocative rules and agenda-setting mechanisms of research funding organizations: the promotion of interdisciplinarity can be undermined if we fail to appreciate its contingent, institutionally dependent existence. Barry describes how such interdisciplinary research institutions 'often have a fragile existence, dependent on political circumstances, or on the patronage and energies of key individuals' (Barry 2007). From a UK perspective, as Lowe and Phillipson explain, the challenge of working across disciplines 'is much more than about disciplinary barriers and crucially implicates the decisions, processes, and structures of research-funding organizations' (Lowe and Phillipson 2009).

This book attempts to support positive incentives to undertake interdisciplinary research and to do that well, and to counter the disincentives that are still so much in evidence in all countries with strong, publicly supported research programmes.

Summary

This chapter has emphasized the excitement and the challenges of doing good interdisciplinary research and also the continuing important role for disciplines themselves. At two extremes we have distinguished between the academically oriented interdisciplinary research that presents fewer challenges to disciplines and to traditional discipline-based structures, and problem-focused inter-disciplinary research that is more challenging to conduct and more difficult to evaluate. In practice a large interdisciplinary collaboration may include elements of both to varying degrees.

We have explored the value of interdisciplinary research in contributing to the evolution of academic disciplines and to the resolution of real-world prac-tical problems, including better policy and/or business decision-making. In all these contexts there is a need to have a clearer idea of what constitutes 'good quality' in interdisciplinary research, including avoidance of biases introduced by poor understanding of discipline-based limitations.

We have shown how the various elements of interdisciplinary research introduced in this book could be combined as part of a virtuous circle that supports and encourages interdisciplinary research and could greatly improve its capacity to generate societal value for money.

Questions

For researchers and research managers

 1 Why do interdisciplinary research?

2 How can you improve your chances of being funded to do interdisciplinary research?

3 How can you ensure that it produces outcomes of high quality?

For institutional leaders

1 How could you improve the research environment to support interdisciplinary research in your institution?

2 How could your institution benefit from providing an improved environment for interdisciplinary research?

For research funders

1 How could you stimulate effective interdisciplinary research as part of a research portfolio?

2 How could you institute criteria and evaluation processes suitable for interdisciplinarity that will select for good quality interdisciplinary work?

3 How could you contribute to improved quality in the interdisciplinary research that is funded?

4 How can greater academic, public and commercial added-value be generated from the increased levels of investment in interdisciplinary research?

3

Planning the Expedition

Designing interdisciplinary research projects

Introduction

Like any expedition, an interdisciplinary project needs to know why it is heading out, where it is going, who is going with the team or supporting it and how it is going to progress. But many interdisciplinary projects will be much more like explorations of virgin territory, so the answers to some of these questions will not be knowable in detail before setting out. There will also be solo expeditions which may raise different challenges. In general, several key steps need to be taken:

- First, a decision has to be made as to whether the research project actually needs to be interdisciplinary in order to advance its goals.

- Then, either a suitable collaborative team needs to be assembled, with selection informed by an understanding of different disciplines' approaches and assumptions and an awareness of the importance of skills, expertise *and* personality, or the individual concerned needs to ensure that they already have, or can acquire, the interdisciplinary capacity to do the research.

- A joint approach to tackling the research question has to be developed and a plan for integrating the contributions of component disciplines needs to be devised, taking into account the extra time and effort required.

- All of this needs to be done with appropriate leadership, reflection and, if necessary, adaptation of the plans as the journey unfolds.

In this chapter we will consider some of the basic challenges of designing interdisciplinary research projects and how these may be overcome, starting off with the basic question, 'Does this research project need to be interdisciplinary?' Chapter 4 will then develop further some of the themes of team-building, project management and leadership.

Deciding on the focus

At the outset, development of a research design entails consideration of whether an interdisciplinary approach is the best way to achieve the research objectives. Both discipline-based and interdisciplinary research are valuable and both are necessary in specific circumstances, but interdisciplinary projects are likely to require greater resourcing and are generally more complex to run than single discipline projects. Given the potential benefits, there are a variety of reasons why a research project should be interdisciplinary. Some areas of study are inherently interdisciplinary, as noted already in chapter 2. Many research fields, such as agriculture, environmental science, ecology or geography, are themselves 'portmanteau disciplines' which are broad, outward-looking and open to other methods (Phillipson *et al.* 2009), and draw on a range of specialist disciplines. For example, information systems analysis may take into account social needs and interface design for specific requirements; development-oriented research will not only take into account different disciplines but will also need to work cross-culturally. In other circumstances, interdisciplinary groups are brought together to address specific research questions that have either proven intractable to monodisciplinary approaches or that require a range of specialisms.

There are various situations when interdisciplinary research may be relevant or indeed vital. The European Commission funded a study of interdisciplinarity in its Fifth Framework Research Programme (II-FP5) (Tait *et al.* 2002), as summarized in Case Study 3.1. The following motivations for choosing an interdisciplinary project were identified:

- the nature of the subject was interdisciplinary (e.g. transport, environment);

- researchers were looking to apply results in the 'real world', so-called 'translational research', or to break down barriers between science and society;

- the research was driven by users, who might be commercial companies, policy-makers or civil society groups;

- research in a single discipline had reached a bottleneck and more disciplines were needed to make a breakthrough.

Types of funding can influence the project design: interdisciplinary research projects may be circumscribed and driven by the needs of research funders and, in particular, by the way in which peers will review those research project proposals. Interdisciplinary research can also be the result of a speculative proposal (where the topic originates from the researcher, termed 'responsive mode' proposals in the UK) or a specific research call requesting an interdisciplinary

Case Study 3.1 Studying interdisciplinarity within the European Commission Framework Programme

Many of the European Union's research activities during 1998–2002 were conducted under the European Commission's Fifth Framework Programme. One of the features of this programme was the encouragement of closer collaboration between different disciplines both within and between the social and natural sciences. We undertook a research project for the European Commission to examine interdisciplinary integration within the Fifth Framework Programme (II-FP5).

We examined a large number of themes in the Framework Programme, ranging from biological sciences (Quality of Life and Management of Living Resources) to information technology (User-friendly Information Society). Our research method included a questionnaire-based survey (with 160 responses), follow-up telephone interviews and 6 detailed case studies. The intention was to understand and learn from the experiences of interdisciplinarity from within these projects including how the research consortium was developed, project management and general experiences of running cross-disciplinary projects. Several of the examples and quotes used in this book, particularly in chapters 3 and 4, have been taken from this research project.

Source: Tait *et al.* 2002; Bruce *et al.* 2004.

approach, or it might arise in the context of working with stakeholder groups or end-user groups. A host of different variables will shape the project design, with the envisioned project falling at different points of the ranges for each one. These variables, some of which we will discuss briefly here, include:

- 'strength' or level of interdisciplinarity;
- focus versus multi-dimensional scope of the problem;
- level of connectivity with prospective users;
- duration;
- size of team;
- number of disciplines;
- number of institutions, number of countries;
- maturity of relationships (including pre-existing collaborations) among team members.

Some studies of large-scale interdisciplinary initiatives suggest that 'collaboration-readiness' for an initiative can be teased apart by looking at multiple factors including 'contextual-environmental' conditions (such as institutional resources, proximity), 'intrapersonal characteristics' (such as leadership or orientation of research) and 'interpersonal factors' (such as size, spectrum of disciplines and prior history of collaboration) (Stokols *et al.* 2005; Stokols *et al.* 2008a; Hall *et al.* 2008).

In deciding if or how to pursue interdisciplinarity, it might help when conceptualizing the research design to use a visual device in the form of a spider plot (Figure 3.1), for example, in order to prompt discussion amongst team members about the degree of interdisciplinarity and/or collaboration readiness, and how the design might influence the conduct of, and outcomes from, the project. By identifying a number of factors relevant to the success of the project (some of which are illustrated in Figure 3.1) and attempting to quantify these, where possible, this may help team leaders and others to conceptualize the research design and assess its strengths and weaknesses.

Inherent in the term 'interdisciplinary' is a concept of degree or strength of interdisciplinarity. Projects may have some integration of disciplines resulting in a small degree of interdisciplinarity, or 'weak' interdisciplinarity. Other projects may have disciplines deeply embedded with each other (and this will often be true of academically oriented interdisciplinary projects as described in chapter 2), giving a high degree of interdisciplinarity, or 'strong' interdisciplinarity. Even within a particular project, it is quite feasible for research teams to start with weak forms of interdisciplinarity and move to stronger forms as the partners begin to understand the potential contribution of different disciplines more clearly.

The term 'interdisciplinary research' covers an array of different approaches. As explained in chapter 2, problem-focused interdisciplinary research projects will bring together unique teams for periods of a few months to a few years; they

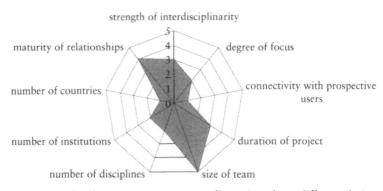

Figure 3.1 Using visual prompts to encourage discussion about different design approaches

can take the shape of relatively circumscribed projects or large, long-term collaborative efforts such as some of the biosphere monitoring programmes where the information from remote sensing technologies needs to be shared among various different scientists (Kwa 2006).

Some projects entail ongoing involvement of users such as developing medical diagnostic technology with the aid of patients; even some knowledge-transfer projects, such as the former UK Genetics Knowledge Parks[1] set up to bring together diverse clinicians and academic and industry researchers to tackle genetic illnesses, could be considered interdisciplinary projects. Interdisciplinary projects can be based in one country such as the Research Councils UK Rural Economy and Land Use (Relu) programme[2] or they can be international, such as the European Commission Framework Programmes.

There is a range of different types of interdisciplinary research project, each with its own unique features, but this chapter will focus on the commonalities that have been found to be important across these types of project. This chapter and chapter 4 consider interdisciplinarity as a team effort, but it can also be conducted by an individual with expertise in more than one discipline – early bioinformaticians, for example, could have been identified as individual interdisciplinary researchers until the discipline became recognized in its own right. This chapter will go on to discuss how to bring together an interdisciplinary team, considering skills, disciplines and individuals. It will then look at conceptualizing the research problem and finally at strategies for integrating disciplines within the project.

Identifying team members

A good interdisciplinary researcher will have a high tolerance for ambiguity. This means not prematurely reducing a problem to a limited set of dimensions, but taking time to explore a range of aspects in order to test several potential boundaries to a problem until the apparently optimum boundary has been identified. These explorations should be part of the teamwork conducted by the project coordinator and the ability of team members to engage productively in this process is very important to the project's success.

The range of disciplines included should be closely tailored to the needs of the project. Thinking through the lines of evidence that would need to be woven together, along with the technologies or data sources needed, can help to define the set of disciplines and specific sub-disciplines to be involved. Some imagination may be required to generate the necessary disciplinary juxtapositions since interdisciplinarity, at its best, can lead to genuine creativity and innovation.

Adding a 'token' discipline, perhaps for reasons of tactical or political expediency, rather than genuinely incorporating it into the project design, is not likely to be fruitful and may result in a great deal of frustration for the person involved. One way of checking for the presence of such tokenism is to examine the budget to be sure resource allocations are appropriate. Tokenism may occur by accident simply because team leaders did not understand fully what a particular discipline could offer to the overall aims of the project. It is therefore worthwhile spending some time exploring with people from unfamiliar disciplines what their contribution might be. This may be a particular issue where one discipline's contribution is viewed as a mere 'support' function by some in the team but is (understandably) viewed as an important research perspective by others.

Various views have been expressed as to whether some disciplines are able to work better together than others. For example, it is sometimes suggested that collaborations among natural science disciplines or among social science disciplines are easier to achieve than across what may seem to be the 'yawning abyss' of the natural science/social science divide. There is some contradictory evidence, however, that it is more difficult to work with a combination of social scientists than across social/natural sciences (e.g. Tait *et al.* 2002; Lélé and Norgaard 2005; Greaves and Grant 2010) as we discussed in chapter 2. It may be that different social scientists rely on very different presuppositions, making it difficult for them to work together. Economists, for instance, may believe the key driver of human behaviour is maximizing material benefits, while some sociologists may believe that it is power, and some anthropologists that it is cultural norms and values (Lélé and Norgaard 2005). These, and other deeply ingrained disciplinary commitments, may make it difficult to accept the saliency of alternative explanations from other social science disciplines. However, partners from distant disciplines may be aware of this distance and therefore pay more attention to the issues of communication.

Another distinction that is often made is between quantitative and qualitative research methods. In the view of some, disciplines which are more quantitative in nature (for example, economics and natural sciences) will work together more readily than, for example, physics and sociology. Phillipson *et al.*, in a survey of ecologists, found that they considered collaboration with social scientists using quantitative methods easier than with qualitative social scientists (Phillipson *et al.* 2009). However, the alternative view has also been expressed, that it is easier to recognize and value the contribution from a very different discipline than from one that is only a little different. For example, an engineer we interviewed for II-FP5 pointed out that he was trained in formal mathematical methods and for him qualitative methods were appropriate for use in social sciences, whereas he felt quantitative approaches were not. In that study, we found that there was little agreement among natural scientists over whether it was easier to work with quantitative rather than qualitative social scientists.

Methodological commitments

Recognition of the different methodological commitments of different disciplines is also helpful when putting together interdisciplinary teams. Methodological commitments (and thus approaches to framing and pursuing questions) can be understood, rather simplistically but we think helpfully, as:

- primarily normative (such as ethics);
- deductive (such as the natural sciences); or
- inductive (such as many of the social sciences).

A normative view is predicated on the understanding that there is some standard that should be achieved. In contrast, some social scientists understand the world in terms of social construction: that a phenomenon exists because people behave as though it exists. An interdisciplinary collaboration including a normative discipline and a social science discipline that is committed to social construction would need to negotiate these two different ways of looking at the world. An awareness of the distinction between deductive reasoning and inductive reasoning can also be helpful. Deductive reasoning demands that valid conclusions are the necessary outcomes of logical argument. This is an approach used in philosophical argumentation but the approach is also relevant to the scientific method where a theory is verified or refuted by empirically testing a hypothesis deduced from the initial theory. Whilst the reality of scientific practice may not fully reflect the aspiration, there is a goal of deduction that is being sought. Inductive reasoning on the other hand occurs when evidence makes a certain conclusion more likely. However, inductive methods do not ensure the inevitability of the conclusion because it is always possible for new evidence to demand a different interpretation. Whilst deductive reasoning is used in the natural sciences, inductive reasoning is more common in the social sciences where it is not usually possible to set up controlled experiments to test social theories.

The challenge of working with different approaches was well captured by one of our II-FP5 interviewees:

> For example, in the physical sciences we normally deal with very much experimental results, so we try to derive all our work so as to be shown experimentally, to provide a solution. In the social sciences (sometimes – not always) it is not to ... How can I put it? Sometimes the *thinking* about different ways of looking at things is important – the argument is the important issue, not a particular solution. (Interviewee, II-FP5 project, Tait *et al.* 2002)

We will return to this question of what counts as quality standards for data and analysis in different disciplines when we consider the issue of interdisciplinary evaluation in chapter 7.

An awareness of these differences in disciplinary commitments can be helpful in putting together an interdisciplinary team. In designing and managing such a team, these differences can be recognized explicitly so that the value of each is clear, rather than individuals from one discipline secretly thinking the others are missing the point. Ideally, brainstorming over the framing of the problem(s) to be pursued, and the pathways for doing so, would benefit from these different approaches bumping up against each other in the planning process; a resultant project design that makes the most of more than one fundamental approach is likely to provide something special compared with a monodisciplinary approach.

Further friction between disciplines may occur with respect to value neutrality (see also Lélé and Norgaard 2005). Value neutrality is the aim of natural sciences. In contrast, in *some* forms of qualitative social science, research that is openly ideological is deemed to be appropriate. Examples include feminist approaches, where the research method critiques traditional perspectives as relying too heavily on a masculine way of viewing the world and as a result failing to reflect female approaches and perspectives (e.g. Punch 2005). Equally, some social scientists would find this problematical, arguing that any research that is knowingly biased by the personal views of the researcher is likely to be of poorer quality, and that research from any discipline (in the social or natural sciences) should strive for 'neutral competence'.

Even within natural sciences, indeed even within one branch, different approaches may occur. As an example within biology, molecular geneticists may work with small numbers of organisms, perhaps hoping to find an exceptional mutation that will shed light on a phenomenon, and for them statistically valid numbers may be irrelevant. In contrast, quantitative geneticists seeking to understand the evolution of pathogenic organisms rely on statistics as a principal source of knowledge. Individual results may easily be disregarded as being beyond the norm and contributing to error rather than being significant themselves.

Each of these differences results in tensions in terms of defining and identifying good quality research. However, simply disputing the basis for 'good quality' between different knowledge domains is unlikely to be fruitful. Each needs to be considered by its own lights even if the approach seems dubious when viewed from another perspective. Definitions of 'good research' have developed over decades in most disciplines and reflect the particular approaches that are possible within that discipline. So, in practice, the members of a team need to be able to trust in the commitment of their colleagues to the same level of quality, whatever that translates into for each discipline; selection of researchers driving themselves to similar standards is a key step at the design phase. As a leader of an Research Development Grant centre commented:

> It is important for leaders to be selective, to vet the possible collaborators, because you only have so much time and so much resource. You want to have a collaboration with others who are successful in what they do, you also want them to have the reputations to be complementary with what you do, to ensure that you get the maximum return. (Meagher and Lyall 2005c: 13)

The need to focus on an appropriate project membership should not be underestimated. Taking part in an interdisciplinary research project is seen as risky by many researchers and success is largely dependent on the quality of the team (Marzano *et al.* 2006). It can be extremely difficult to incorporate new partners at late stages of research proposal development or after the project has started. We return to this issue in chapter 4.

The human dimension

Human considerations are at least as important as the disciplinary component of the collaboration. Being familiar with people, their working styles and the demands and pressures under which they work is an important aspect of any collaboration but in an interdisciplinary project these are crucial. The project is likely to require a degree of trust in colleagues whose methods may not be familiar and whose contribution may be questioned by those who do not understand what constitutes good research in that discipline. Research collaborations that build on existing teams have an advantage here: the team will already have some familiarity with different disciplines and ways of working, and will have developed some degree of trust that partners will deliver the outputs necessary for a successful project. When a new collaboration is brought together there is always the need for preliminary meetings to develop research ideas but in some cases long periods of networking – sometimes several years – have been the prerequisite to developing a successful interdisciplinary research consortium.

Many research projects consist primarily of a group of people who know each other already and have worked together in previous projects. It is common to build on their expertise by bringing in a few new key skills and people to the research consortium. This model is generally preferred to developing a completely novel collaborative team from scratch. Indications are that at least some pre-existing relationships within a project team may be advantageous to effective interdisciplinary work (e.g. Stokols *et al.* 2008b). It is possible to put together a team for a specific purpose such as a research funding bid. It might be tempting to choose a team based on simply the disciplines or sub-disciplines of the members. However, because personal and intellectual 'chemistry' does matter, many would advise first bringing prospective team members together early and informally, perhaps through brainstorming exercises, to explore the 'fit' of the individuals as well as the ideas involved. Our evaluation (Meagher and Lyall 2007a) of a 'seed-corn' grant scheme conducted by Relu concluded that there was real value in this early opportunity for funded activities to help prospective collaborators get to know each other and develop new research ideas. The experiences helped to catalyse interdisciplinarity and community-building, and increased commitment to, and/or competence in, interdisciplinary work.

Research has highlighted the importance of paying attention to personalities as well as disciplinary expertise with aspects such as flexibility, willingness to learn and creativity identified as important (Key Advice 3.1). Interdisciplinary research may particularly attract divergent, or synthetic, thinkers who have the ability to draw on ideas from across disciplines and fields of enquiry, bringing material from a variety of sources to reach a deeper understanding of a problem (Atherton 2010). Repko identifies 15 traits and skills common to interdiscipli-narians (Repko 2008). These range across an entrepreneurial attitude to risk, an intense interest in 'understanding the knowing process' (self-reflection and a love of learning) and 'tolerance for ambiguity and paradox in the midst of complexity'. Although many of the skills he identifies would be widely shared among the research community (e.g. good communication skills and the abil-ity to think abstractly, creatively and in a non-linear manner), it is perhaps the ability to think holistically which typifies the interdisciplinary researcher's need to view a problem as part of a bigger system. The same holds true for col-leagues who are supervising graduate students or mentoring early postdoctoral researchers engaged in interdisciplinary research, as we discuss in chapter 5.

Other key characteristics identified include the need for humility and will-ingness to acknowledge the limitations of one's own disciplinary knowledge and to respect that of others (e.g. Jeffrey 2003; Marzano *et al*. 2006). A leader of an interdisciplinary programme whom we interviewed as part of the Relu project (Meagher and Lyall 2007a) rejected polarization as the defining dynamic of interdisciplinarity, pointing out that 'understanding the common-alities between the members of an interdisciplinary team is as important, if not more, than becoming aware of their differences'.

Research suggests that there is a variety of ways to identify project part-ners (e.g. Tait *et al*. 2002). The most common is word of mouth or recom-mendations from colleagues, but meeting people at conferences and other events is also important. One supervisor of interdisciplinary students whom we interviewed when evaluating an interdisciplinary PhD scheme (Meagher and Lyall 2009) described a very deliberate searching and testing process for identifying colleagues who would be good co-supervisors, attending their conference presentations and engaging them in conversation well before broaching any talk of collaboration. The experience of a Research Network Manager at the Cambridge University Interdisciplinary Research Network tasked with promoting interdisciplinary interactions was that it was desirable to combine directive facilitation of collaborations with organizing events and circumstances where people could meet together in a less formalized way and from which interactions might ensue (Strathern 2005). Partner search facili-ties, such as the database offered by the European Commission, have had a more mixed response. Some people find them useful but many others are uncomfortable with the unknown quality and personality of partners identi-fied in this way.

Evaluating the competence of someone in another discipline can be very difficult and this may be part of the reason why recommendations from others

> **Key Advice 3.1   Useful characteristics in an interdisciplinary researcher**
>
> In interdisciplinary research, personality and attitudes of researchers are at least as important for success as discipline base and specialization. Useful characteristics are:
>
> - flexibility, adaptability, creativity;
> - curiosity about, and willingness to learn from, other disciplines;
> - an open mind to ideas coming from other disciplines and experiences;
> - good communication and listening skills;
> - an ability to bridge the gap between theory and practice;
> - a good team-worker;
> - a willingness to tolerate ambiguity.

are highly valued. It is also worthwhile reading the publications of potential research partners. A clue to a potential research partner's suitability for a larger team effort might be the degree to which they tend to frame their own work within a bigger picture, even if the publication's content is mainly disciplinary.

Another aspect worth considering is the motivation of a potential research partner for joining the collaboration. Why do they want to join the project? What is their goal? What do they intend to do in the project? What might their personal biases be?

The size of consortia can vary greatly reflecting the different needs of different projects. Successful examples can be found of some very large interdisciplinary projects but these have generally spent a great deal of time working together in advance of the specific research project. Generally, once the collaboration becomes larger – more than seven to ten partners – the management required to ensure appropriate progress becomes more demanding and we address some of these challenges in the next chapter.

Interdisciplinary integrators

In structuring a team it is important to consider to what extent the leader, and also perhaps an additional member of the consortium, can fulfil the role of an intermediary between disciplines, facilitating communication and 'translating' between the disciplines (Jeffrey 2003). The required qualities for such an

Case Study 3.2 Are interdisciplinary researchers born or are they made?

The Tyndall Centre is a UK-based interdisciplinary research organization exploring climate change. Its experience reveals that some researchers thrive in an interdisciplinary and interactive environment and adapt their research methods and working habits, while others just dig a little deeper and continue to do things the same way. They report that this does not appear to be related to seniority, nor to disciplinary area: senior engineers may or may not be just as adaptive to an interdisciplinary setting as PhD students. Tyndall raises two interesting questions: 'what are the determinants of inter-disciplinary researchers (are they born or are they made?) and what mix of disciplinarians and inter-disciplinarians is best to do truly creative and useful research?'

Source: Tyndall Centre 2006.

intermediary, according to Jeffrey, are credibility in each discipline and ability to communicate effectively with all parties. The leadership of an interdisciplinary team is a critical role, to which we return in chapter 4, but suffice to say here that any successful interdisciplinary project needs to be led by someone with an appreciation of the perspective of other disciplines and with interdisciplinary integrative skills. However, the ability to span boundaries and mediate between disciplines need not be restricted just to the team leader. In our II-FP5 project, we found an example of this role being played by a PhD student who had no formal integrative responsibilities within the project but who was involved in several tasks and whose field studies of users were an important component linking the researchers. This might lead us to question whether good interdisciplinary researchers are born or made (Case Study 3.2), a theme to which we will return in chapter 5 when we consider the training of interdisciplinary early career researchers.

Conceptualizing the problem

Having begun the process of assembling a team, a key next step is to plan the route in terms of conceptualizing the research problem. This is likely to be an iterative process and any proposed collaborative team at this stage may need to be adjusted to bring in additional disciplines to change the disciplinary focus. Also, as noted earlier, the formulation of the research project may be prescribed by a specific research call or by a client specification for problem-focused research.

Where a research topic is specified by a client, it is important for researchers to give some thought to whether the clients really do understand their own problem. There have been cases where interdisciplinary researchers have persuaded a client to engage jointly in this early problem specification stage, only to find that the potential research contract evaporates as the clients gain a more in-depth understanding of their problem and decide that they no longer need the help of the researchers to resolve it.

Each group of researchers is likely to develop its own preferred method of conceptualizing a research problem. For an interdisciplinary project, a relatively long preliminary research planning phase is recommended, to allow early involvement of all disciplines in formulating the research questions and the overall approach in order to encourage more integrated outputs. If members of the research consortium have not worked together before, this stage may take some time. Developing a common conceptual model for the research and clarifying the contribution of different perspectives will have its challenging moments and a degree of focus along with good 'people skills' will be needed to maintain forward momentum.

Consortium members may vary in the extent of their prior experience with interdisciplinary research. This can result in different levels of comfort with, or commitment to, thorough immersion in interdisciplinarity and it can also result in different expectations. Researchers who have not worked in interdisciplinary projects before may have simplistic understandings of other disciplines, leading to unrealistic expectations. More experienced interdisciplinary researchers may be able to understand better what contribution can be expected from another knowledge domain. The intention is not to turn everyone into a generalist but to recognize and use the different contributions that different disciplines can make to the overall project objective.

Because the universe of exciting interdisciplinary projects is ever-expanding, providing a detailed roadmap for design would be neither possible nor appropriate. We can, however, draw from successful approaches, research literature and our own research and experiences to offer some key points to consider for individuals or teams conceptualizing their own unique problem and planning integration of methods.

Even where a call for funding specifies an interdisciplinary approach, it can be useful to spell out the justification and to emphasize the 'value-added', to think through how joint working can enhance the achievement of project objectives: what can be achieved by integration across disciplines that could not be generated by any one discipline alone? Articulating what could be special about their work can help team members to bond and also to focus on designing for synergy. (As an example, one of us facilitated the growth of an interdisciplinary team which ended up winning significant centre funds from

NASA for work involving plant biology, food engineering and waste management in space; preparation for the reviewers' decision-making site visit led to the team developing the story of how morale-boosting pizza could be made in space; the fun they had with this sparked a new level of team integration that conveyed itself convincingly to the funders.)

Jeffrey suggests that some of the benefits, whether specific to a project or drawing more generally on the potential of interdisciplinarity, include:

- development of new tools which will make further collaborative work more productive;

- appreciation of broader aspects of the problem being addressed;

- learning from the critiques of accepted paradigms and methodological issues voiced by other disciplines; and

- development of a simulation model that can be easily used by people from different disciplines (Jeffrey 2003).

Interdisciplinary projects have an innovative edge over single discipline projects in terms of the interactions between the disciplines. This has two potential consequences. One is that the contribution of each discipline may not be 'cutting-edge' in itself, but the novelty of the proposal derives from the interaction between disciplines. The outcomes of this interdisciplinary edge may not be immediately obvious and may become clearer as the research project progresses. Secondly, the innovative nature of the work often makes it unrealistic to expect an interdisciplinary team's plans to be fully formed on the basis of the research proposal. As researchers learn the strengths of different disciplines during the research process, unanticipated opportunities can arise. Mechanisms for taking advantage of these should be included in the research design. This means that a degree of flexibility will need to be built into the design: if the potential of interdisciplinarity for innovation and creativity is to be achieved, then evolution should be anticipated and valued.

One way of ensuring flexibility is to incorporate it explicitly as a virtue when writing a proposal. While it would be foolhardy to say 'trust us, we'll make it up as we go along', it would be knowledgeable and responsible to say, for example, 'we are including a plan for formative evaluation/critical self-reflection to run throughout the project, so that we can take stock and make informed changes if new opportunities for synergies arise'. Sometimes having an external advisory group, stakeholder committee or critical friend as internal evaluator can provide both a sounding board and credibility should changes need to be made during the course of the project.

Having considered how to conceptualize the research problem, we now turn to the challenging task of designing a research project that integrates disciplines, rather than simply allowing them to work in parallel on the same problem.

Research design strategies

Organizing the work

Ideally, the conceptualization of the research problem will have achieved an overall goal and approach for the project to which each specific competence can make a contribution. In planning for integration to achieve the goal, there are a number of possible ways to organize different disciplines and define interfaces between partners. For example, a classic method of organizing research projects is into workpackages with specific partners responsible for, and committed to, a particular workpackage. However, this method needs careful consideration, as project designs involving several workpackages proceeding autonomously, with the expectation of becoming integrated (only) at the end of the project, tend not to provide strong levels of integration. It is extremely difficult to retrofit an integration of workpackages that have proceeded on the basis of different basic assumptions. Another somewhat similar approach is to define the expected products of the interdisciplinary collaboration, to assign responsibility for each and to specify a budget that allows them to be achieved (Jeffrey 2003). Case studies, with different partners responsible for different cases, are another approach that might be used in some projects. Again, sensitivity to the relationship between components is important. Lingard *et al.*, for example, give a cautionary note about the scheduling of case studies (Lingard *et al.* 2007). Their research consisted of a series of case studies, the first of which was in a medical setting, which they suggested, due to the power and authoritative nature of the medical context vis-à-vis their other cases, framed the issue in medical terms, becoming the authoritative case study with a disproportionate impact on the furthering of knowledge from other case studies.

So, as tempting as tidy compartmentalized approaches to design might be, interdisciplinary integration is a vital and dynamic process that needs to take place at all levels of a project, throughout its lifetime. Of course, even one human mind, let alone a team, requires conceptual organization to progress understanding, so that some division of responsibilities is only sensible. Activities and processes to stimulate integration need to be planned into the project design from the start. In many research projects integration is achieved through an iterative process of working, talking and revising. Meetings and visits are a key component of integration and may include exchanges of staff between organizations for short periods of time. This 'dynamic' approach also provides a degree of flexibility which is particularly desirable in interdisciplinary research projects in order to make the most of unforeseen insights and serendipitous interactions that may arise.

Finally, as noted earlier, integration requires all partners to become and stay committed to the overall objectives of the research project; this can be addressed at least in part by planning for stimulating, interactive events (including celebrations of milestones reached during the expedition). Key Advice 3.2 illustrates key

Key Advice 3.2 Integration activities at key stages of a project

During bid writing

- informal links and networks of researchers;
- cross-disciplinary meetings;
- links among researchers within their own institution;
- links with other research institutions;
- informal links and networks between researchers and stakeholders.

During project

- informal links and networks of researchers;
- informal links and networks of researchers and stakeholders;
- cross-disciplinary meetings;
- cross-disciplinary interactions with stakeholders;
- links with other research institutions.

After award

- interdisciplinary publications;
- informal links and networks of researchers;
- informal links and networks of researchers and stakeholders;
- links with other institutions;
- further joint funding applications.

integration activities at various stages of a project (during proposal writing stage, during the project and post-award) (based on Meagher and Lyall 2007a).

Integration approaches

It is worth reflecting on what is meant by the term 'integration' and how integration can be recognized. Repko suggests that:

- integration involves combining or uniting ideas, data and/or knowledge to create a new whole which is greater than the sum of its parts compared with previous understanding;

- integration must consider the nature of the new 'whole', the cognitive activity involved in the integration process and the contribution of the disciplines to the new whole (Repko 2008).

In Repko's view this is not like fitting together the parts of a jigsaw puzzle (an analogy that is sometimes used). In a jigsaw puzzle, the parts fit together exactly and produce a predetermined picture. In an interdisciplinary project, the parts do not necessarily fit in so well with each other and they do not produce an output that is predetermined or has existed before. (In fact, the director of the UK's £1 billion cross-funder, interdisciplinary Living with Environmental Change initiative, often illustrates interdisciplinarity with a picture of a living slime mould, perhaps unattractive to some but undeniably a dynamic entity as it shifts its shape according to what it comes across in its environment.) Thus, the process of integration is particularly complex and indeterminate but it is, nevertheless, a key factor in enhancing the likelihood that interdisciplinary projects can produce results above and beyond addressing issues in an monodisciplinary way.

A number of different ways of integrating disciplines have been used and suggested. These might include:

- providing an integrated assessment of technologies and systems;
- designing diagnostic measures of system performance;
- offering general perspectives on geographical areas and a holistic analysis of the problems;
- combining research techniques and methods;
- developing approaches to the modelling and monitoring of systems;
- combining social and natural science datasets;
- developing tools, techniques and methodologies to support decision-making;
- facilitating interdisciplinary dialogue and the scrutiny of key concepts (Lowe and Phillipson 2006).

Given the need for greater flexibility in interdisciplinary proposals, where and how should applicants draw the boundaries? Much more than discipline-based projects, interdisciplinary projects have to undergo a preliminary research phase that is open-ended. As we discussed in chapter 2, this is particularly true for problem-focused interdisciplinary projects, compared with more academically oriented interdisciplinary research where it is probably clearer from the outset which disciplines need to collaborate to give the required interdisciplinary outcomes.

This initial phase involves trying out a range of possible boundaries to the problem to see which gives the best 'fit', allowing the outputs of this analysis to determine the disciplines to be involved (for relevant techniques see Flood and

Jackson 1991; Checkland and Scholes 1990). This should be part of the process of developing a research proposal and it should be clear from the proposal:

1 what has been done prior to submitting the bid;

2 that the outcome described in the bid represents a justifiable decision on the project's boundaries.

The outcome of the initial exploratory phase should be:

- a specification of the range of issues that is central to the research problem;

- a description of how they interact with one another to create or sustain the problem;

- a (general) plan for how these interactions can be modified to deliver an implementable, synergistic solution.

The early, relatively open-ended phase at the start of a new project may therefore be quite lengthy and complex.

Cognitive activity involved in the integration process involves perspective-taking (examining the research problem from the standpoint of the interested disciplines) and holistic thinking (Repko 2008: 120–24). Socio-cognitive frameworks proposed to achieve this include common-group learning, modelling, negotiation among experts or integration by a leader (Rossini and Porter 1979). Modelling is often seen as a key approach to better understanding and responding to complex real-world problems where models can be used to synthesize knowledge, to better comprehend unknowns and their consequences, and to provide decision support (Badham 2010). While models can only ever be partial representations of the real world, different models may reveal different facets of a problem's complexity. Both the process of model-building and the model itself may provide a systematic way of developing a more comprehensive understanding of key aspects of the problem (Badham 2010). Thus, as illustrated in Case Study 3.3, the act of model-building can help researchers from different disciplines define a research question, set the parameters for the research and together focus on a shared problem (e.g. Tait *et al.* 2006b; Suk *et al.* 2008; Smith *et al.* 2009).

Yet, as Jeffrey observes, the type of information derived from social scientific observation does not necessarily lend itself readily to the structured, simplified formulation required by modellers (Jeffrey 2003). So the development of mathematical models, for example, might provide one way of achieving synthesis but such models can prematurely close down a research problem. Conceptual modelling/framework development can address some of the challenges of joint problem framing: modelling can simulate futures, help to construct new visions and not just 'fit the facts'. Models can either act to place boundaries or bring in new disciplines.

Case Study 3.3 Modelling as an integrative technique

An interdisciplinary team from the UK, comprising senior researchers drawing expertise from health system economics, economic modelling, health and social care and risk analysis, examined the economy-wide impact of pandemic influenza on the United Kingdom (Smith *et al.* 2009).

The objectives of the study were to estimate the potential economic impact on the UK of pandemic influenza, associated behavioural responses, school closures and vaccination. The research design comprised a computable general equilibrium model of the UK economy which was specified for various combinations of mortality and morbidity from pandemic influenza, vaccine efficacy, school closures and prophylactic absenteeism (where healthy people avoid social contact, including not going to work) using published data. The main outcome measures included the economic impact of various scenarios with different pandemic severity, vaccination, school closure and prophylactic absenteeism specified in terms of gross domestic product, output from different economic sectors, and equivalent variation.

The case demonstrates how the act of model-building can help researchers from different disciplines define a research question, set the boundaries for the research and together focus on a shared problem. Within this study, one person conceived the idea of a computable general equilibrium application for influenza and advised on the modelling and scenario-building; one was responsible for the modelling, the underlying dataset and the construction of the modelling scenarios and shocks; two of the researchers conceived the idea of the transition point based on social networking theory, and advised on the scenarios and vaccination strategies, and contributed to the drafting of the paper.

A qualitative risk analysis framework developed for a UK Foresight study on the Detection and Identification of Infectious Diseases (Tait *et al.* 2006b; Suk *et al.* 2008) played a similar role. This risk assessment covered human, plant and animal diseases in the UK and Africa in the years 2015 and 2030. Through engaging a diverse pool of experts, a model conceptualizing disease spread as the outcome of interactions among sources, pathways and drivers was developed. This model was then used to conduct a Delphi survey of experts. This methodology provided a transferable framework for those who need to integrate a wide range of perspectives and factors into their planning and analyses.

Since models do not always act as integrating forces other approaches to integration might be used. Newell *et al.* recommend the use of a 'conceptual template' to support early developmental stages of integrative research efforts (Newell *et al.* 2005). Their template includes high level-concepts (in their case, essential features of human-environment problems) and more specific concepts such as change, positive feedback and causal loops. They suggest that, when clustered, these latter lists can provide points of connectivity across disciplines, and so can be called 'nexus concepts' ('basic concepts that appear to be different, when seen from existing disciplinary points-of-view, but that turn out to be equivalent when looked at more fundamentally'). In addition to helping in the investigation of the very nature of integrative research teams, Newell *et al.* recommend this as a practical approach to integration processes; for example, in the developmental dialogues of an interdisciplinary project, the conceptual framework can be useful by simultaneously providing a high-level checklist of key major research areas while also encouraging individuals to search for perhaps surprising equivalencies across their fields, and to develop shared language and concepts.

Extra time and effort

It would be naïve and unrealistic to design an interdisciplinary research project without planning to take extra time and effort, relative to work in a single discipline. The Swedish sustainable environment funding programme, MISTRA

Illustration 3.1 Develop a shared language from the start

(Swedish Foundation for Strategic Environmental Research), reminds applicants (Case Study 3.4) about many of these extra efforts, as well as the extra time that will be needed, so that they can design sound, credible strategies for integrating disciplines.

Case Study 3.4   MISTRA: Advice to applicants

Based on experience with previous interdisciplinary research projects, the Swedish sustainable environment funding programme, MISTRA, recommends that future applicants pay special attention to:

- programme-wide meeting places;

- a shared analytical framework and language;

- developing a team spirit;

- conscious leadership;

- interdisciplinary quality control.

Its website also encourages grant applicants to remember that:

- Preparing a proposal that cuts across disciplinary boundaries and boundaries between research and practical use takes time – much longer than most people think. Make time and create places to meet, and invest in developing a team spirit.

- Careful thought needs to be given to how a programme can provide value to users, while still meeting researchers' needs in terms of career development.

- Interdisciplinary research often takes longer than research within a single discipline. Plan sufficient time to allow for this.

- A MISTRA programme often requires experienced researchers with both depth and breadth. There therefore needs to be a balance between senior researchers and postgraduate students.

- Avoid having large numbers of participants involved in the programme on a limited part-time basis, since this makes it more difficult to achieve the shared goals of the programme.

- The programme manager is a key figure in ensuring that the programme achieves its objectives. Being the manager of a MISTRA

Case Study 3.4 *Continued*

programme is generally a full-time job. Think through who the most
suitable person is to take on the challenging task of leading your
group.

- Make every effort to ensure that communication between researchers
  and users is a two-way process. One-way presentations of ideas and
  research results by researchers rarely inspire a sense of involvement
  and commitment on the part of intended users.

Source: MISTRA. The Swedish Foundation for Strategic Environmental Research,
http://www.mistra.org.

Aspects such as team-building and communication need to be addressed
at the project design stage and reappraised regularly as illustrated by a quote
from one of our II-FP5 interviewees:

> At first it took several meetings to synchronise people coming from different
> disciplines. Some tend to see only their own positions. As co-ordinator you have
> to do a lot of communication to bring all partners to a common understanding of
> the problem and a position where everybody accepts everybody without knowing
> in full detail what the other partner has to do. Also definition of interfaces
> between partners and their work is highly time consuming. (Interviewee, II-FP5
> project, Tait *et al.* 2002)

Some of the key aspects for successful interdisciplinary research identified in
the II-FP5 project were:

- the need to build conditions favourable to learning across disciplines,
  implying a trade-off between recognition of individual partners'
  domains of expertise and competence and the organization of
  situations in which other partners can learn from the most expert in
  the field;

- the need for collective decisions at the different stages of the project to
  enrich methods and models, adapt them to the specific needs, perhaps
  providing unexpected results that require reconsideration of some
  aspects of the project;

- the need to set aside specific coordination time to prevent
  misunderstandings, find a clear agreement on the problem focus,
  questions, methods and wording of reports.

This time and effort have to be built into the research design, in particular, to allow integration of disciplines and this has to be planned into the early stages and throughout a project:

> If there is to be integration between scientists and social scientists this should be from an early stage in the research process. This is to ensure that data appropriate for use by all parties is collected. The dialogue between scientists and social scientists should be ongoing, from the involvement of social scientists in the experimental design stages, to the involvement of science in the policy design stages. This is not an easy process but has the potential to prevent some of the difficulties encountered in interdisciplinary working. (Interviewee, Meagher and Lyall 2007a: 20)

Time is needed for learning across disciplines but also for people to express their domain of expertise. But an inevitable aspect of building interdisciplinary research capacity is the realization that no one is an expert. Allowing time to overcome the barriers caused by this discomfort is important when building capacity among researchers who are used to thinking of themselves as 'experts'.

There is a need to make opportunities for collective discussion that allows methods and models to be enriched. A useful tactic may be to plan 'site visits' to 'internal stakeholders' in the various disciplines involved, so that others can learn about each discipline and its approaches (Meagher and Lyall 2007a: 20).

In general, more time and effort have to be directed to meetings and to coordination than in a single discipline project, to generate positive advances, but also to prevent misunderstandings. The consequent resource implications will have to be justified to funders who themselves need to recognize that extra resources are likely to be required if an interdisciplinary project is to be successful. Extra time for deliberate steps to foster sound interdisciplinary synergy is not time wasted if the output means that progress is made in an intractable area, if results are achieved that go beyond anything that could be expected from a monodisciplinary research project, or if the nature of the research itself demands the involvement of many disciplines. This is again exemplified by a quote from our II-FP5 project: 'if we work in a monodisciplinary way, we can work without the extra time, but the problem is that the results are not so interesting in contrast with interdisciplinary results' (Interviewee, II-FP5 project, Tait *et al.* 2002).

There are exceptions, of course: interdisciplinary research may, conversely, speed up the delivery of research outcomes. Sometimes discipline-based research can reach an impasse and bringing in insights from a new discipline may actually save time compared with trying to solve problems within the constraints of that single discipline; interdisciplinary research also has the potential to provide answers where no answer would otherwise be found.

A good interdisciplinary proposal should be goal-oriented and demonstrate synergies between methods and disciplines. More so than a monodisciplinary project, interdisciplinary projects may need to develop and change as they proceed, as noted above. Over-planning could constrain a project's ability to be responsive to change.

Summary

There is a wide spectrum of different types of interdisciplinary project and each will have its specific demands. However, some generic issues exist and this chapter has identified some of the key points to consider in negotiating the design of interdisciplinary research projects.

In considering different ways of identifying possible team members, we have highlighted the need to focus on not only the personalities and needs of individuals, but also a careful examination of the disciplinary composition of the research consortium. In particular, we noted the need to be aware of basic assumptions from within different disciplines in order to be prepared to negotiate these effectively toward collaborative integration. We have emphasized the importance of deliberate efforts to conceptualize a proposal and to enable different disciplines to make their contributions. A key component of a plan for any interdisciplinary project is to ensure that the different disciplines are integrated rather than working in parallel. We have provided some suggestions of methods or mechanisms for doing so, to ensure that a dynamic process of interaction takes place throughout the life of the project. We have highlighted the importance of the research design, particularly for complex interdisciplinary projects, and the need to allow sufficient time to develop sound interdisciplinary plans or proposals while still building flexibility into the research design to allow the benefits of unforeseen outcomes to be incorporated. Some of these points are summarized in Key Advice 3.3.

Key Advice 3.3 Checklist for a good interdisciplinary research proposal/project design

- Specify clearly why an interdisciplinary approach is needed, which type of interdisciplinary approach is envisaged and which disciplines should be involved. (Where this has been based on a formal analysis of the problem domain, describe the process briefly.)

- Describe how the disciplines involved will be integrated and how this relates to the type of interdisciplinarity involved; demonstrate how the quality of integration will be assured.

- Describe the leadership role and management strategy to deliver the desired outcomes.

Key Advice 3.3 *Continued*

- Summarize the interdisciplinary skills of the researchers involved.

- Where relevant, develop a clear plan for the involvement of end users and stakeholders in the project, including contingency plans for recognized pitfalls. Indicate clearly the benefits to stakeholders and the roles of stakeholders in contributing to the project.

- Budget for, and justify, the additional resources needed (e.g. for longer time periods, more interactive meetings and opportunities to reflect and refine strategies).

- Describe how interdisciplinarity will be reflected in the project outputs and outcomes.

This chapter has primarily considered issues that are important during the research planning stage. In the next chapter we will identify successful strategies for building and managing interdisciplinary research projects.

Questions

For researchers

1 How might you ensure that you are networked with the disciplines that you may wish to work with in the future?

2 How would you reassure a prospective funder that your interdisciplinary research design will actually work?

3 How would you reassure a prospective funder that your interdisciplinary research design will deliver added value?

4 How would you balance thoughtful planning with opportunistic seizing of new, creative lines of enquiry?

For institutional leaders

1 How might you provide stimulating events to assist your researchers and their collaborators in developing ideas, designs and proposals for interdisciplinary projects?

2 Do you have a system for 'early alerts' as to interdisciplinary funding opportunities?

3 Do you have qualified and enthusiastic academic-related support staff who can help with the hard work of the early design stage?

For research funders

1 Given the extra effort and resources needed to run interdisciplinary projects, it is only worthwhile doing them if there is a realistic expectation of some sort of pay-off. By what criteria would you make this decision?

2 How would you judge the degree to which the proposed team either has become integrated or is on track to become integrated so as to lead to synergistic results?

4

Making the Expedition a Success

Managing interdisciplinary projects and teams

Introduction

In chapter 3 we considered the planning phases involved in designing an inter-disciplinary project. In this chapter we reflect on what happens once the project begins. While this can be done as an individual (and interdisciplinary careers are considered in chapter 6), it is more often conducted as a team-based activity. We noted in chapter 3 that interdisciplinary teams may involve practitioners particularly where a practical issue is being addressed. Although focusing on predominantly academic interdisciplinary teams, this chapter is relevant to such projects, with particular features specifically related to user engagement considered further in chapter 8. In this chapter we will offer some guidance on:

- getting the project established;
- managing the team;
- key roles and traits needed for success;
- continuing the collaboration.

Achieving successful interdisciplinary integration requires attention not just to the outcome but to the process, or, to extend the metaphor, it is not always the destination but the journey that matters. Among the key challenges we will consider are:

- ensuring that the team is focusing on the same project;
- balancing a commonality of vision with strength of input from multiple disciplines;
- developing leadership and/or co-ordination functions, and institutional supports, that work effectively for interdisciplinary teams;
- facilitating a productive evolution of the work over time.

This chapter will therefore go beyond conventional understanding of generic project management to become a guide tailored to the management of interdisciplinary efforts. Despite differences in scale, the points we raise should prove useful whether the interdisciplinary group is a large consortium or a small team, whether the interdisciplinary effort is a small, focused project primarily based in one institution or a multi-project programme or geographically distributed initiative. We will first consider how to start a project as a well-grounded team effort. Secondly, we will consider how to maintain the project impetus and take it toward successful completion. Then we will consider the nature and function of leadership and coordination in such projects, and we will finish with a few thoughts on evaluation, evolution and sustainability beyond original funding.

Beginning the project

Why this stage matters

In setting off on a prolonged adventure, preparation is key. Usually, several givens are established by the start of the research project that will shape the preparation needed: the budget will be fixed (either by the size of the grant received or perhaps by the research contract or the time available [in the case of a PhD project]) and most of the senior members of the team will have been agreed. The institutional context(s) may already have been determined but should not be ignored. Also, the project goals will have been identified, even if in general terms, along with the general direction to be taken and the overall methods (techniques, approaches to problem-solving). With all this established, where does preparation come in? Where is there scope for enhancing the probability that the project will be successful?

In fact, despite all the fixed parameters, the more closely interdisciplinary teamwork is examined, the more important the early stages turn out to be. The extra time taken at the start of an interdisciplinary project is becoming increasingly recognized, not just as an irritating fact of life but as a critical component of success. As we discussed in the previous chapter, extra time, and indeed extra effort, is needed compared to setting off on a solo journey, in large part because of the need to build trust, understanding and communication capacity across a number of individuals and intellectual approaches. It also takes time to develop a shared vision and to negotiate an explicit allocation of roles and responsibilities within the team, framed appropriately against institutional and intellectual contexts.

Shared vision

The National Academy of Sciences survey of interdisciplinary activity in industrial and national laboratories found that the main reason for failure

Illustration 4.1 Strive for effective teamwork

of interdisciplinary projects was the failure of the team to function effectively together (National Academies 2005). It suggested this was because of individuals placing more emphasis on their own work than the team vision, devaluing the contribution of some team members, or because of lack of leadership. Inadequate time to establish close working relationships and insufficient funding were given as contributory reasons. Lack of support from senior staff members and, occasionally, differences in research culture were given as additional reasons. This survey thus suggests that close attention needs to be paid to these aspects of collaborative research in interdisciplinary projects. Our own II-FP5 case studies (Case Study 3.1) offered a number of key steps towards successful interdisciplinarity (Key Advice 4.1): clearly, while continuing throughout the project, these steps must be taken in the early stages if the project is to succeed.

Most projects are initiated with a kick-off meeting. From this point on, each of the project team members needs to manage tensions between their contribution to the project and their focus on other aspects of their careers. The general view is that integration efforts need to be weighted towards the beginning of the project. This is a crucial time and it is well worth putting in a great deal of effort at the start to create commitment among the group members and ensure a common vision and strategy. Among the interviewees for our II-FP5 project the difficulties of the initiation stage were stressed with the need to 'overcome basic prejudices', understand the language, tools and culture of

---

Key Advice 4.1   Key steps towards successful interdisciplinary team-based projects

- team-building;

- developing a common culture (although sometimes cultural differences can be creative);

- clarifying the contribution of different perspectives;

- developing a common conceptual model for all researchers/ stakeholders;

- developing a common understanding of the language and tools relevant to the project;

- developing a common understanding of the division of labour and how changes are to be handled;

- developing a tolerance for ambiguity;

- achieving a balance between agreement on the 'common purpose' and the creative tension brought about by differences.

---

different disciplines, and arrive at a common view and targets. This process could take more than one year.

There can be a creative tension between the need to achieve a common culture and the richness of ideas that can be brought to bear on a research problem by having several research cultures involved. For academically oriented interdisciplinary research, this common culture could be the starting point from which to build a new academic discipline. In team-based, problem-focused interdisciplinary research, the original tension may remain right to the end of the project with no lasting cultural change for those involved: some individuals may simply return to their home disciplines after a transitory involvement, others may continue to participate in interdisciplinary teams. For a solo project, such as a PhD thesis, and also for some individuals involved in interdisciplinary work, there can be a change in individual worldview that leads to a long-term, interdisciplinary career rich with opportunities.

A number of different actions have been taken to achieve a common project objective. Workshops, off-site retreats, meetings and field trips have all been found to be helpful in creating understanding and trust within collaborations (e.g. Marzano *et al.* 2006; Bruce *et al.* 2004; Stokols *et al.* 2008b). Visioning or brainstorming activities can give rise simultaneously to intellectual stimulation, sharing of assumptions and reframing of conceptual frameworks;

Key Advice 4.2 Interdisciplinary workshops as analogues to interdisciplinary initiative-building

Through both facilitating the development of many interdisciplinary initiatives and designing and facilitating numerous interdisciplinary workshops, one of us (Meagher) has come to see the phases undergone by a carefully designed interdisciplinary workshop as a foreshortened analogue to interdisciplinary initiative-building. Some considerations that go into designing the exercises and flow of such a 'microcosm' workshop might usefully reflect similar stages in longer term initiative development. And, of course, such a workshop should be set in an attractive retreat setting, with plenty of food and opportunities to interact informally, and with the detail of the exercises making them fun and creative. Steps include:

Design: clarification of workshop goals frame the entire design including tone, participant selection, structure and flow, types of interactions, specific exercises, nature of the workshop product.

Charge to the group: leaders (e.g. a 'champion' and the professional facilitator) articulate workshop goals and how they will be achieved so that participants share understanding of objectives and a sense that they have a joint responsibility to create something worthwhile.

Introductions: all participants briefly introduce their interests, demonstrating their array of strengths.

First task/exercise: brainstorming (no wrong answers), future-oriented and deliberately set in no one participant's 'territory' ... allowing participants (accustomed to being experts) to realize that no one is an expert in this new topic, so they can relax and pitch in.

Accomplishing the first task: allows participants to begin to build confidence.

Second task/exercise: a bit harder, requiring more thought and interaction.

Accomplishing the second task: gives a greater sense of confidence and a dawning realization that the mix of people present made it possible.

Third task/exercise: harder still, and drawing on input from all perspectives.

Key Advice 4.2 *Continued*

Accomplishing the third task: gives a sense of intellectual excitement, digging into something challenging, and a growth of mutual respect. (There may well be other exercises to help individuals understand each others' points of view.)

Final task/exercise: bringing all tasks together to generate a tangible 'product' that will be useful in the future (e.g. identification of key research questions that cannot be tackled by any one discipline).

Accomplishing the final task: reminds participants how interdependent they are, with all their input needed to generate that pinnacle product. With a growing commitment to quality, participants (now respecting each other) discuss, negotiate and achieve workable solutions so that differences of perspective are accommodated within an integrated product of which all can be proud.

Follow-up: with workshop results shared, participants are reminded of the solid accomplishment they have created together, and their new history of interactions, so that some may take steps toward future collaboration.

---

ideally leading to genuinely innovative insights or solutions (e.g. Gray 2008 and Key Advice 4.2). The value of meetings that allow 'naïve' questions to be asked has been stressed (e.g. Tait *et al.* 2002). These questions, which may seem naïve at one level, point to some of the taken-for-granted assumptions that have been made and can often open up new angles of thinking for the experts in particular areas. These types of discussions require careful facilitation and leadership to ensure an atmosphere of confidence where no one feels demeaned by not knowing about the other disciplines. Blackwell *et al.*, while acknowledging the usefulness of well-run workshops in early stages of interdisciplinarity, warn that these are often conducted poorly and that, if not run with expertise, they can put an initiative in jeopardy from the start (Blackwell *et al.* 2009).

Starting with an iterative process involving working, talking and then revising ideas (Tait *et al.* 2002) has been used as one approach. The value of informal social gatherings in engendering good working relationships has also been frequently emphasized (e.g. Bruce *et al.* 2004; Meagher and Lyall 2009). Not for nothing has 'breaking bread together' been regarded through the ages as a way to promote bonding.

Another important aspect for research leaders is to create spaces for learning between disciplines (Case Study 4.1) – interdisciplinarity does not happen automatically simply by bringing disciplines together; it requires some specific opportunities to allow disciplines to learn from each other. One suggested approach (Hinrichs 2008) is for each disciplinary partner to select key readings from their own discipline to be read and discussed by the whole team. In this way learning about the contribution of each discipline is enabled. Marzano *et al.* suggest better understanding may be achieved if collaborators attempt to 'teach' their discipline rather than just to 'communicate' (Marzano *et al.* 2006). More radically, Marzano *et al.* also suggest getting people to present on each others' discipline, asking social scientists to explain their substantive knowledge of the topic and natural scientists to explain how they generate their knowledge. This very task is assigned to PhD students studying in the interdisciplinary CHANGE (Certificate on Humans and the Global Environment) programme originating in an NSF IGERT (Integrative Graduate Education and Research Traineeship grant – see also chapter 5) on coupled human and natural systems; matched pairs of students each identify a favourite paper in their own discipline for presentation by their counterpart in a different discipline, and vice versa.[1]

Having emphasized the start of the project, there are situations where it is not possible for disciplines to relate to each other until there are some project results around which to coalesce. For example, an information/engineering project (Tait *et al.* 2002) involving psychologists found that it was difficult to generate a common view of the objectives of the project from the start. The technicians felt they were not able to explain to the social scientists exactly what they wanted to do from the technical point of view and their feeling was that the social scientists were not focusing on the project itself but on very broad questions. Meeting together helped to resolve some issues but real progress in understanding was only made when there were some actual results to discuss, in this case when the first prototype had been developed. It may be that discussion at the start of the project can only go so far in breaking down the communication barriers.

Trust-building

Discussion can lead to conflict and be threatening to team members (Lingard *et al.* 2007). Although aimed at reducing differences, discussion may end up highlighting them (Marzano *et al.* 2006). It may be tempting to skim over conflict in order to proceed with the project but the danger with this approach is that the conflict will re-emerge at a later stage, and may do so with devastating impact and with little time left to resolve the issues. On the other hand, successful interdisciplinary researchers do need to be tolerant of ambiguity and accept that there will not always be agreement within the team: focusing too early on an agreed approach may curtail other, more profitable, avenues of enquiry. Effective leadership should be able to manage this creative tension.

Case Study 4.1   Connecting different disciplines: building a team to develop a new technology

Research and development (R&D) in nanosciences and nanotechnologies challenge scientists and engineers to integrate knowledge from different fields in order to create something new: in this case, in an example of problem-focused interdisciplinarity, the development of anti-viral nanoparticles and their incorporation into various coating materials.

The presence of participants from different disciplines in this project resulted in important and necessary contributions to the development of new anti-viral nanomaterials, including:

1   The development of a shared research object which may never have evolved without close collaboration between material engineers and biologists.

2   The expansion of the repertoire of material engineers, by adding biological (anti-viral) properties to their existing conceptual models of materials.

3   The development of new test procedures where the requirements of one disciplinary group initiated change in the standard practice of the other disciplinary group.

The participants in Sutherland Olsen's study did not share a common history, often regarded as helpful in smoothing the interfaces between different functional groups. This project was fairly typical of many R&D projects in its temporary nature where participants did not have time to establish relationships of trust or formalize ways of working which might have made it easier to learn from one another. The common goal, in this case of creating a new anti-viral material for use in a future flu epidemic, served to pull all the participants together and gave direction to their activities.

Sutherland Olsen demonstrates that history matters and indeed the various histories all exert a great influence on the project by providing the theories and concepts the participants use to interpret and understand, and also the practice with which they are familiar. Looking at the traditions, which have evolved over time in the different disciplines, helps to understand why collaboration between different groups of participants can be problematic.

Looking for shared objects to facilitate understanding can be rather haphazard: developing a more systematic technique when establishing interdisciplinary and multidisciplinary projects would be helpful, as would a greater awareness of the disciplinary differences when trying to resolve conflicts in projects. Both might lead to faster and more reliable solutions.

This suggests that managers of multidisciplinary projects, where there is a high element of exploration, should be aware of the variety in the types of learning going on within teams and acknowledge the different requirements in terms of time, proximity and negotiations which may be necessary depending on the circumstances. They should also endeavour to create an environment conducive to interdisciplinary learning and the development of novel solutions.

Source: Sutherland Olsen, 2009.

McCulloch advocates recognizing that disagreement is an expected stage in a team's development rather than a disruption to be avoided, particularly at the early stages of a project (McCulloch 2007). Thus, the expectation is that the 'storming' phase of the project can quickly move on to the 'performing' phase. However, it is true that ongoing conflict can result in stasis in the research project at its initiation. Particularly when teams are dispersed geographically, trust may pose a particular challenge. Again, face-to-face interactions make a difference, as do behaviours creating an open environment characterized by mutual respect (e.g. Stokols *et al.* 2008a).

Communication and mutual understanding

One of the key issues identified by many in interdisciplinary research projects is the difficulty of communication (e.g. Tait *et al.* 2002; Greaves and Grant 2010; Bracken and Oughton 2006). In addition to the potential divisiveness of specialized jargon, a term used within one discipline may have a very different meaning when used in another. Different 'languages' between the disciplines mean that even when partners think they understand each other it can become apparent later in the research that their understanding differed – and problems in aligning strands of work can have occurred before this belated recognition. The same word may be associated with different concepts in different disciplines, e.g. the word 'model' used in engineering is rather different from an economics model. An example is given in this quote from the II-FP5 project in the context of an information technology project:

> We were talking about interfaces, and when I was talking about interfaces, I was talking about ... the interfaces for how the system would make its operations and functions available for the staff, in the context of the control room. But then, when *they* were talking about interfaces, they were talking both the graphical interfaces,

but also about the interfaces in the computer systems! The interfaces between the different components. All the time you have a kind of different representation of the problem you're talking about. You'll go on for several hours talking about what you think is the same problem. But you're talking about different problems. (Interviewee, II-FP5 project, Tait *et al*. 2002)

A number of different strategies have been advocated for overcoming communications problems, such as developing a project-specific glossary. People would be unlikely to consult a glossary which was simply handed to them, but the process of developing a glossary and the discussions this involved have been found to be valuable (Tait *et al*. 2002). Jeffrey advocates the use of diagrammatic representations, graphs, sketches or other pictorial representations to help clarify ideas and descriptions (Jeffrey 2003). The issue of common language may become less of a challenge as the project progresses and a common understanding is achieved.

As well as the language challenge, interdisciplinary projects need to tackle the question of different disciplinary cultures. Aspects of differing research cultures were touched on in the previous chapter. Addressing issues of different cultures of research may involve appreciating questions such as, 'What counts as research evidence? What are valid research methodologies?' Or, indeed, 'What are important questions?'

The time frames of relevance can be very different, for example, where geologists, dealing with millions of years, work with social scientists who may be dealing with months (see Case Study 4.2). There may be differences in what are regarded as sufficient sample sizes or in the accuracy expected; for example, inputs into economic models may have an error of 50 per cent, which would be completely untenable to natural scientists (Tait *et al*. 2002). Armsworth *et al*. highlight the different approaches to regression analysis techniques adopted by ecologists and economists (Armsworth *et al*. 2009). More generally, standards for what counts as good quality work may not be intuitively obvious across disciplines, again underscoring the importance of team members coming to know and trust each other.

Difficulties may be experienced in explaining the contribution that the different disciplines will make, in regard to their varying epistemologies. Lingard *et al*. note, for example, that in qualitative research, the writing up stage is part of the process of sense-making and not just a reporting of findings (Lingard *et al*. 2007). This approach is different from that of the natural sciences.

Differing project-oriented perspectives can have implications for the research design. Lélé and Norgaard identify the value commitments that may be hidden, for example, in a scientific assessment of the best way of managing forests favouring different kinds of outcome (e.g. biodiversity, fuel wood production, watershed management, timber production, fodder and leaf manure) (Lélé and Norgaard 2005). Similarly, researchers in one discipline may prefer a particular way of categorizing phenomena and may not be open to different ways of seeing the

Case Study 4.2   IHOPE: working on different timescales

Human history and earth system history have traditionally been developed independently, with little interaction among the academic communities. Separate methods of describing these histories have been developed, and there have been few attempts to integrate these histories and information. Recent recognition that current earth system changes are strongly associated with the changes in the coupled human-environment system make the integration of human history and earth system history an important step in understanding the factors leading to global change, and in developing coping and adaptation strategies for the future.

The Integrated History and future Of the People on Earth (IHOPE) is an international network of researchers and research projects that shares knowledge with the intention of ensuring a sustainable future for humanity and the planet. The IHOPE initiative therefore aims to contribute to understanding of climate change through the integration of human history with earth system history, by bringing together archaeological studies of humans interacting with the environment (e.g. in prehistory or Roman times) with (very different) studies based on large-scale highly quantitative models covering millions of years.

Source: http://www.aimes.ucar.edu/ihope.

subject. Again Lélé and Norgaard give an example of this based on agricultural scientists shifting from working on agricultural soils to working on questions of sustainability in forests where categorization of soil-types may not transfer unproblematically from one approach to the other (Lélé and Norgaard 2005).

There may also be imbalances of power within a research consortium. Societally, different disciplines and different interdisciplinary combinations are valued differently, resulting in some disciplines commanding more attention and resources (Lélé and Norgaard 2005). As a result researchers may be either arrogant or defensive, depending on their discipline, in ways that will need to be addressed in a research project (Marzano *et al.* 2006). Many social scientists have felt that they were involved in a project team as a 'token' and only expected to have input on the social impacts of the issue, not to the project as a whole (Tait *et al.* 2002). Marzano *et al.* suggest that defensiveness becomes less of a problem where people are confident because they have experienced due respect from colleagues (Marzano *et al.* 2006), but this kind of trust can only be engendered over time. Again, it is important to begin to foster this kind of attitude at the very start of a project.

Whether or not there are differences in power, there may be differences in responses among different individuals and disciplinary 'sets' of individuals. For example, an empirical study (Stokols *et al.* 2005) found that, within one interdisciplinary centre, Medical School neuroscience investigators reported consistently more positive scores than School of Social Ecology behavioural scientists on: scientific integration, satisfaction, enjoyment and appreciation.

A related issue which could occur in any project is raised by researchers who seek to tailor their research to personal or political objectives, in a way that is likely to lead to bias in the results. This kind of bias may be difficult to detect in any circumstances but the difficulty can be magnified in an interdisciplinary project where researchers may be unfamiliar with the standards expected for the disciplines of some of their colleagues. In interdisciplinary research, a scientist can usually understand social science up to a point, and vice versa, but few are able to evaluate critically the quality of analysis or thinking across this divide. Ultimately the onus is on the team leader to be alert to such influences.

Roles, responsibilities and rewards

While we will dedicate a later section to leadership and coordination roles, it is worth capturing here the need to ensure at the start of a project that all participants know what is expected of themselves and of their colleagues. When recruiting staff for interdisciplinary research centres, research leaders may also reflect on Rhoten's distinction between the 'stars' (those whose work may take centre stage) and the 'connectors' (those interdisciplinary integrators who may operate out of the limelight) for, as she notes, these attributes are not usually present within the one individual (Rhoten 2004).

The grant proposal outline provides a starting point for a shared understanding; specific responsibilities can be made even more explicit, and shared transparently among all team members as both a map and a reference point should issues arise later on. Agreement in principle should be reached as to how changes might be made in the division of labour should the project evolve along new lines, or if a team member fails to pull his or her weight and discharge key responsibilities upon which others depend.

Given the key importance of publication in the academic community, agreeing a publications strategy early in the project is essential. It may be worthwhile to note the different traditions with respect to valuing various positions within an authorship list. In the natural sciences the first author (typically the postdoc on the project) and the last author (typically the Principal Investigator on the project) are the most valuable positions. In the social sciences and humanities, the proximity to the first author is the most valuable position. Sometimes though, authors may be listed in alphabetical order (particularly in the social sciences) if it is difficult to apportion their contribution.

Decisions will need to be made as to whether all project partners are mentioned in all publications (a strategy that has been successfully adopted by some collaborations) or whether a portfolio of publications is placed strategically in a range of different journals to reach particular target audiences, where greater impact can be gained by selectively identifying the most appropriate authors.

While specific publication plans may alter with the life of the project, principles as to who gets credit for what should be agreed early. A news feature in *Nature* even suggests the equivalent of a 'prenup' checklist, adapted from the US National Institutes of Health Office of Ombudsman, which, although focusing on biomedical collaborations, may provoke some useful discussions (Case Study 4.3).

Taking the extra time to prepare

In summary, as we think about setting off on the expedition, rushing into it without preparation can be dangerous. Taking extra time in the early stages of an interdisciplinary project is likely to be a sound tactic. Ideally, this

---

Case Study 4.3 The collaborators' prenup

Ten questions to discuss before starting a collaboration:

1 What do we expect to get out of this?

2 Who is going to do what and by when?

3 Who will have access to our data?

4 Who will give public presentations, and how much data will they reveal?

5 How will we assign authorship?

6 How will we decide when to publish?

7 Who owns the intellectual property?

8 Will we share our reagents with other labs?

9 What happens if one of us leaves the project?

10 What happens if one of us wants to form a separate, but related, collaboration with another lab?

Source: Ledford 2008.

time can be planned for when submitting a grant proposal, as discussed in chapter 3, and recognized as wise by reviewers and funders. Funders themselves might wish to institute two-stage funding such as the seed-corn funding employed by Relu to facilitate early team-building prior to full grant applications (Meagher and Lyall 2007a). Persuading eager individual researchers to go through what may seem to them to be extra steps will be a challenge for the project leader, particularly if the individuals are not used to working in this sort of complex team. However, the extra time and effort taken at the beginning should pay real dividends throughout the course of managing the actual project.

Managing the team

Even with excellent preparation, once the interdisciplinary project has been launched, it will not simply drift with the current to its desired destination; input of energy will be required to steer to success, in the form of sensitive management of the interdisciplinary team. The need for proactive effort is cited frequently by those looking closely at interdisciplinary projects. A growing group of academics in the United States is developing what they call 'the science of team science', as they explore empirically multiple components of success, with strong emphasis on the vital management function (for example, Stokols *et al.* 2008a; Stokols *et al.* 2005; Hall *et al.* 2008): 'The science of team science encompasses an amalgam of conceptual and methodologic strategies aimed at understanding and enhancing the outcomes of large-scale collaborative research and training programs' (Stokols *et al.* 2008b).

Design, implementation and evaluation of such initiatives are foci of attention. Stokols and colleagues have suggested hypothetically (and with some empirical support, for example, in a comparative study of several centres) that important linkages exist among variables within an 'antecedent-process-outcome model'. 'Antecedents' of collaboration include such things as leadership styles, individuals' commitment to team research, shared space, connectivity and history of working together. 'Intervening processes' include 'intellectual, interpersonal and affective experiences as well as observed or self-reported collaborative behaviors, or both' (Stokols *et al.* 2008b: S81). Examples would be brainstorming, dealing with biases and tensions across disciplines, and resolution of conflicts. A definite connection is suggested between antecedents and processes, and outcomes of collaboration that manifest at various stages, such as new conceptual frameworks, articles, training and innovations. Conceptual frameworks are being developed, such as a suggested typology of key contextual factors (e.g. Stokols *et al.* 2008a: Table 2, S109) including intrapersonal, interpersonal, organizational/institutional, physical/environmental, technologic and socio-political influences.

Key contributing variables appear to include, for example, 'empowering-leadership styles, the regularity and effectiveness of team communication, opportunities for informal face-to-face contact, members' readiness and preparation' (Stokols *et al.* 2008a).

Digging into the dynamics of interdisciplinary project management may itself model interdisciplinarity; for example, Stokols *et al.* generated their suggested typology of contextual influences on interdisciplinarity by reviewing: social psychological and management research on teams within settings; cyberinfrastructure studies; studies of community-based coalitions; and studies directly focusing on interdisciplinary scientific studies (Stokols *et al.* 2008a). Pennington attempts a rounded exploration of interdisciplinary collaborations on environmental issues as a learning problem, explicitly considering the possible relevance of three approaches to understanding learning: a framework on motivation, collective cognition and organized learning (Pennington 2008). Considering basic motivational needs, for instance, Pennington offers thought-provoking counterparts for the world of interdisciplinary collaboration: the need for 'security' is translated into the team's need for trust; the need for friendship/family/belonging is translated into the social relationships vital to a team; the need for self-esteem is related to a facilitator's helping all team members to value different perspectives and linkages; and a need for fulfilment of potential moves from the level of the individual to the team.

Fundamentally, throughout the lifecourse of an interdisciplinary project, every participant has to 'win' something. (As one leader of a collaborative research centre in Scotland commented during our evaluation of a scheme: 'Remember that everyone is in a collaboration for themselves, if they get nothing out of it – they will do sweet nothing!' [Meagher and Lyall 2005c]). Wins will doubtless differ across individuals: different members of a team may seek accomplishments of different sorts, so that the full portfolio of perceived benefits might include: novel empirical findings, an innovative technological breakthrough, an elegant quantitative analysis, an integrated model, a unique narrative, support for a paradigm and so on. Effective management of an interdisciplinary team thus entails a continuous balancing act, in which individual participants are assured of endpoints meaningful to them and their careers while at the same time the group as a whole steadfastly pursues a joint vision that none could achieve alone.

If this balancing act is to be maintained, so that progress is made toward the common vision, it is critical that mutual trust be fostered, maintained and grown over time. Many times success in interdisciplinary projects is seen to be related to the building of a team spirit, or culture, with which members identify increasingly over time. A variety of steps can be taken to build and sustain trust and team spirit. Some examples were given above, in discussing the importance of early steps at the start of a project. Mechanisms need to continue throughout the project, making them a key concern for those managing the project.

For example, Chubin *et al.* identified the following as valuable in fostering interdisciplinary research projects:

- draft reports requiring responses from other team members;
- joint responsibility for aspects of the project, e.g. writing a document together;
- field trips; and
- gatekeepers who can spend a great deal of time building and maintaining bridges to professionals outside their own field (Chubin *et al.* 1986).

Providing opportunities during the project to follow the progress of each discipline is also perceived as important. This can be achieved by interim reports, meetings or by using a steering committee consisting of a representative from each of the partner organizations.

Communication strategies require a balance of enough communication but not too much (Tait *et al.* 2002). Inevitably, as aggregations of expertise are put together from across multiple institutions in multiple locations but time and money constrain travel, projects will experiment with or use various technologies to bring team members together virtually. Regular face-to-face team meetings may be supplemented by electronic communication once a collective community has been established. Cummings and Kiesler make a number of suggestions about IT use and suggest there is a need for: tools to manage and track projects over time, tools to reduce information overload and tools to enable ongoing conversations (Cummings and Kiesler 2005). Yet, most would agree that face-to-face mechanisms are too important to forego entirely, if the trust that underpins searching discussions and innovative work is to be maintained (Case Study 4.4).

An empirical comparative study of several interdisciplinary centres within the National Institutes of Health Transdisciplinary Tobacco Use Research Centers programme (Stokols *et al.* 2005) found that in two centres with relatively constrained initial collaboration, leaders went the extra mile to hold a series of brainstorming sessions and retreats to address challenges, improve communication and progress integration. Interviews suggested that individuals found these activities helpful in developing sustained collaboration at the start and, indeed, such activities were often appreciated in later stages as well. One of the centres in particular showed an increase in interdisciplinary activities such as reading journals or going to conferences in a different field, integrating ideas through participation in working groups, or even altering a research plan due to conversations with colleagues.

Yet another key management balance is that of comfort with the edginess of innovation. At one extreme, if everyone on a team approached a problem

Case Study 4.4 Facilitating communication

The UK Tyndall Centre for Climate Change has a three-fold mission – integrative research, informing policy responses and motivating society – and the centre has had to work in areas which may be considered unusual by some academics, i.e. in policy engagement, capacity-building, outreach and dissemination, whilst at the same time maintaining scientific rigour.

According to Tyndall, interdisciplinary research centres appear to work best when there are three approaches applied simultaneously to encouraging interdisciplinarity, communication and integration. These three approaches can be broadly summarized as: academic means; social means; and physical or structural means (including spaces to facilitate researcher interaction). Any one of these approaches to facilitate interdisciplinarity alone does not appear sufficient to promote active interdisciplinarity and problem-focused research and learning.

Tyndall recommends focusing on facilitating communication – both internal communication and outreach. Techniques range from regular face-to-face meetings (can be through videoconference) and greater use of electronic dropboxes to share and review draft papers. But it notes that geographical proximity of the individuals in a research team has a valuable premium, especially when doing interdisciplinary research: while 'virtual centres' have some attractions as an organizational structure for tackling complex research challenges, creative interaction between researchers in such a setting is often limited. Overcoming these limitations is challenging: travel has a high overhead in time, cost and carbon emissions and the use of technology (phone, email, Access Grid) only provides a partial solution.

Source: Tyndall Centre 2006.

in the same way, framing questions and selecting and implementing methods identically, there would seem to be little point in bothering with a complex team, as rather conventional outputs could be expected. So, management of an interdisciplinary team is likely to encourage diversity of approaches, with some deliberate 'cognitive dissonance' and debate in pursuit of innovative insights which may result in 'misunderstanding', 'disagreement' and 'squabbles' (Gray 2008). Fragmentation might occur, especially if individuals are separated physically. For each project, the right balance must be found between 'diversity and debate among investigators on the one hand, and intellectual integration and social support on the other' (Stokols *et al.* 2005). This reinforces the maxim that proactive effort is needed to fuse diverse individuals into a team.

Maintaining the team

Interdisciplinarity gives rise to journeys which may meet more obstacles than conventional, monodisciplinary work: it can help to be aware ahead of time of possible mid-expedition crises and how they might be dealt with in order to maintain a functioning team. Sensitivity to institutional, career or other restraints on various members can also help to anticipate or moderate problems.

The context within which an interdisciplinary initiative arises can vary across several dimensions. It is important, for example, to be aware of institutional constraints that may weigh differentially on team members in different departments or universities. For example, in contrast to discipline-based departments, interdisciplinary collaborations may run counter to institutional allocations of credit, finances, indirect costs or resources. As a leader of a collaborative centre in Scotland noted: 'there is a fundamental tension between interdisciplinary institutes or centres and the university internal management system' – which needs to be recognized (Meagher and Lyall 2005c: 20).

Across institutions practice may vary, but it may be useful early on to set up memoranda of agreement (for example, around the management and sharing of benefits from potential intellectual property) while still protecting the vibrancy of the emerging initiative from bureaucracy-induced paralysis. 'Context' for institutionalized interdisciplinarity can be quite literal: architectural design for buildings housing interdisciplinary initiatives or centres can incorporate common spaces and layout conducive for bringing people together, formally and informally. Even at the planning stage, making the effort to hold some meetings in comfortable, retreat-like settings can help to accelerate a sense of belonging to the same 'community'.

Understanding the institutional environments or constraints (such as career stage or promotion criteria) under which different people are working is an important aspect of maintaining a team during the course of a project. Factors such as sabbaticals, new positions and the need to write books to ensure career progression were identified as influencing collaborators' ability to contribute to the project at different times (Lingard et al. 2007). These kinds of considerations are not restricted to interdisciplinary projects but can be exacerbated by the failure of colleagues from other disciplines to recognize the implications and imperatives of changing professional circumstances.

Research has indicated the value of short-time staff exchanges (e.g. for periods of two to four weeks), joint meetings and visits in facilitating interdisciplinary research (e.g. Tait et al. 2002). These visits help develop relationships but, importantly, also allow a deeper understanding of the working context of partners in the consortium.

Lingard et al. noted the impact that organizational definitions of roles had on the interdisciplinary research collaboration in which they were involved (Lingard et al. 2007). In their case, institutional requirements meant that only one person could be identified as the Principal Investigator with others involved as 'collaborators'. They felt this devalued the academic contribution these 'collaborators' made. Furthermore, they argue that the skills needed may shift during the research project and demand flexibility to allow a different team member to take responsibility for an aspect of the research than originally planned. Thus, they argue that institutions should be able to recognize and reward such shifts in responsibility.

In a review of projects Cummings and Kiesler concluded that there were a number of other organizational barriers to collaboration (not restricted to interdisciplinary projects) including:

- different term times which meant that there were difficulties in identifying jointly suitable times to meet;
- difficulty of negotiating budgets, contracts, intellectual property rights (IP), etc. across different universities;
- different universities were used to using different software;
- partners became tired of travelling to meet others after a time (which, we may add, can lead to tensions in achieving an appropriate work-life balance) (Cummings and Kiesler 2005).

In chapter 3 we referred to difficulties encountered by people being added to the project in the later stages. A good example of this is given by Lingard *et al.* who found that adding a project team member late increased the potential for misunderstandings and resulted in the researcher feeling 'second class' (Lingard *et al.* 2007). Team processes considered as 'common sense', which had been developed during the project, had become implicit in the project and were not made explicit to the new member of the team who, consequently, was unaware of them. Difficulties can also occur if partners feel at the periphery of the project and they are then more likely to drop out (Cummings and Kiesler 2005).

Lest this becomes a catalogue of woes and difficulties, it is timely to remember that there are good reasons for attempting interdisciplinary research and that some very real and interesting benefits may flow from the research: Case Study 4.5 highlights some of these from the II-FP5 project.

Interdisciplinarity can be a wellspring for creativity and economically or socially important innovation. Blackwell *et al.* consider the 'radical innovation' that can be brought about by interdisciplinary teams crossing the 'social boundaries' with which we structure knowledge – not only with regard to academic disciplines but also departmental structures within government, internal divisions within companies, and so on (Blackwell *et al.* 2009). They see building the capacity to generate radical innovation as valuable, since 'interdisciplinary innovation is an essential tool for the future' (Blackwell *et al.* 2009: 3).

Case Study 4.5 II-FP5 interviewees on the benefits of interdisciplinarity

'50 years of research ... has resulted in very little progress in controlling this problem. [The co-ordinator] feels that in the last 2 years in this interdisciplinary project he has learned more than in his previous career.'

'An electrical engineer working with a biologist ... if they worked separately, the work couldn't have been as fruitful, as rapid and as in great a depth as it has been with the two working together. This reduced the time to get the results not by 2 to 3 years but probably by 10 or 20 years in the view of the co-ordinator.'

'we heard about different colours in metro stations – what they can produce in the mind. That was of course quite new for us. We never thought about these issues inside the project. We were just looking for the technical stuff: how many cameras, how to look at the people, the mean speed of a pedestrian and such. And they said, "Yeah, but when you use the colour green, that will calm down the mind of the pedestrian, and when you use red, they will ..." That was the first really interdisciplinary approach.'

'The final result of the project [was] more than 1+1+1=3.'

Source: Tait *et al.* 2002.

Finally, we should note that the degree of interdisciplinarity within a project can vary. Projects can be just a little integrated in terms of interdisciplinarity or they may be heavily interdisciplinary. The degree of interdisciplinarity may well increase with time or as partners learn more about one another and the potential contributions they can all make. This is perhaps one of the reasons where existing research consortia often form the backbone of new consortia (as indicated in chapter 3). Klein suggests that interdisciplinarity is a process, not a subject or body of content (Klein 1990). Part of the art of helping interdisciplinary projects achieve their potential is a healthy dose of flexibility and a willingness to let the particulars of the journey evolve, even while the overall destination continues to be pursued.

Key leadership roles and traits

The key role of the leader in integrating the disciplines is often highlighted (e.g. Gray 2008; Stokols *et al.* 2008a). Metaphors such as conducting an orchestra have been used to describe the role of the project coordinator. In our survey of European Commission projects, the key role of the coordinator in ensuring the success of the project was frequently stressed, as was the demanding nature of what they are being asked to do. This role was variously seen to include (Tait *et al.* 2002):

- understanding the research methods and assumptions of the different disciplines;
- bringing partners together when this seemed useful;
- interpreting and negotiating between researchers;
- listening for signals that one partner was suggesting a different way of doing things and not constraining the approach to any particular discipline's accepted methods.

Generally, coordinators agreed that people who themselves have interdisciplinary backgrounds make the most effective leaders of interdisciplinary teams. One reason given for this was that an interdisciplinary researcher is used to listening to others who come from different backgrounds and have different ways of thinking (Key Advice 4.3). Those involved in this type of work are often 'bitten by the bug', so that they go on to play key roles in subsequent interdisciplinary research. For example, nearly all (over 90 per cent) of survey respondents in an evaluation of the Scottish Research Development Grant scheme (Meagher and Lyall 2005b: 28) said that they were more likely to play leadership roles in future interdisciplinary collaborations than they would have been without the Research Development Grant centre experience. Also, in problem-oriented interdisciplinary research, there is a danger that a single-discipline leader will bias the project towards his/her own discipline. This may be less of a problem for academically oriented interdisciplinary research. Solo researchers, perhaps doing a PhD, may experience pressure from single discipline-based supervisors or other advisers to 'do it their way' and this can be difficult to resist.

Various terms can be used for the roles that need to be played: some of those identified by Interdisciplinary Masterclass participants (described in chapter 5) are listed in Case Study 4.6. It is worth noting that not all roles may be played by one individual.

Skills needed by interdisciplinary leaders, coordinators, facilitators or managers will, of course, sometimes be intellectual – the ability to conceptualize and integrate components of complex problems, and to make new links across disciplines where an approach from one discipline could be relevant to another. But many times vital skills will not be those conventionally recognized in academia; they will fall under the rubric of interpersonal and process skills. Many (e.g. Gray 2008) have noted that without keen process skills somewhere in the mix, interdisciplinary collaborations will have a tough time; skills identified include (but are not limited to) problem-solving, conflict resolution,

Key Advice 4.3   Qualities of a good interdisciplinary research leader

- clear vision for what the project is trying to achieve;

- respect for other disciplines;

- high level of expertise in your own discipline;

- good interpersonal skills such as tact, assertiveness, patience and perseverance;

- being proactive towards partners and not waiting for them to come to you;

- not being too ambitious in your own field;

- interested in a wide range of subjects;

- avoiding constraining the project to the methods of any one discipline;

- ability to absorb information and its implications rapidly;

- open-mindedness and flexibility;

- ability to keep a balance between openness and maintaining the progress of the project;

- structuring meetings so that there is plenty of opportunity for discussion of different ideas, encouraging people to come to a majority view (or consensus) on how to proceed;

- understanding of the structures within which people are working and the pressures they are under, with an appreciation that they work in different systems.

modulating differences in power, aligning different individuals with different aims toward a common goal, translating and facilitating interactions. Gray suggests that there are three categories of responsibilities for leaders of inter-disciplinary initiatives:

- cognitive tasks, such as visioning (stimulating creativity) and framing (helping all involved to participate in a new mental model);

- structural tasks, such as boundary-spanning (e.g. gaining support, building bridges) and brokerage (facilitating linkages and knowledge flow);

Case Study 4.6 What roles does an interdisciplinary leader need to adopt?

- 'Banker
- Cheerleader
- Coach
- Communicator
- Damage limiter
- Diplomat
- Enforcer
- Facilitator
- Fire fighter
- Interpreter
- Matchmaker

- Mediator
- Motivator
- Negotiator
- Peacemaker
- Plate spinner
- Referee
- Relationship counsellor
- Role model
- Salesperson

and ...

- Chocolate provider

(As identified by some of our Interdisciplinary Masterclass participants)

- processual tasks, such as ensuring productive interactions and communication and building trust while mediating conflicts (Gray 2008).

In our evaluation of centres established with a Scottish Funding Council Research Development Grant (Meagher and Lyall 2005b), for example, we were frequently told by professorial leaders that the staff person hired to liaise across disciplines (and institutions) turned out to have been a crucial investment. Often, a key challenge for an interdisciplinary team is to find funding to sustain such a critical person after specific project funding runs out. Some interdisciplinary programmes are so large and complex that the leader of the overall programme must be supported by leaders of constituent interdisciplinary projects, and perhaps also by coordinating or liaison staff at the centre of the programme. Gray, for example, considers differences between small projects and larger, distributed teams, noting the need in the latter for 'innovation networks' managed by multiple unit leaders (Gray 2008). Since every interdisciplinary research effort is different, it may be useful for senior members to cast a critical eye over the sorts of functions described here and double-check to make sure that each role is played by someone, with the responsibilities clearly defined at the start and evaluated as the effort matures.

We ourselves have drawn upon our own efforts in interdisciplinarity, our evaluations of interdisciplinary schemes and the input of participants in our masterclasses on interdisciplinarity to generate what is effectively a checklist of points to consider in management of interdisciplinarity (Key Advice 4.4).

Key Advice 4.4 Tips for interdisciplinary team managers

Conceptualizing the research problem

- ensure that all participants contribute, and contribute to the same standard, even if their methodologies and data differ;

- negotiate roles as necessary; take the time to find a common framework for the research in order to get the right balance of contributions from the component disciplines (so that you achieve a truly interdisciplinary product, not simply a multidisciplinary project);

- plan to take extra time for group working in the early framing stages; facilitate lively interactions that help disciplinary partners explore commonalities and differences, and establish relationships and trust.

Distributing team responsibilities

- develop a systemic framework and agree the common problems and goals from the outset;

- build bridges between the different disciplinary contributions to achieve synergies across disciplines and methods;

- recognize that, despite early planning, interdisciplinary projects may need to develop and change as they proceed – be flexible;

- encourage the research team to be more reflective than they would be for a monodisciplinary project; facilitate frequent, open and positive discussion of the project's evolution;

- designate a dedicated member of staff to carry out coordination, dissemination and knowledge exchange responsibilities, as when such individuals are valued appropriately they can have a significant impact upon success of large-scale projects, programmes or centres;

- when distributing team responsibilities, be transparent so that every member of the team knows who will be doing what, and when;

- identify expertise and assign it appropriately without necessarily expecting everyone to participate fully in all tasks;

- be open to new methods;

- consider how analyses may be structured to integrate different sorts of findings, from different disciplines' methods and data;

- recognize that team responsibilities may go beyond standard/ traditional areas of expertise;

- consider the role and contribution of 'users' or other stakeholders in the team.

Overcoming communication barriers

- expect to expend time and effort in developing a common language within the team;

- be aware that different disciplines have different traditions and styles of working; air preconceptions among partners about different disciplinary paradigms;

- include multiple face-to-face team-working meetings and networking events, especially early in the project and then at project milestones/ decision-making points. Augment (but do not replace) as necessary with regular video-conferencing to tackle geographical separation;

- use social events to help the team coalesce. Joint fieldwork may also be helpful;

- find a way of applying rewards and incentives to teams rather than individuals;

- consider using existing techniques and computational tools for integrating data;

- provide opportunities for team members to write together to encourage integration across disciplines;

- expect some clashes within the team; when possible turn these into new ways of thinking about a research problem, or even new avenues for future research;

- steadfastly and diplomatically, throughout the project refresh team members' commitment to their shared goals.

Bringing it all together

- as early as the research planning stage, consider how work – and credit – can be apportioned fairly when it comes time to publish results;

Key Advice 4.4 *Continued*

- be aware that different disciplines have different traditions in, for example, the sensitive issue of authorship which can sometimes be particularly disadvantageous to junior researchers within an interdisciplinary team;

- discuss a deliberate publications strategy with team members early on, toward the development of a portfolio of publications with different outputs targeted at different types of journals (e.g. various monodisciplinary journals as well as one or more interdisciplinary journals) or other media;

- designate lead responsibility for different publications to different team members depending on their disciplinary standing and their role within the team;

- before you reach the end of the project, you may also want to consider what factors will influence the likelihood of the team staying together and perhaps evolving (by adding or subtracting members to tackle what may be new niche opportunities building on the first round of research) or whether the team should be allowed to disperse and the project die a graceful death.

Continuing the journey

Shaping the nature of the endpoint is another challenge for managers of inter-disciplinary projects. Usually, not all the subtleties and complexities of effective interdisciplinary projects will be completely resolved. However, funding stops at a certain point and individual researchers have to get on with their professional lives, securing other funding and/or pursuing somewhat different research problems. The end of an interdisciplinary project might consist of:

1 the interdisciplinary team dispersing completely (whether or not members have successfully generated integrated outcomes and publications from their work) with only a few individuals – or no one – pursuing the general problem area;

2 subsets of members of the team, perhaps augmented by new colleagues, pursuing subsets of the original problem (these new more focused teams might be monodisciplinary or interdisciplinary);

3   the original team, recognizable but with natural turnover, pursuing either the original problem or a next evolutionary stage/offshoot of that problem.

If sustainability of the investigation is desired – if some or all of the members of the expedition want the journey to continue – the team needs to be managed accordingly, long before the funding is over. For instance, team members will need to feel that their problem area continues to be vital and intellectually stimulating, offering new opportunities even beyond the end of a particular grant. The sorts of brainstorming activities described earlier (Key Advice 4.2), as well as continued networking and team-building, thus need to contribute continuously to the identification of compelling new questions derived in full or in part from work being done. Reflection and (self) evaluation can help the team both to learn continuously about how to behave more effectively in an interdisciplinary context and also to monitor how their problem area is evolving generally, and where corresponding niches of opportunity may arise (Meagher and Lyall 2005b). Chapter 7 discusses various sorts of evaluation, including self-evaluation as a useful tool.

Leaders and coordinators may have special roles in 'succession planning', bringing along others to lead all or some components of the next phase of the work. Capacity-building in junior researchers who can grow to take on more responsible roles, and networking which can bring in new members with different perspectives, also contribute to a healthy evolution. Stokols and colleagues indicate positive influences that successful outcomes of one inter-disciplinary study can have on future collaborative processes, through, for example, team members feeling intellectual satisfaction or an institution supporting future initiatives more effectively (by, for example, providing appropriate shared space) (Stokols et al. 2005). It may well be that the selection of leaders of new initiatives could favour those who have demonstrated requisite personal traits and prior experience of responsible roles in complex initiatives; innovative training programmes or indeed novel targeted training toolkits, can enhance the 'collaboration readiness' of future participants, helping to prepare a new cadre of individuals for roles in such initiatives (e.g. Stokols et al. 2008b; Mitrany and Stokols 2005; Nash 2008). Rhoten offers a compelling argument that mobility may not always be detrimental to the livelihood of interdisciplinary centres:

> while longer organizational life cycles give centers time to improve their research practices and processes, long-term and full-time affiliations can actually limit and not accentuate researcher creativity and productivity ... researchers who felt free to enter and exit collaborative relationships reported more progress with their interdisciplinary projects and greater satisfaction in their professional lives overall. (Rhoten 2004)

In going forward with follow-on proposals or initiatives, it makes sense to balance old and new, both in terms of drawing on findings from the earlier work to propose innovative research and in terms of continuing to involve some familiar faces, with trust already built, along with new ones.

Summary

In this chapter we have addressed the challenges of ensuring that a research consortium consisting of different disciplines can be brought together and focused in a continuing way toward achieving the main aims of the project. In particular, we have emphasized the proactive work that is needed early on to build a good foundation: to embed a shared vision; to build trust and mutual understanding of fundamental assumptions; to achieve good communication in circumstances where the 'language' of one discipline may be understood in different ways in a different discipline; and to allocate fairly and transparently roles, responsibilities and rewards. Time, effort and plenty of social interaction should be recognized as necessary and valuable, so that seemingly slow progress at the start of a project should be expected and acceptable. Ongoing management of interdisciplinary work requires proactive efforts to build upon the early foundation and maintain forward momentum, tackling challenges, adapting as professional circumstances of participants change and maintaining sufficient flexibility to allow informed evolution. Intellectually stimulating activities that help to both foster team spirit and enrich the vitality of the project will be important. Appropriate, effective communication channels will be critical; while these may vary from project to project, they are likely to consist of face-to-face interactions supplemented with electronic communication. All of these critical components underscore the importance of individuals playing leadership and coordination roles to ensure that synergy is achieved, that the project moves beyond individuals working in their own discipline to the creative status of an effort in which individuals genuinely interact with each other across disciplines to achieve new understanding.

Questions

For researchers

1 Interdisciplinary collaborations are often put together under a great deal of time pressure and may be conducted by people who do not know each other (or each others' disciplines) well. What are the key management issues that you need to address when working in these less than ideal circumstances?

For research managers

1 What steps (and in what order) need to be taken to proactively build and manage a team so that it makes the most of the potential value of interdisciplinarity?

2 What roles do you see yourself playing? How will you manage wearing multiple hats? Can you get support to help with any of your roles?

3 What role models do you have for successful interdisciplinary research? Can you find other managers of interdisciplinary initiatives with whom you can discuss issues?

4 In what way does the labelling of research team members in a collaboration (e.g. Principal Investigator, Co-investigator, etc.) influence their role in the team and their responsibilities and benefits institutionally and how might that affect specifically interdisciplinary projects?

For institutional leaders

1 What kind of job security do interdisciplinary researchers have in your organization? How does that compare with disciplinary experts?

2 How are 'teams' rewarded for research – or is all the reward on the basis of individuals?

3 How might this policy impact on interdisciplinary research?

4 Has your organization established any 'environments' conducive to interdisciplinarity?

For research funders

1 How would you evaluate the quality of a research team and the Principal Investigator's proposed management approach for an interdisciplinary research project?

2 Would you consider offering seed-corn funding to launch projects in new interdisciplinary directions?

3 Have you considered how self-evaluation or critical friend formative evaluations could help complex interdisciplinary projects evolve?

4 Would you consider bringing together interdisciplinary researchers to share experiences, approaches, issues and good practice regarding the management of interdisciplinary projects?

5

Permit to Travel

Supporting the next generation
of interdisciplinary researchers

Introduction

Developing the ability to do good quality interdisciplinary work is an activity that can take place at the graduate level but also throughout a researcher's working life. This chapter considers what funders and other institutions are doing to develop interdisciplinary research capacity through publicly funded programmes at a number of different career levels (graduate student, early postdoctoral researcher and beyond). We will discuss issues of graduate supervision, mentoring early career researchers, and the advanced training and development activities that may be required to develop future interdisciplinary research leaders and help them make the transition between the various career stages. Advice on various aspects of interdisciplinary research strategies is an important form of 'training' that can be conducted by mentors from within one's own institution or from the broader community, or by peers. Such guides may also offer vital advice on careers as we discuss in the following chapter. This is especially important in order to build interdisciplinary communities, often spanning multiple networks, as interdisciplinary scholars do not readily develop the same types of 'invisible colleges' as their monodisciplinary peers. Nash recommends 'meta training' to help early career researchers understand and manage distinctive features of their own interdisciplinary education, future work and careers, suggesting that necessary knowledge and skills are best developed through a mix of 'formal didactics, research experiences, and mentorship' (Nash 2008).

Particularly at the beginning of an interdisciplinary career, finding an intellectual community can be a major contributing factor to student success by countering the potential feeling of intellectual homelessness (Golde and Gallagher, 1999). Supervisors and mentors have a key role to play here. In this chapter we consider how they might best advise and guide PhD students and junior colleagues setting out on an interdisciplinary research journey. In the chapter that follows, the focus shifts to early career researchers themselves and the strategies that they might need to develop in order to chart a course for a successful interdisciplinary career.

Other authors have addressed many of the more methodological issues encountered in designing and conducting interdisciplinary research (for example, Oberg 2010; Repko 2008; Szostak 2007) and we have already discussed some of the research processes relevant to designing interdisciplinary research projects and putting together interdisciplinary teams (see chapters 3 and 4). Here we consider what other forms of support may be required in terms of advanced training and career mentoring in order to develop the next generation of interdisciplinary researchers and improve the experience of the current generation.

Building capacity: Some challenges

There have been long-standing and increasingly insistent calls from national and supranational funders (for example, European Commission 2007) for interdisciplinary research, including collaboration between the social and natural sciences, as a means to promote scientific and technological advance and to foster its more effective acceptance and beneficial utilization in society. In the UK, the Economic and Social Research Council (ESRC) has identified interdisciplinary, collaborative research to be a key means of addressing major social and economic challenges (ESRC 2009a). For example, the UK Living with Environmental Change (LWEC) programme is a partnership of organizations funding, undertaking and using environmental research, including the Research Councils UK, government departments and devolved administrations. The ten-year programme seeks to connect world-leading natural, engineering, economic, social, medical, cultural, arts and humanities researchers with policy-makers, business, the public and other key stakeholders. In the policy realm, the UK Department for Environment, Food and Rural Affairs (Defra) stresses the need for increased interdisciplinary research in order to address its major challenges: climate change, food security and ecosystems (Defra 2010). There is, however, less understanding about how capacity-building in interdisciplinary research expertise can be achieved.

The seven Research Councils (covering medicine, biology and biotechnology, engineering and physical sciences, natural environment, arts, humanities and social sciences) are increasingly joining forces to tackle these challenges by funding schemes that seek to foster interdisciplinary research skills in 'next-generation researchers' (for example, the ESRC/Medical Research Council [MRC] and ESRC/National Environment Research Council [NERC] studentship schemes and the ESRC/MRC postdoctoral fellowships).[1] The ESRC's Postgraduate Training Framework (ESRC 2009b) also highlights better opportunities for interdisciplinary training programmes, supporting the long-term ability of the UK social science community to address complex research questions.

However, interdisciplinary training is by no means a mainstream activity in UK universities. Despite attempts to promote interdisciplinary research

---

Case Study 5.1   Interdisciplinary training – sink or swim?

The Tyndall Centre has formed interdisciplinary PhD supervisory boards and created an actively managed network to provide identity to Tyndall PhD researchers. In its academic teaching it has developed a coherent framework for learning and a more problem-based curriculum.

For younger researchers, discussion groups were organized to promote interdisciplinary learning. However, by the Centre's own admission, relatively little effort went into specific training for established disciplinary staff and it was essentially 'learning on the job' and 'sink or swim'!

Source: Tyndall Centre 2006.

---

and collaboration between different natural sciences and between the social and natural sciences, or with the humanities, evidence suggests that existing capacity-building schemes do not yet offer the growing number of early-stage interdisciplinary researchers sufficient opportunities to network and share learning about the considerable intellectual and management challenges of interdisciplinary research (Meagher and Lyall 2005a; Meagher and Lyall 2009).

Nor should graduate students be the sole recipients of such training; continuous interdisciplinary skills development is also valuable and necessary: many mid-career researchers may find themselves suddenly involved in interdisciplinary work, having been provided with no advice on how to do it well (Case Study 5.1). There needs to be recognition of research – and interdisciplinary research in particular – as a craft that should be learned through practice. In addition to traditional face-to-face short courses and annual summer schools, this may include less conventional types of training such as ongoing mentoring to impart skills and work-shadowing or placements in research settings (Wiles *et al.* 2005). In the UK, the interdisciplinary Rural Economy and Land Use (Relu) programme has supported a Work Shadowing Scheme since 2005. By funding placements of between one week and a month, it aims to introduce Relu research staff to the action-contexts in which their research may be used. These contexts have included commercial organizations, voluntary bodies or public agencies.[2]

In the United States, the situation is different. With a much longer tradition of interdisciplinary or at least multidisciplinary undergraduate curricula and a different degree structure, American university students tend not to specialize as early as those in the UK. Nevertheless, we share many common challenges when supporting interdisciplinary research capacity and American funders are also finding non-curriculum-based approaches to supporting early stage interdisciplinary researchers (for example, Case Study 5.2).

Case Study 5.2 Dissertation Proposal Development Fellowship

The Dissertation Proposal Development Fellowship (DPDF), offered by the US Social Science Research Council, is organized to help early-stage graduate students in the humanities and social sciences formulate effective doctoral dissertation proposals.

Each year, the programme offers training within different interdisciplinary fields of study under the leadership of pairs of tenured senior faculty, who define the fields and serve as research directors for groups of 12 graduate students. The students participate in two workshops: one in the spring, to prepare students to undertake summer research that will inform the design of their dissertation research; the other in autumn, to help students apply their summer research experiences to writing dissertation and funding proposals.

Every year the programme is organized around different, interdisciplinary research fields. Examples of past research fields include: Black Atlantic Studies; Rethinking Europe; Religion, Ethnicity, Nation; The Political Economy of Redistribution; Visual Culture; Water Sustainability: Society, Politics, Culture; Animal Studies; Critical Studies of Science & Technology Policy; Human Dimensions of Global Environmental Change; Muslim Modernities; and Urban Visual Studies.

Source: Social Science Research Council, http://www.ssrc.org/fellowships/dpdf-fellowship.

Many commentators, from both sides of the Atlantic (e.g. Golde and Gallagher 1999; Lau and Pasquini 2008), have called for radical changes in the ways in which interdisciplinary scholars of the future are trained. One such approach is the Integrative Graduate Education and Research Traineeship (IGERT) scheme of the US National Science Foundation. This is a publicly funded programme that provides large-scale grants to individual institutions to develop postgraduate training in a particular interdisciplinary area (e.g. language sciences) with the goal of building interdisciplinary human capacity. This scheme is regarded by its evaluators (Abt Associates Inc. 2006) as being successful in achieving this aim (Case Study 5.3).

One of our findings from the Interdisciplinary Masterclasses (described later in this chapter), and from our own evaluation of a UK interdisciplinary studentship scheme (Meagher and Lyall 2005a), is that graduate students undertaking an interdisciplinary PhD can often feel rather isolated unless they are based with like-minded individuals in a centre or department that specializes in interdisciplinary research. The IGERT scheme entails broad programmes within institutions

Case Study 5.3 Evaluation of the IGERT scheme

IGERT (Integrative Graduate Education and Research Traineeship) is the US National Science Foundation's flagship interdisciplinary training programme. Since 1998 the IGERT programme has made 215 awards to over 100 lead universities, providing funding for nearly 5,000 graduate students. The IGERT model supports collaborative research that transcends traditional disciplinary boundaries and requires teamwork, thereby providing students with the tools to become leaders in the science and engineering of the future. The interdisciplinary graduate programmes covered by the scheme vary greatly, spanning disciplines that include: biomedical engineering, environmental economics, nanoscience, sustainability, computational science, molecular biology, psychology, anthropology, political science and materials science. In general, the focus is primarily on what we would term academically oriented interdisciplinary research. IGERT offers a rich seam of learning about how a successful capacity- and community-building funding scheme can support the development of the next generation of interdisciplinary researchers.

Source: Integrative Graduate Education and Research Traineeship, http://www. igert.org. ·

and this seems to address some of the difficulties encountered by more scattered individuals. It is interesting to note early faculty and department chair perceptions of 'stronger departmental and institutional support for interdisciplinary research and education at IGERT institutions than non-IGERT institutions', including, for example, stimulating new course development, and 'to a lesser extent, new degrees and requirements for doctoral students' (Abt Associates Inc. 2006).

One of the concerns about interdisciplinary research can be the loss of quality within individual disciplines (a theme that we shall return to in chapter 7) but quality was not seen as having been sacrificed in the IGERT scheme: for example, 84 per cent of IGERT faculty felt that their students 'are being prepared to know their own discipline in depth' well or very well.

Our analyses of UK-based interdisciplinary studentship and fellowship schemes (Meagher and Lyall 2005a; Meagher and Lyall 2009) have identified the importance of developing a variety of mechanisms for fostering interdisciplinarity among early career researchers (ECRs) funded by such schemes. In the same way, IGERT students when surveyed selected mechanisms such as:

> access to disciplines and expertise outside of home department, opportunities to study multiple disciplines, working on a research project involving multiple disciplines; courses presenting laboratories or research techniques of multiple

disciplines; communicating to people outside your home discipline; attended professional conference outside home discipline; laboratory rotations in multiple disciplines; developed or taught a multidisciplinary/interdisciplinary course or educational effort. (Abt Associates Inc. 2006)

Career development can often be a concern for interdisciplinary early career researchers (ECRs) as we shall discuss in more detail in chapter 6. Perhaps reassuringly for junior researchers, the evaluation of the IGERT scheme found that nearly two-thirds of IGERT students surveyed felt they were being prepared for a wide range of career possibilities, compared with 44 per cent of non-IGERT students. Only 15 per cent of the IGERT students responding to this question were concerned that their interdisciplinary work might 'harm their ability to get a traditional job in their own field' (Abt Associates Inc. 2006). This may be because the focus of this scheme is primarily on academically oriented interdisciplinary research which, as noted earlier, presents fewer challenges to academic disciplines and to conventional academic career prospects.

Our evaluation of the ESRC/MRC scheme (Meagher and Lyall 2009) showed that nearly all supervisor/mentor respondents agreed that they had either to some or a great extent furthered their own interdisciplinarity, with more than half having developed other interdisciplinary collaborations. Showing a similar 'ripple effect', the IGERT evaluation also found that participation in IGERT led to 'an additional shift towards more interdisciplinary work' as reported by academics and department chairs (Abt Associates Inc. 2006).

As former students of the scheme, Graybill *et al.* offer reflections of the Urban Ecology IGERT and put forward six recommendations for both students and institutions undertaking interdisciplinary research and training programmes:

- attend to the processes involved in simultaneously exploring interdisciplinary topics while also addressing the interpersonal dynamics of the groups involved;

- develop students' sense of ownership of the programme;

- garner institutional support, both intellectual and financial;

- plan for your own progress in order to successfully complete an interdisciplinary doctorate;

- create and maintain flexibility regarding logistical issues such as scheduling;

- practise appreciative inquiry in order to understand and appreciate different worldviews (Graybill *et al.* 2006).

Many have discussed how the dominant structures and norms within universities and doctoral education make it difficult to conduct interdisciplinary research (e.g. Golde and Gallagher 1999). The same is also true when developing interdisciplinary capacity within the wider research community. Is it better to approach these interdisciplinary research capacity-building challenges in a way that builds from and across the different disciplinary/substantive bases (Wiles *et al.* 2005) or to adopt a more generic approach that recognizes that many of the research design, development and management issues are universal and largely independent of the particular research topic being addressed? We have attempted to do both with a series of capacity- and community-building activities which we will now describe.

Our response to these challenges

Much of the knowledge that surrounds interdisciplinary research capacity-building is tacit, with practitioners often 'learning by doing' through a process of informal apprenticeship with more experienced colleagues who may not always articulate or explain the good practice they are conducting as a matter of instinct. In this section we will describe how we have sought to formalize and codify our approach to interdisciplinary research and to share this knowledge of how to design, manage, report and evaluate interdisciplinary research with the research community.

Through our long, practical engagement with these interdisciplinary research challenges we identified two skills gaps in the UK. The first was at the graduate level where PhD students in the social sciences are generally taught about a range of qualitative and quantitative research methods, and given the tools with which to construct the research design for their thesis. However, unless students are embedded in a centre specializing in interdisciplinary research, those engaged on interdisciplinary projects are rarely given any specialist help with their research design and are presented with the considerable challenge of drawing on, and integrating, two or more bodies of literature, methodologies and, indeed, research paradigms. The second, related challenge occurs at a later stage in researchers' careers when they are faced with leading an interdisciplinary research team for the first time. This can require a particular set of skills which we believe are not extensively taught at present and are, again, essentially 'learned by doing'.

The origins of this approach lie in our evaluation of the Economic and Social Research Council/National Environment Research Council (ESRC/NERC) interdisciplinary scheme (Meagher and Lyall 2005a). A very strong recommendation of our report (supported by 90 per cent of award-holders who were surveyed) was to bring students together to share experiences, challenges and lessons learned regarding interdisciplinarity. Supervisors also supported this shared learning in order to reinforce students' confidence and abilities as interdisciplinary researchers. We thus developed a range of masterclasses – the University of Edinburgh Institute for the Study of Science, Technology and

Innovation (ISSTI) Interdisciplinary Masterclasses[3] – at two levels. The first was aimed at graduate students embarking on interdisciplinary projects for the first time and sought to improve students' ability to design interdisciplinary research projects, and to give them a better understanding of the issues and challenges of interdisciplinary research spanning the natural and social sciences. The second level aimed to provide new 'interdisciplinary integrators' at the postdoctoral and junior researcher stage with the tools they require to lead successful interdisciplinary project teams in order to develop participants' research management, leadership and supervisory skills in interdisciplinary projects across the social and natural sciences. Some of the teaching materials we developed for these courses have also been used in other training contexts and made available to the wider research community via a project wiki.[4]

These workshops went beyond the usual training in transferable research skills and developed a virtuous training circle: those trained to be interdisciplinary integrators will incorporate their interdisciplinary research management skills into their supervisory roles, thus helping the next generation of researchers to adopt good interdisciplinary practice in their research design and project development. By recognizing that different gaps exist at different levels, we were able to develop a systematic approach to imparting often intuitive, craft-based skills.

The programmes for the Masterclasses consisted of training activities along with an element of sharing of research experiences which we hoped would develop into lasting peer networks useful to interdisciplinary researchers throughout their careers. The Masterclasses examined the motivations for interdisciplinary research and the different modes of interdisciplinary working, in particular one of the most challenging forms of interdisciplinary engagement – the direct involvement of social scientists as collaborators in scientific and technological research.

The graduate Masterclass focused on issues to do with research design and writing an interdisciplinary thesis. The postdoctoral Masterclass focused on developing in junior and mid-career academics the skills needed to be a good interdisciplinary researcher and research manager or leader of interdisciplinary teams. These included the need to understand the languages, research methods and cultures of different disciplines, as well as the way that interdisciplinary research often cuts across systems of reward and resource allocation found in most universities. These workshops addressed the various goals of interdisciplinary collaboration, the ways in which the collaboration may be sustained, the problems that may be encountered and tactics for addressing such challenges.

The workshop programmes broadly addressed:

- sharing of problems and lessons learned about the pursuit and timely completion of an interdisciplinary PhD (including the role of supervisors);

- development of publication strategies;
- networking to become part of a community;
- marketing oneself for posts while maintaining one's interdisciplinary approach;
- career advice (career path challenges facing interdisciplinary junior academics, awareness of non-academic jobs and potential applications of research to policy-making and other stakeholder areas);
- understanding different languages, methods and cultures;
- variety of motivations for, and different modes of, interdisciplinarity;
- maintaining an interdisciplinary approach within discipline-focused institutions and academic reward mechanisms;
- common interdisciplinary research management challenges.

In each case, trainers drew on examples from their own research across a range of disciplinary and interdisciplinary domains spanning the natural and social sciences. Examples of such interdisciplinary work spanned the life sciences, information and communication technologies (ICT), energy, environment and design sectors and we sought to complement generic messages about interdisciplinarity with concrete lessons about its application in a range of 'real' research and policy contexts. Masterclass participants worked on a range of research questions from an evaluation of ICT in healthcare (a project which drew on computer science, medicine, medical sociology, psychology and epidemiology) to social learning about water resource management (combining geography, sociology, psychology and environmental science).

These activities took the form of advanced training rather than curriculum-based teaching and we adopted a residential, workshop-based format. The programme included a number of guest lecturers but focused on interactive training methods, small group-working structured around readings (either short published articles or scenarios that we had written ourselves) and plenty of informal discussions in a social setting. Participants greatly valued the opportunity to network and learn from others' experiences. Feedback from the first event (aimed at graduate students) showed that 82 per cent of participants had thought about interdisciplinarity in at least one new way as a result of the Masterclass and 77 per cent had at least one new insight into overcoming the challenges of an interdisciplinary PhD. In a follow-up survey a year later, almost a third had changed something about their research as a result of the Masterclass and almost a quarter acknowledged that they would benefit from further interdisciplinary training as their career progressed.

How successful was this small-scale initiative in achieving its goals of building and consolidating interdisciplinary skills and mobilizing a relatively new

and growing research community in the UK? The events were certainly oversub-
scribed, with demand outstripping our ability to supply enough events within
the allocated budget. The Masterclasses and related activities have clearly demonstrated a demand for this type of advanced training and community-building
within (at least) the UK context, given the stage of development of interdisciplinary research capacity. Early career researchers (and some of the more
established researchers who participated) benefited from help in stepping back
and learning about the processes involved in interdisciplinary work and the
implications for their university careers. They also seemed to appreciate the
sense of community that can be stimulated by this type of activity.

One of the outcomes from these workshops has been a series of guidance
notes[5] written in association with workshop participants, in particular the
postgraduate students, who were able to share practical advice for mentoring
and supervising interdisciplinary early career researchers which we draw on in
the remainder of the chapter.

Reflecting on aptitudes for interdisciplinary research

It is clear that interdisciplinary capacity-building is not simply a case of teaching single methods or research techniques. Instead, it is about cultivating a
range of cognitive skills (such as differentiating, reconciling and synthesizing)
and promoting interpersonal and intrapersonal learning that will foster an ability to respond to complex questions, issues or problems (Haynes 2002, cited
by Chettiparamb 2007). In developing such abilities we may well be striving
to achieve 'pursuit of a conversation aimed at enhanced understanding rather
than victory for one point of view' (Szostak 2007).

Lau and Pasquini speak for many when they describe the practical obstacles
facing interdisciplinary scholars and the 'common struggle to find a disciplinary niche' or negotiate an identity (Lau and Pasquini 2008), not least because
the boundaries of interdisciplinary research are under constant negotiation.
This issue of building an interdisciplinary identity is neatly encapsulated in
Case Study 5.4 which reproduces a blog by Ethan Watrall, a scholar at an
American university. We will return to this theme in chapter 6 when we discuss
interdisciplinary career strategies in more detail.

Lau and Pasquini discuss how 'the expectations, attitudes, and approaches
of researchers, and their very conceptualizing of interdisciplinarity, are all influenced by their personal backgrounds to a considerable degree, although the
extent of this influence may be neither noticed nor acknowledged', an aspect
they term 'positionality' (Lau and Pasquini 2008). From this they argue that,
the fact that the definition of interdisciplinarity is necessarily under constant
debate, may be in large part due to the myriad 'positionalities' of spectators
of, and actors in, interdisciplinary research. Even committed interdisciplinary

Case Study 5.4 Building an interdisciplinary identity in a (mostly) non-interdisciplinary academic world

Hi there, my name is Ethan and I'm an archaeologist. Well ... maybe not exactly. I haven't run an excavation in years, and I don't teach in an anthropology department. Ok, let's try this again. Hi my name's Ethan and I'm a digital historian. OK, that's a little better, it's got the 'digital', and I also live (mostly) in a history department. But, my PhD isn't in history. Hmmmm ... OK, how about digital humanist? Well, it's got the 'digital', so that's good. I also 'live' in the digital humanities community, work with many people who identify themselves as digital humanists, and have received digital humanities grants. The problem is that I'm not a humanist. Ok, mmmm ... Game designer? No. Serious game designer? Not really ... it's what I work on, not what I am. Oh bother, what the heck am I?

The problem, dear readers, is that I'm an interdisciplinary scholar. I sit on the happy intersection of several domains (both traditional and 'progressive'). As such, it is always a challenge for me, as well as many others who swim in these crazy interdisciplinary waters, to build and maintain an academic identify.

In many ways, the institution is at the root of this problem – not the scholar. Many institutions pride themselves on encouraging interdisciplinary scholarship (I would hold up my institution as an example of this). However, the reality is that it's a heck of a lot easier to have a traditional, one field identity (English, Geology, Physics, etc.) than it is to create and maintain an interdisciplinary identity. The very structure of most universities are based on a model of one scholar = one discipline (the unit of 'discipline' being the department). Departments are usually walled gardens, little islands of thought and practice that are surrounded by moats filled with sharks and patrolled by giant killer robots with instructions to kill on sight (what? your department doesn't have giant killer robots?). Tenure & promotion standards (which guide the activities for junior faculty – as well as many tenured faculty) are based in the department (and usually vary wildly between departments). On top of that, there is a lot of discipline/department-based inflexibility when it comes to teaching in an interdisciplinary space. Departments are often quite territorial about subjects that they see as their own (try teaching a class that has 'Computer Science' in the title when you are in an Fine Art department, for example). Some universities don't even have a mechanism for recognizing team teaching – which is a hallmark of instruction in many interdisciplinary spaces.

You also have to factor graduate education into the equation as well. You are admitted to a department (or perhaps a program), and in that department, you are educated in the arcane arts and secret handshakes of that discipline. In the vast majority of your graduate classes, you only mingle with initiates of your own secret academic society. You become familiar with a specific set of journals and a specific set of conferences. The end result is graduate students (who turn into professional scholars of one kind or another) who are firmly rooted in one particular discipline.

Obviously I've set up a bit of a straw man here. There are many exceptions to everything I've said. There are departments that tangibly embrace interdisciplinary scholarship and teach their grad students (from the ground up) how to be interdisciplinary scholars. However, I would argue that these cases are the exception, and not the norm. Now, it's important to realize that I'm not trying to launch a wholesale indictment of university practice. I am, however, working hard to reveal some of the challenges involved with forging an interdisciplinary identity.

So, what is an interdisciplinary scholar to do? The bottom line is that you have to work hard at building an interdisciplinary identity, and work even harder to maintain that identity. In this context, here are three strategies for doing just that. As is customary, this list is hardly comprehensive. These are essentially the result of my own personal ruminations (some of which I've personally put into practice) – so, take them in the spirit that they are given.

Develop a Brand: Brand is incredibly important. I know this sounds crass and super 'stupid PR marketing speech', but it's true. Lets be honest here, brand is really another word for identity, and identity is what we're trying to get at here, right? Your brand serves as a foundation upon which you construct your scholarly house of cards. In many ways, your brand will serve as your measuring stick when you go to make choices about things like the journals you'll submit work to, the grants that you'll shoot for, and the collaborations & partnerships you'll enter in to. Don't know the best way of coming up with your academic brand? Ok, try this little exercise. Google 'building a brand' (or some such phrase), and you'll get a list similar to the one below. Answer all of these questions (replacing words like 'company', 'product' and 'service with more academic-y words), and you'll be well on your way to developing your own personal scholarly brand.

- What products and/or services do you offer? Define the qualities of these services and/or products.

- What are the core values of your products and services? What are the core values of your company?

- What is the mission of your company?

Case Study 5.4 *Continued*

- What does your company specialize in?

- Who is your target market? Who do your products and services attract?

As an aside, when I was writing this, Tom Scheinfeldt pointed me towards something he wrote on his own blog called 'Brand Name Scholar' (http://www.foundhistory.org/2009/02/26/brand-name-scholar/). The piece has some great points, and is well worth reading in this context.

Give your 'discipline' a name: If you were at a cocktail party (do people really have cocktail parties anymore?) filled with other academics and were asked what you did, you would want to be able to bust out a 2–3 word name for your 'discipline' at the drop of a hat (NB this is really part of the 'branding process', I just thought it should stand alone because of its importance). You don't want to be fumbling around trying to explain what you do. You could be the smartest person in the room, but if you can't tell people what you do (quickly and succinctly), then no one is gonna take you that seriously. So, give your 'discipline' a name, and become practiced at describing it whenever prompted. For me, it's 'Cultural Heritage Informatics'.

Fight for more flexible tenure and promotion requirements: For all the obvious reasons, this is a tough one. On one hand, the ways in which departments reward scholars with promotion and tenure is very closely linked to maintaining an interdisciplinary identity. On the other hand, agitating for more flexible tenure and promotion requirements is often the game of those who've already been tenured.

By way of example as to the impact that tenure and promotion requirements have on an interdisciplinary scholarly identity – one of the most troublesome trends as of late at my institution is that departments are being asked to provide their Dean with a list of the AAA journals in their field. The (not particularly well hidden) subtext here is that if you aren't publishing in those journals, you aren't doing high quality scholarship. And if you aren't doing quality scholarship, your chances of being promoted or tenured aren't particularly good. The problem is that the journals that are usually added to such a list are what you would call 'traditional core journals'. The result is that many of the journals relevant to *your* particular out of the way interdisciplinary patch of academic ground won't garner the same level of respect or 'tenure credit' as you might get if you were publishing in one of these core journals. What's worse is that your work might be completely inappropriate for any of these journals. So, what are you supposed to do? Fight for more flexible tenure and promotion requirements, that's what!

Source: Reproduced with author's permission from a blog first posted by Ethan Watrall, 1 April 2010, on http://www.ProfHacker.com (Tips and Tutorials for Higher Ed) and now available from http://chronicle.com/blogPost/Building-an-Interdisciplinary/23080/ [accessed 15 January 2011].

scholars fail to recognize the degree to which their academic positionalities (including in the case of the geographers they studied: specialism, age, training and possibly gender and seniority) affect their stances to, and understandings of, interdisciplinary research (Lau and Pasquini, 2008).

We discussed likely personality traits of successful interdisciplinary researchers in chapter 3. In a similar vein, good interdisciplinary supervisors and mentors are likely to be open-minded, willing to learn from other disciplines and have a broad appreciation for the languages, research methods and cultures of different disciplines. In many ways, personality may be more significant than discipline base: interdisciplinary supervisors are likely to have a high degree of curiosity beyond the boundaries of their own discipline so there is little point in taking on an interdisciplinary student if one has no interest in the other contributing discipline(s).

Supervising an interdisciplinary PhD

As we showed in chapter 2, interdisciplinary research is not a single, homogeneous entity but takes different forms depending on the research question. Interdisciplinary research can be within the social sciences, within the natural sciences or between the social and natural sciences. As previously discussed, we have subdivided these into:

- research which aims to further the expertise and competence of academic disciplines themselves, e.g. through developments in methodology which enable new issues to be addressed or new disciplines or sub-disciplines to be formed (*academically orien...* *interdisciplinarity*);

- research which is problem focused and addresses issues of technical and/or policy relevance with less emphasis on dis... academic outcomes (*problem-focused interdisciplinarity*).

These two models of interdisciplinary research are appropriate to different types of research questions and the criteria for the choice of disciplines to be involved in a project will also differ in each case. The research may even represent a mix of the two modes. Those new to interdisciplinary supervision may wish to learn more about the different modes of interdisciplinary research and identify which mode of interdisciplinarity applies to their student's research in order to help them think through the implications for the research design and the nature of supervision. For example, if the research tends more towards academically oriented interdisciplinarity, the supervisor may wish to find co-supervisors who are also working in that emerging sub-discipline. If the research is to be more problem-focused, the supervisor may need to help the student ensure that the thesis has a sufficiently theoretical grounding to satisfy the traditionalists.

In the next sections we discuss in more detail the various stages and aspects of supervising an interdisciplinary PhD: developing a supervisory team; framing, structuring and writing the thesis; and integrating the student into appropriate research networks.

Developing and maintaining a committed supervisory team

Supervision is an important aspect of any PhD project, but the complexities of interdisciplinary research make appropriate supervision even more important. Close supervision and guidance are particularly important for interdisciplinary students in order, for example, to encourage genuine integration and prevent students from slipping back into monodisciplinary comfort zones. On the other hand be open to the really smart student, who knows exactly what he/she wants to do, is very capable and will respond best to light-touch supervision.

Given the range of subject matter to be covered, it is common for interdisciplinary PhD projects to be supervised by a team where individuals have different disciplinary strengths. This does not, of course, preclude the supervisors themselves being interdisciplinary researchers. Supervisors need to develop strong team-working with co-supervisors if students are to benefit rather than suffer. Supervisors, co-supervisors and students need to meet regularly, with sufficient clarity and continuity of communication, that such issues as methodologies, format and focus of the thesis, are agreed mutually and explicitly at an early stage and that inevitable fine-tuning of the developing thesis takes place through ongoing dialogue.

Care needs to be given to the selection of co-supervisors (or PhD committees in the United States) in terms of collaborative compatibility as well as ability to commit to regular meetings with the whole team. More so than monodisciplinary supervision, the commitment of the secondary supervisor(s) is crucial: ·y are not simply nominal appointments but should bring complementary, discipline-based expertise and networks to the project. (The larger PhD committees in the United States may lend themselves more readily to mixes of perspectives and expertise, but even so care needs to be taken not to include overly traditionalist views that might seek to restrict the research design or execution.)

The lead supervisor should facilitate an initial meeting between all parties. It may be helpful to ask each supervisor to bring copies of their key publications and for the student to bring a summary of their master's thesis and outline PhD proposal to begin to foster some shared understandings of each other's work. It may be helpful for the supervisors to hold occasional 'pre-meetings' to discuss their common response before key meetings with the student.

Building foundations and setting boundaries

Disciplines have survived for so long in the academic world in part because they serve the very useful function of constraining what the researcher has to think about. They set a boundary on the parameters of interest (what to include and what to leave out) and dictate the range of methodological approaches that are relevant. They thus provide a clearly defined starting point for a project. In interdisciplinary research, where this framework is partially or wholly removed, students can be overwhelmed by the resulting complexity. A key role for supervisors is therefore to help the student set some boundaries to their research while achieving an appropriate balance between breadth and depth. By definition, interdisciplinary students will not be specialists – and they should not feel as if they are failing because this is true; they cannot try to become experts in all fields involved.

More than monodisciplinary projects, interdisciplinary research has to initially test out a range of possible boundaries to the problem to see which gives the best 'fit'. This should be part of the process of developing a research proposal. It should be clear that the outcome represents a justifiable decision on the project's boundaries. An interdisciplinary student may require particular help in framing a research question that is manageable, suitable and reflects their interests. This will require discussion with all supervisor(s) to agree the level and scope of the research and, in particular, realistic timescales.

Structuring and writing an interdisciplinary thesis

Students must for their survival (and successful completion) stay focused, knowing what part of which disciplines they will use to answer which research questions. More planning is likely to be needed for interdisciplinary projects than for disciplinary projects.

There are different conceptions of what constitutes a PhD thesis: the natural sciences classically have a greater focus on publishing papers, so that each thesis chapter may correspond to a paper, whereas a social science thesis more usually resembles a monograph. Interdisciplinary students need to be given early guidance on whether to follow such a route or develop a distinctively interdisciplinary approach. Extra effort is needed to promote the formation of a cohesive thesis that combines inputs from several knowledge domains. An active strategy is thus needed to integrate the different disciplines and different models in an interdisciplinary project. To this end, supervisors need to encourage integrated rather than 'compartmental' writing. In order to achieve this, at least one member of the supervisory team needs to commit to reading everything that the student writes and ensuring that the student is writing in a way that is accessible to readers (especially examiners) from all contributing disciplines.

Building an interdisciplinary network

Supervisors wield considerable influence over the student's early professional life and play a key role in 'socializing' the student (Golde and Gallagher 1999). An

Illustration 5.1 Encourage integration, not compartmentalism

important success factor for an interdisciplinary student is the development of an interdisciplinary research network but students may have a strong incentive to follow the research direction set by the supervisor: depending on the supervisor this may reinforce disciplinary specialization (Golde and Gallagher 1999). Cross-discipline meetings, seminars, etc. will help the student to build interdisciplinary networks. An interdisciplinary supervisor therefore has an important role to play in helping the student to identify appropriate workshops, conferences and other networking opportunities both within and beyond their own institution. This is likely to require extra effort when the default approach of a supervisor might be to introduce a student to the community of just their own discipline.

Key Advice 5.1 gives some tips to prospective interdisciplinary graduate students when considering their choice of supervisor. Many of these suggestions apply equally when choosing a mentor or even research collaborators (Chuck 2008) as interdisciplinary careers progress. (The traits of good interdisciplinary researchers, identified in Key Advice 3.1, might apply equally to good interdisciplinary supervisors.)

A vital part of the supervision process is the early identification of appropriate examiners, who will be sympathetic to the interdisciplinary approach. This is likely to require more careful consideration and may need to be started at an earlier stage than for a monodisciplinary student.

Key Advice 5.1   Questions to consider when choosing a supervisor

- Have you read their work? Do you have a clear idea of why you are approaching them?

- Does this person share your commitment to interdisciplinary research?

- Will they help you to use interdisciplinarity to build a bridge to a new discipline if this is your ultimate goal?

- Can this person teach you the skills you need to complete your PhD (e.g. research methods, research management techniques, integrative approaches to interdisciplinarity)?

- Will this person facilitate access to appropriate (interdisciplinary) networks and other career opportunities?

- Is this person committed to your success as an interdisciplinary PhD student and able to deal with the inevitable challenges that this will bring?

Developing a publications strategy

Early career researchers need to pay particular attention to getting their work published appropriately and in a timely fashion. In the UK, until recently the Research Assessment Exercise produced quality profiles for each submission made by higher education institutions, and the four Funding Councils used these profiles to determine their grant to the institutions. The tendency of the Research Assessment Exercise (and, as seems likely, its successor the Research Excellence Framework) to concentrate on single-discipline quality indicators has, in the past, made it more difficult for interdisciplinary researchers to publish their work in high quality publication outlets as these are more often regarded as having a monodisciplinary focus (e.g. McCarthy 2004). Ethan Watrall's blog (Case Study 5.4) would suggest that the situation is quite similar in the United States.

This means that interdisciplinary researchers – and especially those at the early stages of their career – need a publications strategy that encompasses both interdisciplinary and more conventionally esteemed monodiscipline journals. This may mean that interdisciplinary students have to be more creative in order to publish in a range of well-regarded journals. Supervisors therefore need to encourage interdisciplinary students to plan a strategic portfolio of different types of articles: theoretical, interdisciplinary, policy, etc. Moreover, interdisciplinary work may require more time to reflect on the potential connections between different aspects of the research. It may be harder for interdisciplinary students to publish during their doctoral studies than, say, monodisciplinary students in the natural sciences whose work may be part of a team-based research project leading to earlier publication opportunities with more experienced members of that team.

Postdoctoral researchers working in project teams should also be encouraged to develop publications strategies which lead to portfolios incorporating both publications in single-discipline and also interdisciplinary journals, a theme that we shall return to in the following chapter.

Mentoring and career guidance

Part of any supervisor's role is to encourage and promote the student's personal and academic growth so as to facilitate their development into a mature and independent researcher. This may involve guiding and assisting the student in structuring their own research ideas and exploring interdisciplinary career opportunities. Increasingly, the Research Councils UK are offering postdoctoral funding for interdisciplinary research opportunities but students who ultimately wish to pursue an academic career should be aware that such a career trajectory is not without risks, as we discuss in the next chapter.

It may be appropriate to encourage activities that can be useful in terms of career development (e.g. teaching experience) provided that this does not interfere with the student's ability to complete their PhD thesis in a timely fashion. Interdisciplinary students may need particular guidance with time-management: interdisciplinary theses may typically take longer to complete given that students need to read across different bodies of literature, possibly learn multiple research methods and wrestle with the issues of integration.

Long-term research collaborations begin to develop at this stage in a researcher's career and are built upon a strong foundation of communication and mentoring. Before embarking on such a professional and, in many cases mentoring relationship, early career researchers should be encouraged to ask themselves some fairly searching questions about the benefits of such a partnership. Chapter 6 will develop this type of self-reflection further from the early career researcher's perspective. But for supervisors and mentors further consideration might be given to offering mentoring opportunities (either with senior colleagues or peers) to give junior staff an opportunity to share experiences, career development plans, etc. As these early career researchers will very rapidly become mentors and supervisors themselves, some training in supervising and examining interdisciplinary PhDs may also be welcome.

As we shall discuss in chapter 8, interdisciplinary research often involves research users to some degree. Early career researchers may benefit from communication training in order to target their language to different audiences and reach a range of different stakeholders and research partners effectively. Training in interpersonal skills such as facilitation, stakeholder engagement and mediation may be particularly valuable for interdisciplinary researchers.

We conclude with a short summary of the dos and don'ts of interdisciplinary supervision and mentoring that we have identified in this chapter (Key Advice 5.2).

Summary

In this chapter we have discussed some of the challenges of building interdisciplinary research skills, not just in the early stages of a research career but also as a form of 'continuous professional development'. We have described our own efforts to support such learning in the UK through our series of Interdisciplinary Masterclasses.

In addition to facilitating peer learning, these Masterclasses have highlighted the importance of community-building by giving early career researchers from different institutions the opportunity to get together. Readers have been encouraged to reflect upon their aptitudes for interdisciplinary research (both as

Key Advice 5.2 A checklist of dos and don'ts for interdisciplinary supervisors and mentors

Aptitudes to interdisciplinary research

- Do be open to new methods from other disciplines.

- Do take the opportunity to read some interdisciplinary papers if this is a new area.

- Do be alive to epistemological differences between the contributing disciplines.

- Do be prepared to question assumptions of your own discipline.

- Do reflect on which mode of interdisciplinarity is appropriate for the particular project.

- Don't assume that there is only one way to conduct interdisciplinary research.

- Don't assume that different approaches are complementary or mutually exclusive.

Developing a committed supervisory team

- Do initiate and maintain dialogue within the supervisory team (including your student).

- Do set and adhere to a timetable for regular, future meetings.

- Do formalize the involvement of each supervisor, reviewing as necessary, as your student's requirement for inputs from each specialist may vary as the thesis progresses.

Helping to structure the research

- Do probe (sensitively) your student's understanding of the foundations of your discipline.

- Do provide your student with introductory and essential references.

- Do help your student to identify any training needs, e.g. research methods.

- Do encourage your student to seek advice from other relevant experts.

- Don't expect an interdisciplinary student to read everything.

- Do help your student develop an integrated strategy for structuring the thesis.

- Do ensure that your student's writing style will not be an obstacle for examiners and other readers coming to the work from different perspectives.

Mentoring and career building

- Do facilitate networking experiences for your student.

- Don't wait till the end to choose examiners, and don't select examiners based solely on outstanding strength in (only) one of your student's disciplines – try to find someone with a track record showing sympathy with interdisciplinarity.

- Do discuss realistic expectations about when and what publications to produce.

- Do impart an understanding of different audiences and writing styles.

- Do promote your student's growth into an independent researcher.

- Do help your student identify and position themselves for interdisciplinary career opportunities.

researchers and supervisors) and we have offered some tips on supervising and mentoring interdisciplinary graduate students and young postdoctoral researchers. We have suggested that such supervisors/mentors need to focus not just on the research but on the particular forms of professional support and mentoring required by inexperienced interdisciplinary researchers in terms of career guidance, network-building and the development of publications strategies.

Questions

For researchers

1 Where do you want to make your contribution? (Publish within one or across several fields; create new interdisciplinary fields; lead in the development of creative solutions to a critical problem?)

2 What support and training do you need in order to achieve this?

For research supervisors and managers

1 Would you say that you and your colleagues (team members, co-supervisors/mentors) have had the opportunity to step back and think through issues and processes related to the generation of high quality interdisciplinary research?

2 Are there opportunities to attend masterclasses or other focused events to learn more?

3 How might it help you and your team members to participate in a dispersed community or network across which practical learning about interdisciplinarity could be shared and extended?

For institutional leaders

1 How could you go about creating an environment conducive to interdisciplinarity among early career researchers?

2 In what ways could you support researchers and research managers through continuous professional development, so that they have the freedom to be creative combined with a supportive infrastructure?

3 How could you celebrate interdisciplinary successes and otherwise send positive messages throughout your institution?

For research funders

1 What steps could you take to catalyse or support long term capacity-building? Through formal degree training? Through short courses or other events focused on the processes of interdisciplinarity?

2 Are there ways in which you could help interdisciplinary researchers develop networks and communities?

6

Charting a Course for an Interdisciplinary Career

Establishing and sustaining interdisciplinary careers in and beyond universities

Introduction

Interdisciplinary careers can come in many shapes and guises. The nature of interdisciplinarity will vary among individuals, and their fields, topic areas and career paths. The degree or intensity of interdisciplinarity can change over the course of a career. Charting a course for an interdisciplinary career may more effectively lead to desired destinations if tactics are developed deliberately with awareness of this range of possibilities.

For many, interdisciplinary careers will involve working in teams. Some will view their careers as interdisciplinary by virtue of occasionally participating in multidiscipline teams. Others will seek out the opportunity to work in multidisciplinary teams more often, as an ongoing element in their research portfolio. Their commitment may arise because they enjoy the intellectual dialogue and/ or because this represents a route toward tackling 'favourite' complex problems. They may or may not think of themselves as interdisciplinary researchers but they do pursue interdisciplinary (or transdisciplinary) understanding.

Among these frequent flyers, some will relish, in particular, the process of integration across a team's disciplines. They may thus view themselves as more actively interdisciplinary than others who 'simply' contribute a discipline-based component. Sometimes called 'boundary spanners' or 'knowledge intermediaries', they may act as facilitators of dialogue and synthesis. Over time, this active role may transform into a fully fledged leadership role, one that involves identifying opportunities for interdisciplinary research, putting together teams and bids, and managing teams to achieve interdisciplinary understanding.

Some of these individuals will come to affiliate themselves more with interdisciplinarity than with a particular discipline; they may even find it constraining to return to their home discipline. Instead of this evolution over time, some will see themselves as interdisciplinary from the very start of their careers; strategic charting of a career path may be most critical for these researchers as they challenge the academic status quo.

Through their PhD, postdoctoral and subsequent research, individuals develop their own intellectual worldview, their underlying approach to tackling problems. Their position in the range depicted in Figure 6.1 may change at different stages. Some may pursue interdisciplinarity at every career stage, from pre-PhD onwards. Yet, when considering the risks of an interdisciplinary career, for example, an individual starting out might decide strategically to: play down their interdisciplinarity early on in their career; 'earn their spurs' in a discipline; and then, gradually and with increasing intensity, become involved in interdisciplinary research. Less strategically, those with vague leanings toward complex problems might simply find that, over time and with the security of an established position, they become more involved in interdisciplinarity. Some will find themselves moving into a newly emerging field, which draws from more than one parent discipline.

All of these different paths can be encompassed by the term 'interdisciplinary career'. The set of questions provided at the end of this chapter (Key Advice 6.3) may help readers reflect upon what sort of interdisciplinary career (if any) is most appropriate for their future.

Types of interdisciplinary careers

Just as the problems tackled by interdisciplinary research can vary all across the map, so can the nature of interdisciplinary careers. Some individuals span short or long 'distances' between disciplines (e.g. two different areas of biology representing fairly 'close' interdisciplinary distances, versus arts and engineering or social sciences and environmental sciences representing a greater span). Some are very single-mindedly problem-based, while others are more broadly exploratory with their interdisciplinarity, and yet others employ interdisciplinarity inherent in new emerging fields (conservation biology, environmental economics, synthetic biology) (see for example, Case Study 6.1). To appreciate

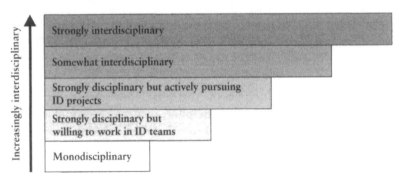

Figure 6.1 Degree of interdisciplinary involvement

the heterogeneity of possible interdisciplinary careers and to gain a sense of how they can develop over time, brief profiles of seven people who have incorporated interdisciplinarity into their careers are included at the end of this chapter (Case Study 6.5).

Case Study 6.1 From collaborative interdisciplinarity to individual interdisciplinarity

Systems biology approaches have increased in profile over recent years and are a good example of academically oriented interdisciplinarity, the development of a new discipline. Systems biology involves integrating data from the molecular level to produce computer-based models of biological systems. Knowledge from different disciplines is needed in order to understand and integrate data. Sometimes knowledge and problem-solving skills from very different domains (such as astrophysics) need to be encompassed.

Jane Calvert has tracked the development of systems biology in the UK and United States and the changes that have taken place in individuals' disciplinary identity. On interviewing senior scientists in systems biology she found that most did not identify themselves as systems biologists but rather along their original disciplinary lines, often referring to their training as a biologist, physicist or computer scientist. A few indicated that they no longer identified themselves with their original discipline and one identified himself as in 'purgatory' between mathematics and biology. However, more junior scientists were generally more comfortable with identifying themselves as systems biologists and their training was less monodisciplinary. First year PhD students in systems biology hoped to be able to identify themselves as 'systems biologists' once they had finished their training. Intriguingly, one postdoc used multiple disciplinary identities depending on the context. In talking to someone outside the research organization he would describe himself as a systems biologist but within the organization he would call himself a bioengineer working in the field of systems biology, thus maintaining the dual identity of systems biologist and bioengineer.

Interdisciplinary careers can therefore result in a multitude of different directions and stages: from collaborative interdisciplinarity through to holding multiple disciplinary identities, to a liminal place between disciplines and to individual interdisciplinarity and identification with a newly formed discipline.

Source: Calvert 2010.

Career risks and benefits

Despite the enthusiasm of these devotees of interdisciplinarity, the route toward an interdisciplinary career is not always plain sailing. Awareness of possible hazards that may show up along the way can help when charting or indeed steering a course. Several sorts of risks may arise. What role(s) might you play in ensuring that researchers who do excellent interdisciplinary work progress in their careers?

An important possible risk, especially but not exclusively for someone starting out in their career, might be lack of institutional advancement. For many good reasons, the institutions of academia have long been geared toward disciplines and monodisciplinary work, whether these institutions take the form of departments, faculties, universities, professional bodies, journals or esteem measures such as membership in key societies. If promotion or selection processes, criteria and judges are all oriented toward evaluation of worth as measured by contribution to a single discipline, an individual who participates in more than one discipline may be disadvantaged by this 'dilution'. Illustrating this is the very practical point of authorship: participation in interdisciplinary team projects typically leads to publications with multiple authors, yet single authorship is looked upon more favourably in certain disciplines and author order can sometimes be a tricky issue to negotiate. Even when part of an interdisciplinary person's research contribution is to their parent discipline, other components of their research may be simply disregarded, thus decreasing the perceived volume of their effort. And, of course, if reviewers in a position of power are in a different discipline, then contributions may be undervalued. For example, a lone social scientist in a medical school might not be promoted, without colleagues knowledgeable about his/her work to speak up for him/her in competition with medical colleagues whose attributes would be more familiar to decision-makers.

In fact, there is a risk that overt interdisciplinarity of a young researcher could deter potential academic employers at the start of a career, prior to any promotion processes. For example, in a study we conducted of an interdisciplinary capacity-building scheme for the UK (Meagher and Lyall 2005a), one professorial head of school was extremely complimentary about the calibre of interdisciplinary PhD students produced by the scheme. Yet, when asked if he, personally, would hire such a product of the scheme into a standard academic track, he paused and then quite sheepishly admitted that he probably would not, as priority would inevitably be placed upon individuals seen to be able to teach introductory courses in that discipline. A survey on interdisciplinarity by the National Academies captured this sort of risk across multiple US universities: promotion criteria were the highest ranked impediment to interdisciplinary research, as ranked both by individuals and by university provosts (National Academies 2005: 264–5).

The winning of research grants is intimately interwoven with career prospects at all stages. There is a financial risk taken by interdisciplinary researchers when they attempt to compete with conventional bids submitted within the accepted parameters of a discipline. In most cases, senior bodies of reviewers such as the Research Councils UK's Peer Review Colleges are composed of professors who have won their seniority by rising through the ranks pursuing one discipline. The worldview they and, most often, any other reviewers bring to evaluation is thus couched within the context of one discipline. Since an interdisciplinary bid is by nature bound to include components beyond any monodisciplinary reviewer's purview, much of the calibre and content of the bid may be ignored, misunderstood or at best discounted. (An exception may exist if an appropriate range of interdisciplinarity-aware reviewers are selected for bids submitted to an explicitly interdisciplinary scheme.) We discuss challenges of evaluating interdisciplinarity at various levels in more detail in chapter 7.

More broadly, the way an individual is viewed professionally is often influenced by the company they keep, which has inherent implications for career advancement. Most monodisciplinary researchers, for example, will give talks and network at conferences dedicated to their discipline; they become known in that circle, which can lead to invitations to give seminars and keynote presentations, submit and review articles, participate on review panels and so on. For a researcher pursuing multiple interests, there is no one comfortable circle of colleagues. On the other hand, there may be a wide circle for whom that person is their 'token interdisciplinary researcher', leading to excessive pressure to participate in a wide range of interdisciplinary roles and further dilute the depth of their influence in any one area.

Rather than deterring people from interdisciplinarity, perhaps some useful lessons can be drawn. For those venturing into interdisciplinarity, decisions as to which conferences to attend and which communities to join become strategic. Does one, for example, give a 'straight' disciplinary talk each year in a conference devoted to one's home discipline and then also another talk at an explicitly interdisciplinary conference dedicated to a favourite complex problem? How does one pursue networks, and of what sort? What is the best context to become known in, as someone who does excellent work or has important insights, perhaps even as a leader? One way to acquire a more permanent network of colleagues is to participate preferentially in a particular area of application, e.g. risk, rural development or innovation.

With these institutional, financial and community-building risks comes a personal risk. There is certainly the potential for stress or even depression if an interdisciplinary career does not progress as quickly or positively as

Illustration 6.1 Feel secure in your interdisciplinary identity

surrounding disciplinary careers. An individual pursuing interdisciplinarity may feel quite isolated, particularly if he/she is the only one with that orientation in a department. More extensive personal effort, in terms of proactive reaching out, may be required to build a sense of community with other kindred spirits, who may be located far away rather than a neighbourly walk down a corridor. Another lesson, relevant to any researcher but perhaps vital to interdisciplinary researchers at any career stage, is to believe sufficiently in what one is doing that it is possible to create for oneself a core equilibrium and thus project the confidence that will make others listen to what one has to say, with or without a conventional disciplinary persona.

Participants (primarily early in their careers) who attended one of the Interdisciplinary Masterclasses described in the previous chapter offered suggestions as to risks and benefits associated with interdisciplinary careers

RISKS	BENEFITS
• Methodological confusion	• Interesting, exciting and satisfying work
• Lack of focus/clarity, danger of losing focus	• Flexibility
• Absence of common goal (chance of some being 'outsiders')	• Diversified, larger portfolio of methodological tools
• Inability to evaluate quality	• Multiple, creative approaches (or combinations thereof) to a problem
• Lack of theoretical rigour and a discipline base	• New perspectives, disposing of myths
• Lack of integration, complexities	• Good exercises in communicating with wider audiences (and related improvement in self-understanding)
• Fewer outputs (e.g. fewer high quality interdisciplinary journal outlets)	• Real-life, practical relevance
• Disagreements over ownership of intellectual property, novel ideas, findings	• Improved understanding of complex phenomena
• High risk of failure	• Novel, exciting breakthroughs, achievement of complementarity
• Bottlenecks due to interdependencies among team members (complexity of some playing key roles at different stages, with others dependent upon them)	• Over the long-term, cost-effectiveness due to synergies saving time and energy
• Wasting time on management and administration rather than doing one's own work	
• Mission drift	

Figure 6.2 Risks and benefits of interdisciplinarity. Implications for research and future careers
Note: many benefits can be identified as the positive side of risks, e.g. high risk of failure can also imply opportunity for genuine innovation

(Figure 6.2). For many, despite the potential for rough seas, working in an interdisciplinary way allows them to enjoy the journey as they move along in their career. Incentives include the intellectual challenge of dialogue with others who may have very different perspectives, ways of tackling problems and even ways of framing questions. It can be enjoyable to test one's assumptions regularly and to expand one's view.

Closely related to this may be a personal enjoyment brought about by working in a team with others. In a sense, one interdisciplinary team, or more broadly an interdisciplinary network focused on a common problem, can a as a personalized community, potentially more tightly knit than a far-flung discipline.

A significant motivating factor for many embarking on interdisciplinarity is the satisfaction arising from making a contribution to society. The complexity of many problems facing society today, with sustainability (environmental, economic and social) being just one example, cries out for interdisciplinary work. As discussed in chapter 8, many people who employ interdisciplinary approaches in their career are especially proactive in attempts to exchange knowledge with those outside of academia who might make positive change happen.

Finally, particularly when attached to a societal challenge, willingness to participate in interdisciplinary work may lead to funding for research, with correlated advantages for career progression. With increasing emphasis by research funding bodies on visible generation of societal impacts, opportunities for interdisciplinary funding may grow in the future. For example, the Research Councils UK (RCUK) see interdisciplinarity as a goal, noting at their July 2009 International Stakeholder Meeting that, as one of their four ways of 'shaping a strong science base', they 'encourage research across discipline boundaries'. Examples cited of RCUK Interdisciplinary Programmes, each supported by multiple funding bodies, illustrate the weight of investment now being put into interdisciplinarity in the UK (Table 6.1; see the List of Acronyms at the beginning of the book for full names of the councils).

Making the decision to embark on the journey

Given that the road to a successful interdisciplinary career may, at times, be more of an obscure track road than a major highway, the choice of that career goal deserves some deliberation. A useful first step may be that tried but true one of self-reflection, knowing oneself and understanding what motivations will act as drivers in building a career. Taking some time to think through questions such as the checklist in Key Advice 6.1 or the mental exercises in Case Study 6.2 might be helpful in that regard.

Adding value to different career dimensions through interdisciplinarity

One way to think about prospects for an interdisciplinary career is to think about how interdisciplinarity might add value to different aspects of a career.

Table 6.1 Research Councils UK investments in interdisciplinary research (2008–2011)

Programme title	Programme funding	Lead Research Council	Research Council partners
Ageing: Life long Health & Wellbeing	£486m	MRC	EPSRC, BBSRC, ESRC, NERC, STFC, AHRC
Living with Environmental Change	£363m	NERC	EPSRC, BBSRC, ESRC, STFC, MRC, AHRC
Energy	£319m	EPSRC	BBSRC, ESRC, NERC, STFC
Global Uncertainty: Security for All in a Changing World	£114m	ESRC	EPSRC, BBSRC, NERC, STFC, MRC, AHRC
Digital Economy	£53m	EPSRC	AHRC, ESRC, MRC
Nanoscience through Engineering to Application	£51m	EPSRC	BBSRC, ESRC, NERC, STFC, MRC

Source: http://www.rcuk.ac.uk/cmsweb/downloads/rcuk/international/
RCUKpresentationJuly2009.pdf [accessed 25 February 2010].

Undergraduate teaching

Some would argue fervently that undergraduate teaching can benefit from an interdisciplinary approach. The liberal arts tradition in US higher education, for example, often translates into institutional requirements that students learn in some depth about the content and approaches to problem-solving of at least two or three quite different subjects. Many times, courses are added to the curriculum that are inherently interdisciplinary. Many leading institutions place a positive value on interdisciplinarity. As just one example, Middlebury College,

Key Advice 6.1 Understanding interdisciplinary motivations: Some questions to ask yourself

1 Why are you interested in pursuing an interdisciplinary career? Which of the possible incentives or positives speak to you? What sort of career example resonates with you? Why?

2 Do you want to solve complex problems, and interdisciplinarity is the only viable pathway you see?

3 Do you get an intellectual buzz from working with people who take diverse approaches?

4 Does working in only one discipline, and only with others from that discipline, seem 'flat' to you?

5 Are you yourself so attracted to two or more fields that you want to conquer both – and look for synergies between them?

6 Or do you have some other reason?

7 Do you see yourself working primarily or exclusively in an interdisciplinary way? Or primarily in a discipline, with a portion of lively interdisciplinarity at the edges?

8 Do you feel driven to spend your whole career in an interdisciplinary mode or do you have a sense that it is 'a phase you're going through' such that you'll come out the other side focusing on one discipline, perhaps different from your starting point?

Case Study 6.2 A thought experiment

Imagine you are at a retreat with a number of individuals you don't know, who are from a variety of different fields. The topic of the retreat is to be a multifaceted exploration of the rapidly growing phenomenon of addiction to personal communication technologies. The actual meeting doesn't begin until tomorrow, so tonight is just a social time. There is a fire in the fireplace, plenty of nibbles and beverages are available, but you are a bit late and people already appear to be clumped in four corners of the room.

The retreat organizer welcomes you in and mentions that people appear to have assorted themselves into four groupings, which she describes as:

- a group of biologists of mixed disciplines: neurobiologists, evolutionary biologists, animal behaviourists, some geneticists;

- a group of geneticists, each pursuing a slightly different approach to addiction and behaviour;

- a highly heterogeneous group, which appears to have one of each of widely divergent disciplines: an anthropologist, a Human Computer Interface scientist, a psychologist, an animal behaviourist and an electronics engineer; and

- a group of people with an overview perspective who are interested in but have not specialized in this area: a senior staffer for a key policy-maker, an ethicist, a counselling psychologist, a communications company market researcher and a representative of a newly formed support group.

Say, for the purposes of this thought-exercise, that you are a geneticist exploring the molecular basis of behaviours like addiction. Which of the groups would you naturally gravitate toward? What would be your second choice? Why?

Source: Inspired by Bolles 2010.

itself one of the top five US liberal arts four-year colleges, as ranked in 2010 (US News & World Report 2010), highlights interdisciplinarity as a core element, requiring that courses taken encompass seven academic categories and offering an array of interdisciplinary programmes which provide undergraduates with opportunities to 'synthesize and connect what you learn in many different departments'.[1]

Even in the UK, where a far greater narrowing of focus is traditional, some inroads are being made into interdisciplinarity at an undergraduate level. Sometimes the fiercest battles can be fought across seemingly closely related disciplines; yet at other times a virtue is made of creating bridges to help students learn. For example, an integrated exposure to biological anthropology, physical anthropology and archaeology is extolled as a hallmark of Cambridge University's 'unique', 'broad-ranging' Tripos in Archaeology and Anthropology.[2]

Individual courses or modules can offer undergraduates a tantalizing glimpse into interdisciplinarity; since they are often taught by teams, such courses require effort but also provide academics with intellectual stimulation

(Shearer 2007). It is not impossible to imagine that even a course/module within a particular discipline might capture students' attention by setting it within a broader context, or providing examples of relevant problems that can best be tackled by collaboration with other disciplines.

In the United States, calls for more interdisciplinary researchers to be developed cite the need to address this at an undergraduate level: '*Undergraduate students* should seek out interdisciplinary experiences, such as courses at the interfaces of traditional disciplines that address basic research problems, interdisciplinary courses that address societal problems, and research experiences that span more than one traditional discipline' (National Academies 2005: 4). On the other hand, some might argue that people who have had a discipline-based education up to first degree level make better interdisciplinary researchers, perhaps because they have a better idea of what constitutes academic rigour, whether applied in a disciplinary or interdisciplinary context.

PhD supervision

Usually the bastion of disciplinary continuity, PhD level education has begun to experience breaches by interdisciplinarity. Challenges and opportunities involved in supervision of interdisciplinary PhDs are discussed in chapter 5, but there is clearly an increasing need for individuals who can provide such supervision. Certainly, as new fields emerge at the crossroads of traditional fields, up and coming PhD students are seizing opportunities. Furthermore, funding bodies that support PhD students have begun to experiment with interdisciplinary PhD studentship and postdoctoral support. This is sometimes, although not always, associated with an orientation toward knowledge exchange beyond academia.

Sometimes this occurs within the context of a research centre or a large interdisciplinary research initiative. For example, the UK-based Tyndall Centre, tackling the complexities of climate change, instituted interdisciplinary supervisory teams for its interdisciplinary PhD students and also developed a research network for them; this was so popular that even post-PhD researchers come back to gatherings for short courses and 'community' (Tyndall Centre 2010). As another example, through its Research Development Grant (RDG, now Strategic Research Development Grant) Scheme, the Scottish Funding Council has supported a wide array of centres in emerging areas ranging from computer games to science policy advice to integrated microsystems, with the intention of building leadership capacity within Scotland in these promising problem areas; over 500 'next generation researchers' were associated with the 38 RDGs of Phases 2 and 3, most of which involved some form of interdisciplinarity (Meagher and Lyall 2005b). As discussed in chapter 5, the US National Science Foundation, through its IGERT initiative, funds large-scale capacity-building in interdisciplinarity by supporting significant numbers of PhD students at an institution (or set of partner institutions) around a particular broad subject (e.g. the science of language at Johns Hopkins University, the solar economy at Purdue University, and food systems and poverty reduction at Cornell University).

Experimental support for interdisciplinary capacity-building has occurred in the UK across funding bodies with different missions and constituencies. This trend might grow. For example, the combined Research Councils UK launched a fellowship scheme in 2004 in order to 'provide attractive and stable research career paths for promising researchers' and funded 800 fellowships, of which 300 were interdisciplinary; given the scheme's emphasis on innovation, nearly 40 per cent of the fellowships crossed the arenas of two or more Research Councils.[3] Other examples include the ESRC/NERC and ESRC/MRC schemes which supported interdisciplinary PhD students integrating social and environmental sciences, and PhD students and postdoctoral fellows combining social and medical sciences, respectively.

These experiments have shed light on the critical importance of effective team supervision, and appropriate external examination, for interdisciplinary students, such that interdisciplinary expertise may lend real value to a prospective supervisor: 'Variability in student experiences with supervision and co-supervision suggest that ESRC/NERC provide guidance (e.g. a good practice handbook) for supervisors. Perhaps even more urgently, development of guidance on expectations of interdisciplinarity within this scheme is recommended for External Examiners (who in any event must be chosen carefully, quite possibly drawing on experienced Scheme supervisors)' (Meagher and Lyall 2005a: 43).

For example, one supervisor involved in another interdisciplinary postgraduate scheme (Meagher and Lyall 2009) mentioned that finding such external examiners is one of the most difficult tasks, with selection of examiners often high-risk for students, such that she has her students include in their theses a clear statement of their ground and the difficulties of interdisciplinarity to help examiners see how and why the thesis has developed. She, herself, has been asked to play the external examiner role many times across Europe, due not so much to her specific field of expertise but to her sympathy regarding the importance of intellectual linkages and the appropriate structuring of an interdisciplinary thesis. Clearly, an interdisciplinary background would add strength to supervisory and examiner roles regarding others' interdisciplinary work.

Synergistic collaborations

Some indications would suggest that more, rather than fewer, interdisciplinary research collaborations may be funded in the future, as funding bodies such as the UK's Research Councils place strategic emphasis on this (for example, ESRC 2009a). The existence of a number of interdisciplinary initiatives in the UK alone – including but far from limited to the Extending Quality of Life initiative, Flood-Risk Management Research Consortium, People at the Centre of Computers and Information Technology (PACCIT) or Designing for the 21st

Century – would suggest that value is being placed increasingly on individuals who can work effectively in the teams required to implement the vision for such initiatives. In the United States, examples of inter-agency interdisciplinary initiatives include the Climate Change Science Program (CCSP) and the National Nanotechnology Initiative.

One very significant example of UK investment explicitly valuing the crucial role to be played by interdisciplinarity is the Living with Environmental Change (LWEC) programme, a ten-year programme that will invest £1 billion in its first five years (via its many Research Council and other partners) toward aims that clearly need to involve interdisciplinarity (Case Study 6.3).

Case Study 6.3   Goals of UK Living with Environmental Change (LWEC) programme

Through interdisciplinary research activities, knowledge exchange actions and training opportunities, Living with Environmental Change aims to deliver:

- whole-system assessments and risk-based predictions of environmental change and its effects on ecosystem services, health (human, plant and animal), infrastructure, economies and communities on local-to-regional and timescales ranging from seasons to decades;

- integrated analyses of the potential social, economic and environmental costs, benefits and impacts of different mitigation and adaptation responses;

- guidance for more effective sustainable management of ecosystem services, as a foundation for resilient economic development and social progress;

- improved human well-being and the alleviation of poverty by ensuring a sustainable supply of food and water;

- new technology and infrastructure solutions in the management of environmental change;

- a more research-informed dialogue and debate about the environmental challenges and choices we face in the future, and their economic and social consequences.

Source: Living with Environmental Change, http://www.lwec.org.uk/about-living-environmental-change/aims.

Knowledge exchange and consulting

In chapter 8, we will discuss at some length the potential of interdisciplinary research to contribute to knowledge exchange with individuals and entities beyond academia. Here, we would just point out that the complex problems faced by people in 'the real world' seldom if ever align themselves neatly to academic disciplines. Instead, most often they demand integration across perspectives. Furthermore, we would suggest that individuals who possess expertise in communicating and working with people in other disciplines may well possess a distinct advantage when it comes to the collaborative processes required for effective knowledge exchange with stakeholders of varying perspectives and backgrounds. Numerous funding schemes have been established to facilitate collaboration between academics and people in industry. In the UK, just a few examples include: CASE studentships, Knowledge Transfer Partnerships and Scotland's Proof of Concept awards. Even the UK's Research Councils, traditionally the source of funding for basic research, now seek evidence of impact beyond academia, whenever possible (e.g. Research Councils UK 2006; Research Councils UK 2007; ESRC 2009c), and consultation on the next centralized UK-wide assessment of research quality across all departments of all universities includes reference to incorporation of impacts as a parameter to be weighed (HEFCE 2009). Given this context, an increasing number of academic departments may move toward the encouragement of knowledge exchange, through funded research and also consulting; interdisciplinary researchers may be particularly well-suited to respond effectively.

Careers beyond academia

Academia is far from the only setting in which interdisciplinary careers can be pursued. Given that more individuals work outside of academia than within it, and also that industry and non-academic research centres tend not to emphasize disciplinary divides, it may be encouraging to note that interdisciplinary working is an approach that runs throughout a great many careers in industry, government or not-for-profit/third-sector organizations:

> In addition, most graduate students who acquire PhDs in science and engineering will find career opportunities in non-academic research settings, where most of the new research positions are likely to be created over the next few decades. For today's students – who may eventually work not only with researchers in different science and engineering fields, but also in development, marketing, law, economics, ethics or other non-research activities – it is doubly important to hone their skills in communicating with people in other fields and to gain exposure to IDR (interdisciplinary research) in nonacademic settings through cooperative programs, summer jobs, and other opportunities. (National Academies 2005: 42, citing COSEPUP 1995)

Industry

A wide range of industry sectors depend upon innovation. Not for nothing do politicians around the world refer to 'the Knowledge Economy'. Generating, modifying and adapting innovation draws upon research, whether conducted in a company per se or gathered and translated from other sources. While in some cases researchers working in industry can focus on a narrow specialism, perhaps when an extremely technical role must be provided, far more often they are expected to work in teams. Furthermore, these teams are often structured flexibly, composed across expertise to solve one problem and then re-aggregated in different configurations as other problems arise. Team-working skills, mental agility and an orientation toward the integration of lines of evidence, along with a priority on problem-solving, will all contribute to effective roles in industry – these attributes may sound very familiar to someone naturally oriented toward interdisciplinarity:

> Our work in Pfizer in discovering and developing new medicines is critically dependent on integrating advances in many other fields from physics, chemistry, materials sciences, and engineering to computer modeling and information technology. By sharing ideas from these fields, our scientists are able to create a critical intellectual mass that increases the creativity, the capacity, and the speed of innovation at Pfizer and other companies like us. (William C. Steere, Jr, chairman of the board and chief executive officer, Pfizer, Inc., cited in National Academies 2005: 44)

In addition to conducting research, some individuals in industry gather up knowledge generated in a variety of other places, recombining bits of understanding to form something new. Wide-ranging interests and integrative tendencies could also be useful in conducting knowledge exchange, or acting as a knowledge intermediary, working on behalf of industry.

Government

Interdisciplinary individuals can also add value to government. Policies, strategies, regulations and other activities of government all are likely to depend on more than one type of evidence. (Indeed, governments will pay heed to input other than research, such as politics or public opinion). Particularly given the mantra of 'evidence-based policy-making', individuals who can evaluate evidence from a wide range of sources will be useful. Even more valuable than the ability to bring one's own expertise to a policy issue is the ability to communicate with others who bring different expertise, and then join up diverse types of evidence into a recommended policy or solution. Opportunities exist to gain experience with government, for those wondering if that may be the right path. Sometimes this can take the form of sitting on a committee or inquiry, responding to a government consultation or working with a professional society to help policy-makers. Sometimes shadowing or visiting can provide real two-way insight. For example, one of us held a short-term fellowship to contribute to policy-making (Crossland 2010) while learning first-hand how policy is made at the UK's Department for Environment, Food and Rural Affairs (Defra), which has highlighted the need for more inter-disciplinarity in its recent Evidence Strategy (Defra 2010). In the United States, the American Association for the Advancement of Science offers Congressional Fellowships for academics who want to participate in policy-making.[4]

Perhaps mission-oriented bodies are particularly likely to put an emphasis upon interdisciplinarity. Consider, for example, the making of policy regarding sustainability or climate change – complex goals involving consideration of the environment, the economy and society. As an example of a growing demand for wide interdisciplinary understanding, a project funded by the Scotland and Northern Ireland Forum for Environmental Research (SNIFFER) on social dimensions of climate change (Meagher 2010) generated a new level of aware-ness among various governmental agencies across the UK as to the possibility for differential effects of climate change, and capacity to adapt to such change, among various sub-populations of society. Certainly, positions in governmental bodies can draw upon interdisciplinary skills and capacity.

Variously named, national laboratories or 'public sector research establish-ments' are, in a sense, a one-step-removed subset of government. In review-ing a variety of US national labs that address large-scale needs, the National Academies noted that:

> IDR (interdisciplinary research) has been important to all national laboratories since their foundation. They all use large, multidisciplinary teams to attack problems that require a wide array of skills, often in both science and engineering, and that are too complex for research teams based in any single disciplines ... Because of the interdisciplinary nature of their work, national laboratories tend to hire people who want to work on teams. (National Academies 2005: 52)

Increasingly, government-related research bodies strive to bridge between social and natural sciences in their mandate to contribute to evidence-based policy-making. The Macaulay Land Use Research Institute in Scotland, for example, is a main research provider for the Scottish Government and clearly embeds interdisciplinarity within its aims and self-definition (Case Study 6.4).

Third Sector

A wide range of organizations exist in the 'third sector', including charitable or voluntary organizations and foundations. Very often, the goals they seek to address are complex, involving multiple strands of change. Many draw upon natural science or medicine as they attempt to change society, making social science understanding vital as well. Another role for spanners of interdiscipli-nary boundaries might lie in the increasingly prevalent role of 'science commu nicator' which, broadly defined, seeks to engage the public in debates abc and understanding of, the natural sciences.

Case Study 6.4 Macaulay Land Use Research Institute

Founded in 1930, the Macaulay Land Use Research Institute is an international centre for research and consultancy on the environmental and social consequences of rural land uses. Interdisciplinary research across the environmental and social sciences aims to support the protection of natural resources, the creation of integrated land use systems and the development of sustainable rural communities.

With an annual income from research and consultancy of over £11 million, the Macaulay Land Use Research Institute is the largest interdisciplinary research organization of its kind in Europe.

Within the Institute, the water catchment management work illustrates the workings of interdisciplinarity in tackling a multifaceted issue that is both technical and of socio-economic importance. Catchment management research at the Macaulay Land Use Research Institute focuses on understanding the processes which affect water and water resources from the mountains to the sea. Work on catchment systems researches the social and economic aspects of water management, as well as trying to understand the biophysical processes which occur within and between different ecosystems. This seems to be a good example of constructive boundary setting that *enables* interdisciplinary integration.

As the leader of the team, Bob Ferrier, observes:

> Environmental problems start and end with people. Without integrating disciplines we really aren't delivering on the important issues, which are about engagement, equity, empowerment, etc. In many situations it is changed behaviour based on a strong biophysical science support that will effect real-world solutions ... Taking time to understand how disciplines work and communicate is a skill and does not fit comfortably with everyone. It is however how we adapt to face the challenges ahead.

Source: Personal communication, September 2010; http://www.macaulay.ac.uk; http://www.macaulay.ac.uk/videos/wup.

Your personal career development strategy

Whatever the sector chosen, each person will need to craft his or her own balance of disciplinarity and interdisciplinarity at any one time and over the years of a career. This will take self-knowledge as to intellectual drivers as well as assessment of the career risks posed by interdisciplinarity, especially early in a career. Thinking through your own motivations and likely opportunities is an inescapable step of reflection if you are to manage your career actively. The checklist of questions in the 'reflection guide' (Key Advice 6.3) at the end of this chapter may be helpful. Considering the profiles provided in Case Study 6.5, or alternatives such as the scenarios in Key Advice 6.2 may also help.

Chapter 5 discussed many key steps and tactics in forging an interdisciplinary career, primarily from the perspective of a supervisor or mentor helping an early career interdisciplinary researcher. Perhaps the key message specifically for an early career interdisciplinary researcher is that you, yourself, will need to take charge of your career path. Others who take the disciplinary route will probably follow a more straightforward career path, complete with conventional road signs along the way. Breaking your own trail is not impossibly hard, but it will take effort, as well as reflection at particular turning points. You may proceed a bit more slowly as the ground will not be trodden smooth ahead of you. You don't have to be alone as you pursue this path; but you will create your own individualized 'community' of fellow travellers. Because more

---

Key Advice 6.2   Career development scenarios

Scenario A
Are you absolutely driven to do full-scale interdisciplinary work right away, no matter what, even if your career is not yet established? If so, you might look for departments or groups/centres within departments that share your commitment and/or involvement in your particular subject. Try to figure out what steps you would need to take to find a home affiliated with one of them.

Scenario B
Or, you might have sufficient interest in one discipline that you might choose the 'safer road' of developing a 'mainstream' reputation with nearly or most of your early work in that one discipline. To keep your interdisciplinary interests alive, you might perhaps at the same time cultivate a 'side-interest' in an interdisciplinary project or two. Or, you might make a point of participating in a relevant conference each year, while building a network of like-minded interdisciplinary colleagues concurrently with your building of a monodisciplinary network.

Scenario C
You might only occasionally publish interdisciplinary articles in your first years, but then gradually become more involved and develop interdisciplinary work and articles as an increasing proportion of your professional portfolio.

proactive effort will be demanded of you at each stage, you will know without a doubt that the journey is distinctly your own.

The exhortative US National Academies report is so committed to the national need for interdisciplinary individuals that it encourages people to seek out interdisciplinary experiences at all stages: undergraduate, postgraduate, postdoctoral, and researcher/academic, as well as educators at all levels (National Academies 2005). One of the pragmatic recommendations for postdoctoral scholars (which might be relevant to interdisciplinary researchers at any stage), for example, is that they should seek positions at institutions that:

- have strong interdisciplinary programmes;

- have a history of encouraging mentoring relationships across departmental lines;

- offer technologies, facilities, or instrumentation that further one's ability to do interdisciplinary research; and

- have researchers and faculty members with whom the postdoctoral scholar interacts who place a high priority on shared interdisciplinary activities (National Academies 2005: 81).

Whether sited physically in the same location, or 'virtually' via proactively formed national or international networks, a sense of community with others of an interdisciplinary orientation may prove helpful at any career stage. Just one example of this sort of desirable context might be the Modeling Interdisciplinary Inquiry Mellon Foundation Postdoctoral Program of Washington University in St Louis[5] which aims to:

broaden and enrich the training of a select group of newly qualified Ph.D.s by placing them in an environment with highly developed expectations of trans-disciplinary research and teaching. Modeling Interdisciplinary Inquiry seeks to address the cultural and institutional nature of interdisciplinarity itself and to create conditions in which interdisciplinary approaches to work in the humanities and social science can more easily flourish both within and outside the departmental traditions of a research university.

Whatever your interdisciplinary career goals, you are likely to need to demonstrate to prospective employers several key attributes, including (but not limited to):

- research skills;

- analytical skills;

- writing and presentation skills;

- curiosity;

- the ability to learn deeply about a subject;
- the ability to communicate and integrate across different lines of evidence; and
- the ability to argue a case for funding.

You can, in a sense, validate your interdisciplinary approach by seizing opportunities to demonstrate these attributes, particularly if you do so in the recognized 'currency' of academia – publications and grants. And, if possible, you may find it very useful to be able to present some credentials sited within one conventional discipline, giving comfort to the many prospective employers and colleagues who will feel more at home with these, and thus, perhaps, be more willing to recognize the validity of your interdisciplinary work as well.

It may take some sleuth work and informed opportunism to find funding opportunities for interdisciplinary research, although more grants and capacity-building schemes are beginning to emphasize this. You will probably want to develop a strong publications portfolio, with perhaps a mix of monodisciplinary and interdisciplinary publications (which may be in journals of different 'ranking'). A collection of talks at various conferences will demonstrate your confidence in your ability to contribute to understanding. Development of a cadre or network of colleagues, and even perhaps an interdisciplinary mentor or two, can help your confidence when you articulate the value of what you do, as well.

For some audiences, you may want to stress the way in which your interdisciplinarity respects but enhances what individual disciplines do; for other audiences you may want to illuminate the way that interdisciplinarity can cope with complex problems; and for those few audiences of the unrepentant interdisciplinary enthusiasts, you can share the intellectual excitement of your interdisciplinary work.

Case Study 6.5 Interdisciplinary career profiles

Carole Crumley
Professor of Anthropology, University of North Carolina at Chapel Hill & Research Director, IHOPE

Professor of Anthropology at the University of North Carolina, Chapel Hill, Carole Crumley is currently a Guest Researcher at the Stockholm Resilience Centre (SRC), following her involvement in its early stages of development. The SRC was founded in January of 2007 as 'an international

Case Study 6.5 *Continued*

centre that advances transdisciplinary research for governance of social-ecological systems with a special emphasis on resilience – the ability to deal with change and continue to develop'.

Intrigued during her teenage years by C.P. Snow's 'Two Cultures' theory, Carole was irritated at the thought that she would have to 'choose' one area over another. She went on to gain a BA and a PhD in anthropology, as well as an MA in archaeology and specialized training in classical studies and also environmental science fields (ecology, geology, climatology). She is now viewed as a pioneer of emerging sub-disciplines, historical ecology and landscape archaeology, that blend different sorts of enquiry.

Carole plays a leadership role in a variety of international initiatives attempting to span disciplines and gain understanding of the past in relation to the present and the future of people in the environment. For instance, she is currently Research Director of the Integrated History and future Of People on Earth (IHOPE) initiative. She has been on steering committees for the International Geosphere-Biosphere Programme (IGBP), PAGES (Past Global Changes) and Analysis and Integrated Modelling (AIMES) – as well as the US National Committee for DIVERSITAS. While she sometimes works with modellers who aim to bring together information from various disciplines, she is also actively involved in developing other approaches to integration, such as the generation and use of a common conceptual framework by an interdisciplinary team (e.g. Newell *et al.* 2005).

Reflecting on choices in career journeys, Carole observes:

> You really have to basically strike out on your own and see some sort of scheme in which all that you are interested in can work together. For me, that was archaeology. Archaeology is a natural science until you get back from the field and suddenly it is a human or social science. Archaeology lets you go back and forth across that divide all the time.

Source: Personal communication (July 2010); http://www.stockholmresilience. org/contactus/staff/crumley.5.7cf9c5aa121e17bab42800043232.html [accessed 15 January 2011].

Ravi Kapur
Founder and Managing Director, GovEd Communications

Ravi Kapur is the Founder and Managing Director of the entrepreneurial company, GovEd Communications, 'an interdisciplinary media, education, communications & technology company'. Its three principal thrusts are: digital media production (for schools and others); a consultancy in education, media, design and management; and standalone ventures in technology, digital media and sustainability. Ravi has long been aware of the interdisciplinary nature of much of his work and, from experience, likens his current role to that of a documentary film producer:

> You have to be driven by your own curiosity in a subject, go with the flow of your instincts to find the most interesting opportunities and back up with your skills. You need to pick up detail very quickly, absorb data and information, learn new 'languages' and distil it all into something that can be applied ... so 'television producer' describes me fairly well.

Boundary-spanning (across sectors as well as disciplines) and synthesis are key parts of his job, along with leading mixed teams to deliver innovative solutions.

With a range of interests, he left academia after initially studying physics at university and went on to become involved in film-making: 'The journalists' dimension of documentary film-making was a very natural outlet for satiating curiosity. You have a licence as a filmmaker or journalist to gain access and research things in incredible detail.' His career evolved through a combination of serendipity, curiosity and determination, with a bit of direction from him, but not by pre-emptive planning: 'I can't honestly tell you what, ultimately, I am. At heart I am still a film-maker, but that experience has opened up many other opportunities.' He moved from television to science communication to education and social policy (fields now covered by his company), and he also launched a fund for social innovation at the National Endowment for Science Technology and the Arts (NESTA) in the UK.

Ravi describes his company as being like a 'translucent die'; any one client may see just one face of the die (perhaps production of a film) and may only glimpse the other faces, but it is actually these other sets of expertise that will add value to any particular piece of work: 'Interdisciplinary knowledge and expertise can also enable quite focused service provision.' Similarly, someone who has spanned various sorts of activities and gained diverse insights can bring special capability to a focused role: 'Outside of academia, there is a strong link between interdisciplinarity and being multi-skilled; and this is the way the world is moving ... Keep your options open; mixed skill-sets can open up unexpected opportunities and career paths that you can't predict.'

Why is an interdisciplinary approach satisfying for Ravi? 'I have inherent curiosity, a need for knowledge and a set of instincts that almost

Case Study 6.5 *Continued*

compel me to choose projects and opportunities that cross disciplines. The promise of doing interdisciplinary work is that it is almost an excuse to learn new "stuff". And the process of learning new stuff itself enables delivery of interdisciplinary work.'

Source: Personal communication, September 2010; http://www.goved.co.uk [accessed 15 January 2011].

Dr Roger C. Prince
ExxonMobil Research and Engineering Company

A prominent scientist based at the ExxonMobil Research and Engineering Company, Roger Prince has contributed to both advances in science and to important real-world challenges. From his PhD onwards, his special focus has been on biological chemistry – oxidation reduction chemistry and understanding of bioenergetics. This underpinned, for example, his 1989–90 role as lead scientist for Exxon in the Bioremediation Monitoring Program conducted after the Exxon Valdez oil spill in Alaska, which demonstrated for the first time that the newly emerging technology of bioremediation (degradation by micro-organisms) is an effective way to clean up oil spills. His PhD work at Bristol University on the energetics of bacterial photosynthesis led to a career-long strand of research; Roger is now participating in the exploration by ExxonMobil of the potential of photosynthetic algae to efficiently produce biofuels. Roger sees no barrier between doing good science and solving real problems, saying, 'Most of us would like to be useful, and there was an opportunity for our work to be very useful with the oil spill. It was a tremendous pleasure to discover that the science one wanted to do was really relevant.' He feels fortunate that, while many people doing corporate research are expected to change the direction of their work as needs arise, he has been able to generate questions for his own work. Although his work has addressed diverse problems, it has always been underpinned by his focus on energy in biology.

Since he views all of his work as being aimed at biological problems, Roger does not quite think of himself as 'interdisciplinary', despite the description written for his 2007 New Jersey American Chemical Society Lifetime Achievement Award: 'His work is fuelled by an intense interest in the physical, biological and chemical processes that impact the fate of materials in the environment and has involved skilful interaction at the interface of chemistry, physics, biology, geology and oceanography.' Instead, he says of himself in language that most self-avowedly interdisciplinary researchers would recognize: 'I am a great collaborator and team player because it's fun and there is great pleasure in the personal interaction of like-minded colleagues with different backgrounds and in the potential beauty of what you produce.' Roger is emphatic about the importance – and challenge – of collaboration between people: 'Interactions between people who are different is necessary to get things moving.' Different bits of a collaborative effort will give each participant the most 'joy'.

Practical advice for any collaborative team: 'You only ever want to collaborate with someone who will do a bit more than their fair share (including yourself!). Otherwise there is no pleasure in collaborating with them. Most collaborations work well and everyone gets out more than they put in.' 'Interdisciplinarity is not a production line with sequential roles played by each discipline; you need overlapping expertise.'

Regarding careers: 'I wouldn't ever be scared of doing something you want to do because you think it might harm your career. I think that is flawed because you can never predict your career. Always do the thing you think will be the most interesting.' 'What should drive you is "positive fun" ... What is fun is to learn new things and then see it being put into practice ... having collaborators who share the same goals from different viewpoints – that's when it's really good fun.'

Source: Personal communication and http://www.njacs.org/2007-Prince-Lifetime-Award.html [accessed 15 January 2011].

Mark Baldwin
Artistic Director, Rambert Dance Company

Artistic Director of the Rambert Dance Company in London, Mark Baldwin puts together teams of individuals with diverse expertise to create new works. For example, to commemorate the 200th birthday of Charles Darwin and the 150th anniversary of the publication of *On the Origin of Species*, Mark created the dance piece 'Comedy of Change' which toured in 2009–2010. He provided the choreography, a composer created the specially commissioned score, a leader in contemporary art came up with the production design, a former taxidermist turned costume designer created the costumes and a biologist provided key insights into animal traits such as camouflage that have evolved over time. This unusual and thought-provoking blend of science with dance received support from UK science funders.

Born in Fiji, Mark received a scholarship to study fine arts at the University of Auckland, but on his own also studied at ballet school; he

Case Study 6.5 *Continued*

saw commonalities between fine art and dance and decided early on to be a choreographer. After dancing in New Zealand, Australia and the UK, he created many works as a choreographer gathering numerous awards. In his current role he commissions and creates works that involve collaboration between dance, music and design.

Mark's reflections on the creativity that can be achieved by interdisciplinarity, particularly the process of creating the Darwin-inspired 'Comedy of Change', may well resonate with attempts to achieve more academic creativity:

- 'You can do something powerful by working with others.'

- 'Collaboration is really about opening up; keep questioning. Sometimes, you need to try something even if initially you don't think it will work.'

- 'With collaborators, you are looking at ideas; when you work out what the idea is, you're off.'

- 'If you stick with it and hang out together, eventually you'll come up with a common language.'

- 'Even if half an idea is provided, it can make the difference between the team's work being better or not. It was the subtleties and the tiny things that the scientist said that made a difference as to how I thought about the "Comedy of Change" piece ... Not one earth-shattering moment, but a subtle build-up of a picture before you feel it comes together as one thing.'

- 'The set or costume or dance or lighting or stage or music will come into force at different points in the journey, but they are all still part of an overall piece.'

- 'Trust is important ... Control is very difficult to give up, but you have to. You have to know when to let go and let them (other team members) do it. It may not be the way you imagined it but it may be more powerful and may work. That's why I like happy accidents ... You need to trust yourself that you'll spot those moments, those happy accidents. If you envisage it too strictly, you're bound to be disappointed.'

- 'It's the journey and the creativity that is in many ways helping you look for that new thing, that new approach. Try to start with a clean slate and go for something completely different with each new project. When it all comes together and "works" it is very satisfying. But you need the team to try to get that project to "work", to find the commonalities, the associations and to build one picture out of all the ideas the collaborators have offered.'

- 'Remember if you're a collaborator, it's not about you; it's about the project you're working on, and the construction of the One Picture.'

Source: Personal communication, September 2010, and http://www.rambert.org.uk/about_rambert/artistic_director [accessed 15 January 2011].

Professor Tom Inns
Chair of Design, Duncan of Jordanstone College of Art & Design, University of Dundee, Scotland

As Professor and Chair of Design at the University of Dundee, Tom Inns is particularly fascinated by emergent roles for design; in fact, his particular interest is in the use of design approaches, design thinking and visualization for the facilitation of interdisciplinary team efforts involving academics (and stakeholders). Through his recent role as the Director of the 5-year cross-council AHRC/EPSRC Designing for the 21st Century Research Initiative, Tom was able to catalyse and facilitate a diverse range of approaches to understanding the changing uses of design thinking, in some 41 research projects conducted across the UK. The two resultant volumes he edited (Inns 2007; Inns 2010) are a rich resource of reflective snapshots into actual experiments in interdisciplinarity. The first figure in the latter demonstrates the provocative power of visualization, with Tom showing currents, streams and straits in 'the Interdisciplinary Design Delta' travelled by the 41 'research ships'; with the Delta leading to the future's 'Gulf of Complexity' and 'Ocean of Uncertainty'.

Tom began his own journey by studying as an engineer; discovering 'design', he went on to the Royal College of Art, where he learned about the process of thinking, and methods and techniques (including visual approaches) to facilitate or structure thinking in different situations. For his PhD, he developed ways to evaluate the impact of design on drivers of success for small businesses. He went on to direct a design research centre at Brunel University, where he worked collaboratively on various projects – designing seatbelts for dogs, for instance, entailed work with an animal behaviourist whereas working on recyclable products called for other disciplines. Since moving to Duncan of Jordanstone College of Art & Design, he shifted from product design to workshop design, 'designing

Case Study 6.5 *Continued*

interdisciplinary spaces for people to inhabit'. Now he applies the core skills he learned from design (such as knowledge of processes, stages and trade-offs) to the new context of facilitating interdisciplinarity, helping to design interactions, promote communication, encourage speculation and generate 'prototype ideas' to be tested as innovations: 'What really fascinates me as a research area is the designer's role in interdisciplinary space.'

Tom sees research funding bodies as being driven increasingly by governments' desire for resolution of society's issues, which are interdisciplinary. Universities will need to change and even restructure to react to this: 'the only place to be in, if you are going to be a functioning university, will be an interdisciplinary space'. He describes himself as 'T-shaped', with the vertical bit grounded in his home sub-discipline of 'co-design' with its skills and approaches, and the horizontal bit being the breadth in which he can use these. As enthusiastic as he is about working to catalyse interdisciplinarity ('I love it, being in this space'), Tom feels the need to return periodically to his core, communicating with similar people. He commends this to others involved in interdisciplinary work: 'You have to be T-shaped, with something core to yourself that you can add to the mix; you can't turn into grey mush.' While you need this to operate within an academic environment, at the same time, 'you have to be an agile entrepreneur'.

Source: Personal communication, September 2010.

Anna-Louise Reysenbach
Professor, Portland State University, Oregon, USA

Anna-Louise Reysenbach's research centres on 'extremophiles', microbes that have evolved in environments like hot springs and volcanoes on land and deep-sea vents at the bottom of the ocean. Her travel to remote sites includes undersea expeditions in submersibles like 'Alvin'; she finds and studies new micro-organisms and investigates very unusual ecosystems. Her niche, and her ability to work with other disciplines, has led to her advice being sought by those setting directions in a variety of science-related areas. A subject editor of *Geobiology*, she serves on the NASA Planetary subcommittee: her integrative research on microbes' interaction with/impact on geochemistry in extreme environments is relevant to looking for signs of the evolution of life on other planets. Other examples of her range of interdisciplinary activities include a committee otherwise composed of engineers advising the National Science Foundation (NSF) on the next-generation Alvin submersible, and NSF workshops on the future of systematics and taxonomy.

Anna-Louise studied microbiology and botany for her undergraduate degree in South Africa, and earned a PhD in microbiology. Growing up, she spent many family holidays out in nature, especially at the seaside; she learned to scuba dive as a teenager. 'I was born interdisciplinary, and curious about many different things from the sciences to the arts. I have always been this way, a bit of a naturalist. Growing up, I liked rocks and plants and was pretty good at math. I have always had the ability to think big. Also, I had a very strong broad education, which helped.'

Anna-Louise feels that her focus on microbes in extreme environments 'compels interdisciplinarity' because she needs geochemistry and geology to understand them: 'I achieve interdisciplinarity through collaboration with others who can talk my language and I can talk their language.' She is not just interested in what other disciplines can provide for her: 'What really makes my science fun for me is when I can see the impact my work has on different disciplines, and vice versa.' She feels that her career has been helped by the fact that she is herself 'interdisciplinary within biology' as well as between biology and geochemistry.

Anna-Louise is enthusiastic about and encourages interdisciplinarity:

> To understand the whole of a system, you have to be willing to draw on all the other disciplines. I actually believe that some of the most unexpected discoveries one might make are discovered at the interface of disciplines. You can appreciate a problem from a different perspective and sometimes that opens your eyes to something else. It is a non-myopic way of looking at things.

For those pursuing interdisciplinarity, she advises: 'Realize you can't be a master of everything, so if you are interested in doing interdisciplinary science and that's how your brain works, you do need to find good colleagues in other disciplines who can also think interdisciplinarily.'

Source: Personal communication (September 2010) and http://pdx.edu/admissions/profile/meet-professor-anna-louise-reysenbach [accessed 15 January 2011].

Sir Peter Crane
Dean, School of Forestry & Environmental Studies, Yale University

Dean of Yale University's School of Forestry & Environmental Studies, Sir Peter Crane says of his role:

> Leading this School is the biggest interdisciplinary challenge I've ever faced ... and the diversity of our subject matter is one of the things that interests me most about my position. I find it stimulating and demanding, because of its complexity. The School is highly diverse,

Case Study 6.5 *Continued*

with a wide range of social scientists, ecologists and biologists, as well as people who face toward engineering and industrial applications, people with a policy focus, and people who reach out to law, business, public health or even divinity. As a modern school of the environment, our vision is to add value by bringing these disciplines together in a culture of mutual respect and give-and-take that balances the disciplinary with the interdisciplinary. For example, early steps in the development of our Master's level curriculum included the development of both interdisciplinary courses and a recommended spectrum of more discipline-oriented introductory courses.

In his former role as Chief Executive and Director of Kew Gardens in the UK, Peter helped the world-famous botanical garden take on a more proactive, recognized role in plant conservation, and also reach out into policy, as an integrative undertaking across various sub-disciplines. Indeed, he was knighted in 2004 for services to horticulture and conservation. Earlier, as Director of the Field Museum of Natural History in Chicago, he developed the interdisciplinary Center for Environmental Conservation Programs to draw on the expertise of the traditional disciplinary departments of Anthropology, Botany and Zoology.

Peter has found that his leadership in interdisciplinary areas has benefited from the integrative nature of his own research, linking understanding of fossil and living plants: 'I am fundamentally a botanist even though work I've done can be said to be at the joining point of the biology of living plants and geology.' In high school he became very interested in archaeology, what one could learn from plant materials to understand the environments in which ancient peoples lived; this was part of what led him into botany: 'The way my career panned out has been a reflection of these things that go quite a long way back.' After studying botany (with some zoology and geology) as an undergraduate, Peter made a career decision to do a PhD in the integrative area of plant palaeontology, studying plant fossils; his reaching out to geology from botany, coupled with 'a few "Aha!" moments', made him realize there was a new sub-field that could be created.

In Peter's view, thinking holistically is key to tackling our current environmental challenges:

> We all tend to naturally tackle problems a piece at a time; it is just easier to work this way but the downside of this, especially in the environmental arena, is that everything is interlinked. So, we need people who have the breadth of understanding to take a broader view.

We need people who can see multiple dimensions, the bigger picture, especially in the environmental arena. If you break everything down into different pieces, some very bad policy decisions are often the result.

To manage some of the risk often inherent in interdisciplinarity in academia, Peter recommends: 'take advantage of good mentors who can give you good, sound, non-idealistic advice'. Also, 'You have to show substance; the core of what you describe as your work has to be unimpeachable.' Yet, rather than tactics driving career decisions, Peter recommends asking, as for any researcher: 'Is this where your interest really is? Is there something worthwhile and important to do in this area? If you answer these questions in the affirmative, then go for it! *Then* think carefully about tactics.'

Source: Personal communication, October 2010, and http://environment.yale.edu. magazine/spring2009 [accessed 1 October 2010].

Key Advice 6.3 A reflection guide: Questions to consider when contemplating an interdisciplinary career

1 What does it mean to have 'an interdisciplinary career'?

2 What are some examples of interdisciplinary careers?

3 How can interdisciplinary careers develop over time?

4 What hazards might lie ahead?

5 Can the voyage be rewarding?

6 How do I know if interdisciplinarity will motivate me?

   a. Why might I be interested in pursuing an interdisciplinary career? Which of the possible incentives or positives speak to me? What sort of career example resonates with me? Why?

   b. Do I want to solve complex problems, and interdisciplinarity is the only viable pathway I see?

   c. Do I get an intellectual buzz from working with people who take diverse approaches? Does working in only one discipline, only with others from that discipline, seem 'flat' to me?

Key Advice 6.3 *Continued*

    d. Am I so attracted to two or more fields that I want to conquer both – and look for synergies between them?

    e. Or do I have some other reason?

    f. Do I see myself working primarily or exclusively in an interdisciplinary way? Or primarily in a discipline, with a portion of lively interdisciplinarity at the edges?

    g. Do I feel driven to spend my whole career in an interdisciplinary mode or do I have a sense that it is 'a phase I'm going through' such that I'll come out the other side focusing on one discipline?

7 How could interdisciplinarity add value to my career and where might this lead?

    a. Within academia? What value could I envision my interdisciplinarity adding, where, how?
       i.   Undergraduate teaching?
       ii. PhD supervision?
       iii. Research? Synergistic collaborations?
       iv. Knowledge Exchange? Consulting?

    b. Where might the road to interdisciplinarity take me beyond academia? What value could I envision my interdisciplinarity adding, where, how?
       i.   Industry (e.g. problem-solving, teams)?
       ii. Government (e.g. synthesis, use of multiple lines of evidence)?
       iii. Third sector (e.g. reaching out to diverse communities)?
       iv. Knowledge Intermediary? Other?

8 How can I begin to plan for a career involving interdisciplinary research?

    a. Is it possible to be 'a little bit interdisciplinary'?

    b. Should my personal 'interdisciplinarity' grow apace, alongside each stage of my career's maturation … Or is it better to be interdisciplinary only at some career stages, not others? Earlier but not later? Later but not earlier?

    c. What balances between disciplinarity and interdisciplinarity would I want to achieve, when?

9   What can I actually do to forge a successful career path involving interdisciplinarity?

   a.   How can I best prepare for a career that entails interdisciplinarity?
      i.   at the PhD level?
      ii. at postdoc level?
      iii. early career?

   b.   What tactics would serve me well?
      i.   publication strategies?
      ii. pursuit of funding?
      iii. networking, finding a community, other activities?
      iv. utilizing mentors, peer support?

10 How can I convince others of the value of my career path?

   a.   How can I make the case for getting the career posts I desire?

   b.   To what audiences?

   c.   How might I articulate my rationale in terms of the positive value of interdisciplinarity?

   d.   What sorts of validation could I deliberately acquire?

Summary

In this chapter we have considered what it means to embark upon an interdisciplinary career. We have stressed heterogeneity of approaches to interdisciplinarity, degrees of interdisciplinarity and career stages at which interdisciplinarity may be undertaken, as well as the diversity of possible careers within or beyond academia. We have pointed out possible risks posed by interdisciplinary work, yet we have also suggested ways in which interdisciplinarity could add value to a number of components of an academic career, including undergraduate teaching, PhD supervision, synergistic research collaborations, knowledge exchange and consulting. At the same time we have noted the natural fit of interdisciplinary outlook and transferable skills with the demands of many non-academic careers in industry, government and the third sector.

Perhaps the fundamental message of this chapter is that the decision as to whether or not to undertake an interdisciplinary career journey is a highly personal one. We recommend rigorous self-reflection to inform this decision, and we offer some guiding questions and possible thought exercises that may help.

Questions

For researchers

1 How can you tell if interdisciplinary work is for you?

2 What tactics can you imagine employing to make sure that interdisciplinarity adds value to your career rather than making you vulnerable?

3 If you were to pursue your ideal interdisciplinary career, how in five words or less would you describe yourself to: a prospective employer? a student?

For research managers

1 What steps could you take to ensure that less-established individuals who participate in your interdisciplinary teams rack up achievements that will 'count' in academic promotion currency?

2 Can you develop a strategy for a portfolio of outputs, so that everyone in the team benefits?

For institutional leaders

1 What message(s) do you take from this chapter regarding promotion, support, community-building or other ways of treating interdisciplinary researchers at your institution?

For research funders

1 If you believe that the future academic landscape should include (though not be limited to) interdisciplinary research, what sorts of funding opportunities could you make available so that interdisciplinary careers are viable?

2 What role(s) might you play in ensuring that researchers who do excellent interdisciplinary work progress in their careers?

7

Assessing the Route

Evaluating interdisciplinary proposals, programmes and publications

Introduction

Improved evaluation criteria and processes are the key to achieving a more stable and consistent role for interdisciplinary initiatives of various kinds within academic and research-based organizations, and for improving the intellectual status of interdisciplinary research. As noted in chapter 2, sensitive and appropriate evaluation of interdisciplinary research can also play a role in delivering improved value for money for the investments being made in this area.

Individuals, evaluation panels, funding agency staff and university leaders are increasingly placed in positions where they are expected to judge interdisciplinary work or plans and they often struggle to find defensible ways of differentiating levels of quality in interdisciplinary projects and their outcomes. Since the flipside of interdisciplinarity's ambitions and vision is an increase in risk, evaluators will be aware of the need to behave accountably but perhaps also uncertain about how to achieve impartial balance and fairness in evaluations. Likewise, for researchers developing interdisciplinary proposals or attempting to publish interdisciplinary work, uncertainty about evaluation processes can leave them feeling disadvantaged.

Evaluation of interdisciplinarity occurs in a variety of situations. The criteria appropriate to evaluation of academically oriented interdisciplinary research may often be different from problem-focused projects and programmes. Within each of these categories, the range of issues to be considered will differ according to the context – the type and scale of a project or programme, the organizational setting, the kinds of actors involved or the kind of publication being reviewed (Feller 2006). This chapter is written from the perspective of the evaluator, which should resonate with research funders and university managers, but we also consider how interdisciplinary researchers and research managers themselves can benefit from a better understanding of evaluation processes and use these insights to develop proposals that are more likely to succeed, or to write papers that are more likely to be published, and thus advance interdisciplinary careers.

This chapter discusses challenges inherent in the evaluation of interdisciplinarity, as perceived by numerous researchers who have published on this subject, supplemented by some of the authors' own experiences. In particular, we highlight two key aspects of evaluation:

1 the quality of interdisciplinary proposals and research outcomes; and

2 the quality of the evaluation processes themselves.

We make some suggestions as to how different types of evaluation of inter-disciplinarity might be approached:

- evaluation of interdisciplinary research proposals from individuals or small teams, including postgraduate or postdoctoral research;
- evaluation of major interdisciplinary programmes, centres and funding schemes;
- evaluation within institutions;
- evaluation of interdisciplinary submissions for publication;
- self-evaluation.

Some of these evaluation occasions come before the fact (*ex ante*) so that doors are opened, or not, for interdisciplinary initiatives. Some arise after interdis-ciplinary work is done (*ex post*), to check on the effectiveness or impact of ventures such as interdisciplinary programmes or entire funding schemes pro-moting interdisciplinarity. Some occasions may occur sporadically, as when, for example, a university develops a research strategy and surveys its own work when placing relative weighting on interdisciplinarity for its future.

None of these evaluations takes place in a vacuum and approaches to evalu-ation of one type will have implications for others. However, Feller suggests that, even though all interdisciplinary evaluations will share some core val-ues such as commitment to new knowledge, different contexts will respond at different rates to interdisciplinarity:

> The set of assessment questions about quality and the metrics used to produce answers are not always the same ... across subsystems different, contradictory, and divergent answers may be given to the same questions. These fractionated definitions and metrics of what constitutes quality account in part for the checkered and uneven pace of commitments to and acceptance of interdisciplinary research within federal science agencies and research universities. (Feller 2006)

Inevitably, as evaluation is intimately bound up with funding, career advancement and strategy development, issues arising here may draw upon, and have implications for, foci of the other chapters. We hope to shed some light on practicalities of a) improving evaluation of interdisciplinarity, and b) enhancing recognition that interdisciplinarity can in fact be subject to respectable rigour, and thus to contribute to tackling the barriers that evalua-tion at various points can pose to interdisciplinary ventures.

We have argued elsewhere that, if programmes and funding schemes are viewed as experiments, their evaluation can in a sense be viewed as formative evaluation, capturing lessons learned along the way so as to enhance future effectiveness (e.g. Meagher and Lyall 2005a). Given the relatively short history of interdisciplinary research as a recognized phenomenon, and the even shorter trail of self-aware, explicit evaluations of interdisciplinarity, this chapter can be seen as contributing to reflection, informed experimentation and long-term capacity-building in the evaluation of interdisciplinarity.

Whatever the evaluation situation, interdisciplinary work overall is done no favours if evaluation is not rigorous. However, achieving shared definitions of rigour and quality across a range of settings takes extra effort. The distinctiveness of the challenges posed by interdisciplinarity should be recognized, planned for and accommodated.

Judging quality in interdisciplinary proposals and outcomes

Peer review is an essential component of evaluation of discipline-based projects and must also be the cornerstone of evaluation of the quality of interdisciplinary proposals and outcomes. However, the criteria adopted by disciplines do not translate well across to interdisciplinary initiatives. Indeed, because interdisciplinary research does not yet have its own widely recognized criteria for identification of quality this can leave its quality open to debate (Feller 2006).

Lamont has studied peer review in many forms and suggests that evaluating interdisciplinary research well and fairly, and achieving consensus, is a significant challenge, as seen in several of her observations on criteria and multiple layers of evaluation:

- 'The standards used to evaluate interdisciplinary research are not a simple combination of the standards of single disciplines. They are a hybrid, and an emergent hybrid at that – one that has developed through practice and deliberation.'

- 'Interdisciplinarity often brings about a broadening and multiplication of evaluation criteria, which makes both individual judgment and group agreement much more difficult.'

- 'The lack of canonized agreement about how to evaluate interdisciplinarity gives researchers more leeway concerning how to go about their work, but it also creates greater uncertainty about how to establish the resulting project's quality.'

- 'Combining traditional standards of disciplinary excellence with interdisciplinarity presents a potential for double jeopardy.'

- 'Not surprisingly, given the emergent quality of the standards of evaluation for interdisciplinary genres, panelists readily fall back on existing disciplinary standards to determine what should and should not be funded. This may mean that at the end of the day, interdisciplinary scholarship is evaluated through several disciplinary lenses.' (Lamont 2009: 208–211)

In directing attention to the challenges of evaluation regarding interdisciplinarity, the journal *Research Evaluation* covered a range of insights from a meeting that convened experts including research administrators, editors of journals and social scientists to discuss quality assessment in interdisciplinary research and education (Boix Mansilla *et al.* 2006). An underlying premise was the need to find the most helpful and least damaging ways to evaluate interdisciplinary research. The group concluded that 'there is no single quantifiable formula to measure quality in interdisciplinary research' but offered instead a set of four 'hot spots' that merit attention in evaluation of quality by asking, does the research:

- focus on 'the right shared problem'?

- establish social conditions for good work?

- meet multiple disciplinary standards?

- reach effective syntheses? (Boix Mansilla *et al.* 2006)

We expand upon these questions in Key Advice 7.1.

Key Advice 7.1 Questions to ask when assessing interdisciplinary quality

- Does the topic/problem posed require an interdisciplinary approach?

- Does the topic/problem and approach lend itself to robust, high quality research (albeit non-conventional) for which there will be outlets (albeit possibly non-conventional)?

- Does the work show rigorous problem framing, data collection, analysis and drawing of reasonable conclusions?

- Is the work consonant with/grounded in its source disciplines/ methodologies or is it likely to develop novel methodological approaches?

- Has the work added or will it add to understanding, albeit in a non-conventional way?

In the same volume, Boix Mansilla also notes that:

1 discipline-based criteria can be insufficient for evaluation of work that steps beyond disciplines;

2 desired transformative impacts may well take longer and be spread across multiple areas rather than clearly changing one discipline;

3 dependence on standard indicators of quality such as publication or funding relegates responsibility for evaluation to the 'black box of peer review'. (Boix Mansilla 2006)

The lack of agreed indicators of quality may be one reason why a question mark often hangs over the academic value of interdisciplinarity. For example, Feller refers to considerations of quality having become a 'tripwire' in evaluations of interdisciplinary research (Feller 2006). Others have referred to a crucial obstacle for interdisciplinarity being that posed by heterogeneity in perceptions of quality (Oberg 2009; Boix Mansilla 2006; Defila and Di Giulio 1999). This is, in part, due to the inevitable idiosyncrasy of interdisciplinary efforts which tackle such a wide range of problems but the lack of accepted criteria derives also from the inherently complex nature of interdisciplinarity. Interdisciplinary research draws upon two or more disciplines in unpredictable combinations of methods, expertise, content and types of knowledge. This leaves evaluators, at whatever level, in the uncomfortable position of judging something that is at least in part unknowable through their own expertise (Case Study 7.1).

In contrast, the disciplines which serve as academic homes for most evaluators are subjected to a coherent set of discipline-specific, and agreed, criteria. Over time, this evaluative lens has become refined and polished so that judges of quality in a particular discipline are all looking through the same instrument as they focus upon a particular effort within a discipline. This well-crafted telescope allows evaluators within a discipline to feel confident that they can see clearly the path ahead, whether it is a road to publication or a conduit to funding. This system also provides clarity for discipline-based researchers as to the criteria by which their efforts will be judged.

This relative clarity may also (incorrectly, we and many others would argue) reinforce the convictions held by some that monodisciplinary work is necessarily more rigorous than interdisciplinary work. It also explains why discipline-based evaluators may find it less problematic to evaluate academically oriented interdisciplinary research where the contribution of individual disciplines to an overall academic objective may be easier to specify and to accommodate within conventional frames of discipline-based thinking.

For governmental and some other funding bodies identification of quality is not only an academic question. The Swiss Priority Programme Environment

---

Case Study 7.1 The organization of research in the UK

The organization of research in the UK has traditionally favoured a single discipline approach. Consider, for example, the fate of a research proposal on crop-protection decision-making submitted for funding in the late 1980s. It was submitted to the then Science and Engineering Research Council (SERC) and Social Science Research Council (SSRC, now ESRC) Joint Committee. They had, at that time, narrowed their terms of reference to exclude agriculture so sent it to the SERC Biology Committee; the Biology Committee felt it was also outside their area and sent it to the Agricultural Research Council (ARC); the ARC did not at that time fund 'social science' research and sent it to the SSRC; the SSRC thought it was too agricultural for them but, as it had already been to the ARC, decided to forward it to the Natural Environment Research Council (NERC); NERC also felt it was outside their terms of reference and sent it back to the Biology Committee of the SERC, who advised the applicant to withdraw the proposal.

This was not an isolated occurrence. Such tales were commonplace among those attempting to do cross-disciplinary work at the time. Although the UK's Research Councils were restructured in the early 1990s, the seven new councils retained their traditional spheres of influence. Despite major efforts to transcend disciplinary boundaries with cross-council research investments, they have found it challenging to abandon their monodisciplinary heritage.

Source: Tait 1987.

(SPPE) sought deeper understanding of criteria that could be used to evaluate interdisciplinary and transdisciplinary research projects. Seeing each evaluation as distinct and having to adapt to its own focus, Defila and Di Giulio developed a modular approach with possible building blocks and 'criteria catalogues' in order to stimulate discussion about methods and criteria (Defila and Di Giulio 1999). They suggested, for example, specific objectives for evaluation at key stages in a programme evaluation sequence: proposal evaluation, three interim evaluations, a final programme evaluation and impact evaluation.

In promoting the value of interdisciplinary work in the United States, the National Academies recommend regular review of funding organizations' evaluation criteria to ensure that they are appropriate for interdisciplinary activities (National Academies 2005: 6). Boix Mansilla identifies four possible indicators of interdisciplinary quality: peer review, journal prestige, citation patterns and successful patent filings (Boix Mansilla 2006). These criteria are applicable to any project and are not specific to interdisciplinary research. Indeed 'journal prestige' and 'citation patterns', when used as comparative quality indicators, selectively disadvantage interdisciplinary research. Importantly, this study also uncovered an additional three criteria that address epistemic dimensions of interdisciplinary work, such as the role played by active balancing processes that are specific to interdisciplinarity:

- 'the degree to which new insights relate to antecedent disciplinary knowledge in multiple disciplines involved';

- 'the sensible balance reached in weaving disciplinary perspectives together';

- 'the effectiveness with which the integration of disciplines advances understanding and inquiry'. (Boix Mansilla 2006)

From our review of the literature there is clearly no lack of appreciation of the central role that evaluation of the quality of interdisciplinary research plays in ensuring value for money from the research investment and in improving long-term credibility of interdisciplinarity in general. However, there are relatively few positive suggestions for criteria that would form a robust set of quality indicators for interdisciplinary research. Most of those referred to above, for example, are not unique to interdisciplinarity and are indeed criteria that would usefully be applied to any research project. Developing a set of criteria and indicators that effectively delineate quality in interdisciplinary research will have to be a collective project led by interdisciplinary researchers themselves and cannot be an output from any single group of researchers. Given our involvement with interdisciplinary research evaluation over a considerable period, we have developed a set of criteria that has proved useful in evaluations we have conducted across a wide range of contexts. The recommendations set out in Key Advice 7.2 are relevant for both academically oriented and problem focused interdisciplinary initiatives.

Judging interdisciplinary evaluation processes

Well-specified criteria for judging the quality of interdisciplinary research will only be helpful if they are embedded in an equally effective evaluation process. Lamont *et al.* have commented that 'Interdisciplinary panels can be said to be sites where new rules of fairness are redefined, reinvented and slowly recognized' (Lamont *et al.* 2006).

The choice of evaluators, their disciplinary and interdisciplinary backgrounds, and their relative roles in the evaluation process need to be considered carefully. Interdisciplinary researchers often lack a fixed peer community.

Key Advice 7.2 Quality criteria for interdisciplinary research

1 A proposal for a new initiative should indicate what are the expected synergistic outcomes from the combination of disciplines and approaches involved, what are the likely benefits for disciplines (in the case of academically oriented interdisciplinary research) or what are the societal or business benefits (in the case of problem-focused interdisciplinary research). Bear in mind that elements of both may be incorporated in the same project.

2 Do not expect a problem-focused interdisciplinary initiative to contribute to enhancement of the knowledge base of any of the individual disciplines involved. Any single project is unlikely to deliver discipline-related breakthroughs as well as the other synergistic benefits of integrating disciplines. To expect to find both in a single proposal is to make unrealistic demands on the researchers.

3 Look for a good understanding of the disciplines involved, and of their limitations, and a clear justification for the choice of disciplines based on the needs of the research questions.

4 Look for evidence that the researcher or the research team have understood the challenges of interdisciplinary integration, including methodological integration, and the 'human' side of fostering interactions and communication, and have developed an effective strategy to deal with this.

5 More than for a monodisciplinary project, interdisciplinary projects may need to develop and change as they proceed. The proposal should therefore be set out in broad steps but with a flexible timetable that recognizes that the ordering might change: while the end goal should be clear, the routes to achieving it might be subject to revision as the project progresses.

6 In evaluating published outcomes of interdisciplinary research do not include journal prestige or citation patterns as criteria as both actively disadvantage interdisciplinary research outputs.

7 In evaluating researchers themselves, links to excellent discipline-based research can be an advantage, but much more important is evidence of past success in conducting or leading interdisciplinary research. Where young, inexperienced researchers are involved, an integrative mindset is important and this can often be judged from the style of writing. The kind of focused mindset that can excel in a

> discipline-based context can be a disadvantage for interdisciplinary research.
>
> 8 Well before the event, make it clear to those being evaluated the quality criteria by which their work will be judged.

For those being evaluated, interdisciplinary teams and researchers who are not well known to referees may be disadvantaged by the review process. Referee choice is less problematic in well-established interdisciplinary areas such as Science and Technology Studies (STS) where there is already a pool of known, interdisciplinary referees. (Ironically or perhaps inevitably, STS is beginning to show some of the characteristics of a discipline in that there is an established set of methods and topics, and projects that do not conform to the expected pattern tend to be criticized.) The problem is acute for proposals that are trying to put forward a novel interdisciplinary project where there may not be a recognized set of other academics who are individually qualified to referee it. Although the potential for creativity can be the hallmark of interdisciplinarity, ambitious interdisciplinary proposals can seem risky to many reviewers (e.g. Lamont et al. 2006; Langfeldt 2006).

It is important that we continue to build capacity and confidence among interdisciplinary evaluators, developing an 'invisible college' that can be relied upon to undertake such evaluations fairly and with a good understanding of the important issues. Currently, as interdisciplinary research becomes increasingly favoured, there are too few such people to meet the demand. Ideally, as we have indicated in chapter 5, this will change as a new generation of interdisciplinary researchers matures and takes on these functions.

It is common for interdisciplinary review panels to tackle this problem by including an appropriate range of disciplinary experts and one or two token interdisciplinary reviewers. One of the authors of this book was involved in a review panel for a UK Research Council and was the only interdisciplinary expert on the panel. As lead evaluator for an interdisciplinary proposal she judged that it met all the quality criteria outlined in the previous section and met the requirements of the call, and should be funded. However, each of the disciplinary experts on the panel counselled rejection because the project, although competent in their respective disciplines, did not contribute to their advancement. The numerical weight of these comments (perhaps reinforced by the disciplinary prestige of the commentators) prevailed and the project was rejected. This kind of outcome can be avoided by giving clear guidance to panels as to how they should weight disciplinary and interdisciplinary contributions, and

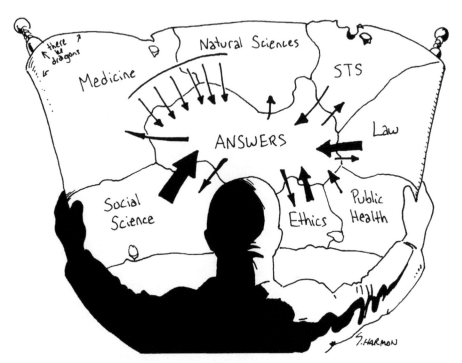

Illustration 7.1 Be prepared to revise the route

by ensuring that the panel chair is alert to these biases. In a similar example –
a study of a European Young Investigator Awards Scheme – applications that
did not fit with the disciplinary structure of the panels were less successful.
The quality criteria had included 'track record' and 'project feasibility', which
suited discipline-based proposals but which may have accentuated the perceived risk of interdisciplinary proposals (Langfeldt 2006).

Individuals affiliated with different disciplines, orientations or interests may
weight various factors differently, even when they agree on the use of a common indicator, and they may also differ as to what they consider worthy of
exploration. By definition, any one reviewer is unlikely to encompass appreciation for the entirety of the 'package' put forward in an interdisciplinary proposal or manuscript and may even see as less than scholarly interdisciplinary
attempts to utilize some but not all of the tools and tenets of their discipline.
The National Academies, for example, in making recommendations toward
interdisciplinary research reaching its full potential, included the importance
of adjusting the peer review process: 'Reliable methods for prospective and
retrospective evaluation of interdisciplinary research and elucidation programs
will require modification of the peer-review process to include researchers
with interdisciplinary expertise in addition to researchers with expertise in the
relevant disciplines' (National Academies 2005: 3).

Panels evaluating problem-focused interdisciplinary initiatives often also include non-academic evaluators representing policy, business or citizen stakeholders; this can be seen as contributing to the objectivity of the evaluation process since they do not share professional networks with the applicants. However, these non-academic experts are also usually in a minority and they are often allocated specific roles in the process, for example to judge the quality of the proposed stakeholder engagement. In our experience, they generally defer to academic evaluators over questions of research quality and so have a limited influence on the overall grade allocated to an interdisciplinary initiative.

Ideally, review panels will act together in a process that is not dissimilar to the collaboration needed for a good interdisciplinary team. Individually or in panels, reviewers are presented with similar challenges of integration to those that they are evaluating. Negotiation will be a part of this process, and the Lamont *et al.* study of the treatment of interdisciplinary proposals by review panels explored behaviours such as deference to colleagues' expertise in a context where no one is actually fully expert – they note that internal tensions between 'blind faith and critical collegial evaluation' occur but tend not to be recognized (Lamont *et al.* 2006; Lamont 2009). Similarly, 'methodological pluralism' (temporarily assumed equality among methods) may be employed by panel members to avoid conflicts that might lead to judgements unfair to the applicant (Lamont *et al.* 2006).

The process of finding appropriate peers to review interdisciplinary work is thus a frequently cited challenge for those managing evaluations and often a source of deep frustration for interdisciplinary researchers subjecting themselves to such judgement and for interdisciplinary evaluators appointed as members of a predominantly discipline-based team. Equally important is the management of the process of evaluation, with informed staff giving clear guidance to panels on how to evaluate interdisciplinary initiatives and appointing a panel chair with a good understanding of what is required and a strong enough control over the process to ensure that the guidance is followed. Case Study 7.2 describes the evolution of interdisciplinary evaluation for an interdisciplinary programme at the US National Science Foundation (NSF) and illustrates the deliberate development of a common culture among panel members.

In the United States, both the NSF and the National Institutes of Health (NIH) have used special panels or study sections when considering interdisciplinary initiatives where programme managers may be asked to identify academics who will be 'empathetic' to work that crosses conventional disciplines (Feller 2006). A study of assessment of interdisciplinary and disciplinary research by the Academy of Finland revealed the importance of assessment practices, including the initial identification of panel expertise and a later 'calibration' process across multidisciplinary panels that appeared to lead to more consensus as to quality, in terms of both merit and relevance (Boix Mansilla 2006, citing Bruun *et al.* 2005). Boix Mansilla also mentions

Case Study 7.2   National Science Foundation: Dynamics of Coupled Natural and Human Systems

Following a series of experimental calls to stimulate inclusion of social, behavioural and economic sciences within global change studies, in 2001 the US National Science Foundation (NSF) identified 'Dynamics of Coupled Natural and Human Systems' (CNH) as a targeted area of interest within competition for funding on Biocomplexity in the Environment. The emphasis is on research that will advance knowledge of the dynamics of interactions and feedbacks among human and natural systems, with both of those central and partners expected to be co-equals. In 2007, the NSF Biological Sciences; Geosciences; and Social, Behavioral, and Economic Sciences directorates agreed to establish a standing multi-directorate programme explicitly targeted to these interdisciplinary goals. The three directorates all contributed funds, with the 2010 CNH programme budget totalling $17 million. Programme officers also continued their integrated approach to managing the programme.

In many ways, the management of the programme reflects good interdisciplinary practice. As one of the three programme leaders, Dr Thomas Baerwald, who has been involved in CNH since its beginning, says, 'If we expect the teams we support to be truly integrated interdisciplinary teams, we as Program Officers need to manage in that kind of way'. Each of the three directorates has named a specific programme manager for CNH and they rotate leadership every year, so that each directorate has equal ownership. In addition to working together, the three leaders also consult with a wider 'Big Team' of about two-dozen interested programme officers from the three collaborating Directorates as well as other NSF units. Big team members alert their respective research communities about CNH, suggest reviewers, attend the advisory panel meeting and participate in discussions that narrow down lists of competitive proposals. Over time, the cross-Directorate group has evolved, achieving a collective vision and also 'a broader mindset regarding what is exciting in other fields'. Despite the challenges, CNH has been cited by NSF as transformative in the way it has pushed research beyond normal boundaries.

The CNH review process is managed deliberately to match the needs of interdisciplinary evaluation:

1 written reviews from both the natural and the social sciences are secured;

2 in selection of panel members, programme officers consciously look for people with broader outlooks and expertise across a range

of areas (people who are comfortable evaluating the breadth of proposals received); and

3 at the beginning of each advisory panel meeting (which lasts two-and-a-half days) at least one hour is spent talking about the philosophy of the programme, to make sure all panellists have a common understanding.

With this 'coaching', each panel develops a collective view, interacting through stimulating discussions and ensuring that both natural and social science components of proposals are sound.

Source: Personal communication and http://www.nsf.gov/funding [accessed 15 January 2011].

experimental mechanisms such as: the NIH's Roadmap initiative's inclusion of 'interpreters' on review panels; growing use of ad hoc expert committees; allowing funding applicants or prospective authors to suggest possible reviewers; and/or allowing them to interact with the review process (Boix Mansilla 2006).

As with quality criteria, there has been some academic analysis of interdisciplinary review processes, with some consensus emerging about the nature of the problems experienced in such evaluations. There is still scope for more practical advice on what should be done to resolve these problems although funding bodies are now much more aware of the issues and many are conducting useful experiments with alternative evaluation approaches (Case Study 7.3).

One issue is that of expertise – the question of what range of skills and experience needs to be represented on a review panel, or among individual evaluators. Another issue is the question of what processes should be used to achieve consensus about the quality of interdisciplinary initiatives. We have noted above that referee choice may be less problematic in well-established interdisciplinary areas such as STS where there is already a pool of known, interdisciplinary referees. But very often there will be no one obvious set of reviewers for a genuinely innovative, interdisciplinary project. In such a case, a review panel and its chair will have an important role in judging the contributions of individual evaluators and in reaching consensus about how to reconcile divergent opinions based on different areas of expertise. Our guidance on effective interdisciplinary review panels (Key Advice 7.3) builds on the insights of others and our own experience.

Case Study 7.3   The sandpit approach to developing
interdisciplinary proposals

Developed in 2004 by the UK Engineering and Physical Sciences Research
Council, the 'sandpit' is an approach to allocating funds for transformative
academically oriented interdisciplinary research that crosses traditional
disciplinary boundaries. Each 5-day sandpit brings together around 30
selected researchers from different disciplines. Selection to attend the sandpit
is competitive and the selection process attempts to identify individuals
who will be temperamentally suited to interdisciplinary collaboration. The
goal is to foster intense discussion around a predetermined research topic
(e.g. synthetic biology) and encourage creativity in working collaboratively
with people outside one's own intellectual comfort zone. The endpoint is
to generate specific research proposals which are peer reviewed in real
time before the conclusion of the sandpit (Mervis 2009).

The week starts with team-building exercises then, in an iterative
process, teams of researchers present their proposals to the larger group,
receive feedback, make revisions and present it again, up to six times
in total. By the end of the week, the lucky winners receive, in principle,
agreement from the Research Council to fund their research idea.

As one sandpit participant comments (Randle 2009), cross-disciplinary
language can be daunting as words can be open to interpretation across
diverse disciplines: at one sandpit, 'matrix' was a mathematical array,
a physico-chemical substrate, a biological extracellular medium, a
technological audio-decoder, a management style and a Keanu Reeves film.

And not everyone finds it easy to embrace the sandpit approach
(Corbyn 2009). Different personalities and different academic cultures
and disciplines clearly respond differently to this technique and some
believe that interdisciplinarity does not occur in this managed fashion.

Evaluating interdisciplinary research proposals from early career researchers or small teams

This section picks up points that are particularly relevant to the evaluation of
smaller interdisciplinary projects, involving a few researchers and a limited
number of disciplines. The projects will often be developed in response to
an open, not specifically interdisciplinary, call for proposals, or will be competing for PhD studentship funding, in which case they may find themselves
being evaluated in comparison with straightforward discipline-based projects.

Key Advice 7.3 Tips for effective interdisciplinary review panels

For those managing interdisciplinary peer review processes

- The make-up of an evaluation panel is probably the most important factor in ensuring maximum potential fairness in the process, so that better quality interdisciplinary projects are funded and poorer ones rejected. The choice of panel members will depend on the context of the evaluation: a set of individual small-scale projects or a major interdisciplinary programme; *ex ante* or *ex post* evaluation; academically oriented or problem-focused interdisciplinary research.

- Discipline-based experts should be chosen on the basis of the breadth of their disciplinary understanding rather than their expertise (no matter how prestigious) in one narrow area of a discipline.

- In all cases it is desirable to have at least one-third of the panel members with a successful track record in interdisciplinary research.

- Ensure that evaluation panel members are provided with guidance on how to evaluate interdisciplinary proposals, including clearly specified criteria, as outlined above. The panel should also be advised on the processes to be adopted, including how to deal with disagreements on the value of different disciplinary contributions and what weight to give to disciplinary contributions in relation to overall interdisciplinary quality.

- The role of a panel chair will be crucial in ensuring that any such guidelines are implemented by the panel, and not sidelined in favour of traditional disciplinary criteria as is so often the case.

For individual reviewers

- Consider personal biases and the implications this might have for evaluation weighting and ultimate decisions

- Be willing to engage in dialogue and respond to others' views.

Some fellowship schemes are targeted specifically at interdisciplinary capacity-building, as in the IGERT scheme in the United States (see chapter 5) and the ESRC/NERC PhD Fellowship Scheme and the ESRC/MRC Fellowship Scheme in the UK (Meagher and Lyall 2005a; Meagher and Lyall 2009), the latter two bridging separate Research Councils with different mandates. This is the most challenging context for interdisciplinary research evaluation and yet it is often faced by the most inexperienced researchers.

Researchers developing an interdisciplinary research proposal, report or publication should find out as much as possible in advance about the review process and the evaluation criteria to be used in order to tailor the proposal accordingly. It is unlikely that the choice of evaluators will be made with inter-disciplinarity in mind so the panel will also need to be given good guidance on how to evaluate interdisciplinary proposals and how to balance judgements so that they do not unfairly discriminate against interdisciplinary proposals. Interdisciplinary proposals can be disadvantaged relative to disciplinary pro-posals if they have to be sent to two panels rather than one (Langfeldt 2006) while Lamont *et al.* found that interviewed panellists struggled to assess whether proposals presented the 'proper balance between breadth and originality on the one hand, and depth and empirical rigor on the other' (Lamont *et al.* 2006).

Doing an interdisciplinary PhD project raises some very specific issues for the evaluation of interdisciplinarity, particularly given the key role played by supervisors who may come from more than one disciplinary background and who may be much less enthusiastic about, and competent in, interdisciplinary research than the student. Just making the student aware that others have faced and overcome such problems can go a long way to alleviating the stress that this situation can generate in the student, and institutions should be open to providing an interdisciplinary advisor for the student in such situations.

Supervisors of an interdisciplinary PhD student have responsibility for the ongoing evaluation of the student, in terms of their framing of the research problem, selection of methods, development of the argument, integrated analy-sis across contributing disciplines' methods and other considerations, and writ-ing of the thesis in a way accessible across disciplines. The supervisory team may themselves have to engage in a dialogue and negotiation to ensure guidance toward an acceptable level of quality. A final responsibility is the choice of exter-nal examiner, who should have empathy to interdisciplinarity and who should be briefed as to the interdisciplinary nature of the thesis. We address a number of these issues in more depth in chapter 5 (see especially Key Advice 5.2).

Early career researchers (PhD students and junior postdoctoral researchers) will be more likely to develop proposals for smaller scale interdisciplinary research and a number of specific quality criteria should be considered in this context. Working on these early stage, smaller interdisciplinary projects is the most challenging and often the least well supported of all types of interdisci-plinarity. Support arrangements for young inexperienced researchers are thus particularly important, e.g. whether there is a team of co-supervisors or co-mentors who are in communication with each other and who are committed to the intellectual pursuit to be undertaken by the researcher(s).

Recognizing the importance of contributions to interdisciplinary integration rather than to specific disciplines can be particularly difficult at the PhD level and needs to be fostered by institutions and supervisors, including contribut-ing to the general understanding among a young researcher's peers about the different challenges involved in interdisciplinary research. Peer-group pressure from discipline-based researchers can seriously undermine the confidence of interdisciplinary researchers at this early stage. Development of a community or network of similarly interdisciplinary young researchers might help to counter this pressure. Young interdisciplinary researchers are often responsible for significant interdisciplinary methodological innovations but may be unaware of the importance of what they have achieved, unless alerted to the value of such outcomes by more senior colleagues.

An individual can do good interdisciplinary research, even though the depth of their knowledge in any one discipline will inevitably be limited and this should be acknowledged. Indeed, researchers who go through this learning process as individual researchers are more likely to become the interdisciplinary research leaders of the future than those who restrict their role to providing specific disciplinary contributions to a larger interdisciplinary initiative.

As discussed in chapter 3, personality traits of the researchers are extremely important. What we would call a high tolerance of ambiguity is an important positive characteristic and, in matching interdisciplinary projects to candidates, evaluators should take this into account. However, this characteristic can also lead to a reluctance on the part of the researcher to focus the area of investigation to manageable proportions. Interim reviews of a project should take account of this tension, placing a large responsibility on supervisors and other reviewers to manage this creative tension. This issue will be much less important for academically oriented interdisciplinary research where there is likely to be a narrower overall disciplinary focus starting from the earliest stages of the project.

With early stage research at doctoral or postdoctoral level, it is less likely that a researcher will have had the opportunity to gain previous experience of interdisciplinary research so this quality criterion should not be applied too rigorously. Indeed, there is anecdotal evidence from experienced interdisciplinary research leaders that those who do interdisciplinary undergraduate degrees and do not pursue any one discipline to an advanced level may find it more difficult to be rigorous about quality standards when it comes to interdisciplinary research. Again the criterion of previous experience should not be used to reject any individual or project, but could serve as an indication of special support that will be needed at these early doctoral or postdoctoral training stages. Key Advice 7.4 suggests some points relevant to the evaluation of such proposals.

Evaluation of interdisciplinary programmes, centres and funding schemes

The increasing number of major programmes and other funding initiatives dedicated explicitly to interdisciplinary research can help to shape research,

---

Key Advice 7.4   Evaluation processes for smaller scale and early career research projects

* It is particularly important in this context to have review panel members who are informed of, and sensitive to, the needs of interdisciplinary research, even if they are not themselves expert in this area. Where discipline-based and interdisciplinary projects are being reviewed simultaneously, the process needs to ensure that each type of project is evaluated according to appropriate criteria and interdisciplinary projects are not required to meet all the discipline-based criteria, with an additional set of requirements imposed beyond that.

* Where interdisciplinary proposals are specifically encouraged as part of a call, the evaluation criteria need to be specified in advance, including an indication of how they will differ from the criteria applied to conventional research. As part of this process instructions/briefings to reviewers should be framed so as to avoid accidental bias against interdisciplinarity.

* Applicants could usefully be able to nominate reviewers for their project, although it will be essential for some independent reviewers also to be involved. It is also useful to give interdisciplinary applicants the opportunity to respond to reviewer comments.

* Communicating openly about how rigorous standards of quality have been applied appropriately and fairly to interdisciplinary as well as monodisciplinary research should be a key feature of the process.

Those evaluating PhD theses may additionally wish to consider:

* Whether the work shows rigorous problem framing, data collection, analysis and drawing of reasonable conclusions.

* Whether the work is consonant with/grounded in its source disciplines and methodologies.

---

through availability of funding. For problem-focused interdisciplinary research, this may take the form of encouraging individuals, teams or new centres to invest their careers and their organization's resources in contemporary, complex issues important to society, such as the multi-partner, £1 billion Living with Environmental Change (LWEC) initiative in the UK.

Likewise, research funding organizations have invested major sums of money in academically oriented interdisciplinary research with a view to stimulating the emergence of new interdisciplinary research areas in subjects such as nanotechnology and synthetic biology. Funding of synthetic biology has been described as 'part of what has become a normal process of disciplinary development whereby, in life sciences, disciplines are being engineered and re-engineered to respond to a variety of pressures rather than being allowed to evolve more "naturally" as would have been the case in the past' (Tait 2009). For such academically oriented interdisciplinary research, concurrent development of appropriate quality criteria can help to facilitate growth of a new subject area or a new discipline from multiple disciplinary roots. The National Academies, in describing the 200-year evolution of biomedical engineering, noted that an important step in consolidating it as a field with its own academic programmes was taken in the early 1960s by the US National Institutes of Health, which: created a committee to evaluate programme-project applications, many of which involved biomedical engineering; established a biomedical engineering training study section that would evaluate applications for training grants; set up two study sections on biophysics; and had a special 'floating' study section to review applications in biomedical engineering and bioacoustics (National Academies 2005: 133).

Funding schemes directed explicitly toward interdisciplinary goals allow evaluators to pay attention to the value that proposed interdisciplinary work is intended to add while also developing standard indicators of quality. So, for example, the National Academies recommend balancing traditional, discipline-based criteria with those more appropriate to interdisciplinary research goals, such as contributions to emerging fields or societal issues (National Academies 2005: 201). Evaluators of such interdisciplinary schemes could benefit from briefings, awareness-raising as to issues and/or open dialogue with other reviewers and funding officers.

One part of the evaluation process takes place prior to the start of interdisciplinary work and most funding bodies will also seek to evaluate the impacts of interdisciplinary programmes they have funded. In such cases, they will want to know if interdisciplinary work has been of equivalent quality to comparable disciplinary work, and if the scheme or programme has actually added value through its interdisciplinarity. Blackwell *et al.* note the importance for the knowledge economy played by long-term benefits which are 'seldom attributed to the investments from which they result' (Blackwell *et al.* 2009). The portfolio of metrics they recommend to funders include 'informal as well as formal outcomes, across a spectrum of outcomes, capacity and processes', even though the qualitative and attitudinal nature of some of these could make evaluation challenging.

We find it possible and important to capture 'lessons learned' from past endeavours to help participants (funders, researchers, research managers and stakeholders) in future such schemes (e.g. Meagher and Lyall 2005a). Insights into important processes of interdisciplinary work in explicitly interdisciplinary schemes can also be captured by sensitive formative evaluation throughout the life of the programme or centre. For example, Hargreaves and Burgess have mapped connections among individuals and project teams, identifying individuals who acted as boundary spanners and highlighting areas where interdisciplinary connectivity could be enhanced (Hargreaves and Burgess 2009). In acting as a 'critical friend' evaluator for a new major interdisciplinary initiative to improve the design of medical devices (CHI+MED),[1] we are building in continuing assessment of evolution of interdisciplinarity and knowledge exchange along with capturing lessons learned. Those evaluating *formatively or retrospectively* explicitly interdisciplinary centres, programmes or funding schemes may wish to consider the quality indicators listed in Key Advice 7.5.

Key Advice 7.5 Points to consider for larger interdisciplinary proposals or programmes

For those reviewing proposals

- aims of the funder relative to interdisciplinarity, any briefings/criteria provided;

- likely quality, robustness of work to be generated;

- importance of the problem focused upon;

- likely effectiveness of interdisciplinarity workings, approaches to building trust, common language, distribution of responsibilities, negotiation over methods, etc;

- explicit attention paid to interdisciplinarity as a process, a goal, and a way of generating value beyond what individual disciplines could accomplish;

- leadership and presence of a liaison role, management plans;

- appreciation by the applicants of the issues that face interdisciplinary ventures;

- interdisciplinary track record of one or more leaders;

- degree of consideration as to how to educate (and advance careers of) next generation or junior researchers involved in interdisciplinary research.

For those evaluating interdisciplinary programmes/funding schemes either formatively or retrospectively

- aims of the funder, principal investigators, centre/programme directors;

- value added through interdisciplinarity;

- tangible outputs (and quality thereof) of interdisciplinary work (e.g. joint publications);

- less tangible results, e.g. development of lasting professional relationships, networks, changes in attitudes/approaches;

- key processes promoting interdisciplinarity, or affected by it;

- roles of various players in promoting interdisciplinarity and related interactions, communication, etc;

- lessons learned/good practice regarding interdisciplinarity that could be useful to others undertaking similar ventures.

Evaluation within institutions

As we discuss in chapter 9, interdisciplinarity presents challenges to leaders of universities and other research institutes who want to craft strategies to promote this approach. Some research bodies may seek to develop an institutional 'persona' of openness to change generally, or interdisciplinarity specifically; some will pursue leadership positions in emerging interdisciplinary niches of importance to society that are likely to receive funding. Some institutions will find upon self-examination that they may have more interdisciplinary work springing up than previously realized; others may find that they have, perhaps unwittingly, consolidated barriers to interdisciplinarity. And few institutions can afford to ignore the increasing number of funding options that target interdisciplinary research initiatives. Whatever the motivation, institutional leaders will confront vexing issues of quality and process in the context of interdisciplinary research.

The Council of Environmental Deans and Directors has prepared guidance for individual academics and academic administrators related to six key career stages for an interdisciplinary scholar with implications for academic quality criteria and evaluation processes (Council of Environmental Deans and Directors n.d.). These are useful institutional support mechanisms, which is why we include them in this section, but they are also more generally applicable in terms of the overall process of interdisciplinary evaluation that we have

---

Key Advice 7.6 Considerations for institutional evaluation and strategy

- Current level and types of interdisciplinary activity at the university.

- Quality of the research itself as judged by criteria outlined in previous sections.

- Real and perceived barriers to interdisciplinarity.

- References to interdisciplinarity in promotion procedures, decision-making.

- Track record of rewarding (or not) interdisciplinary academics.

- Availability of charismatic, committed individuals who could develop plans for and lead interdisciplinary ventures.

- Goals of the university in relation to interdisciplinarity (e.g. desire to solve a particular complex societal problem, desire for leadership in emerging niche areas).

- Depending on the aims of interdisciplinary initiatives, applying the appropriate evaluation criteria in each case:

  - for academically oriented interdisciplinarity this might mean providing insights that lead to the evolution and progress of discipline-based knowledge and understanding

  - for problem-focused interdisciplinarity, contributing to understanding and resolution of practical problems and effective knowledge exchange

---

already discussed above. Further quality criteria that should be considered when evaluating interdisciplinary institutions are summarized in Key Advice 7.6.

1 *Structural Considerations* can make a difference, so, prior to hiring, institutions need to ask themselves questions about the conditions they would provide for someone interdisciplinary.

2 *Position Creation and Institutional Acceptance*, with diverse individuals involved in developing the description of the position and performance expectations in order to gain consensus about goals within the faculty, departments and administration.

3 *Search and Hiring*: a Memorandum of Understanding can play a crucial role in ensuring common expectations among everyone concerned, including committees making decisions on career advancement. (A checklist for such an MOU is provided as an Appendix to the guidance.)

4 *Junior Scholar Development, Mentoring and Protection* can present different challenges for interdisciplinary academics that create difficulties in the tenure and promotion process (e.g. assessing contributions to multi-authored publications).

5 *Dossier Preparation and Evaluation* processes need to acknowledge the ways in which interdisciplinary academics often work, particularly when they work in teams. Strategies recommended by the document include annotation of CVs and provision of guidance to writers of reference letters.

6 *Senior Career Development* can be facilitated by resources and rewards targeted by university leadership to interdisciplinary activities. (Council of Environmental Deans and Directors n.d.)

The National Academies point out the relationship between what is 'tested' and what receives institutional investments noting, for example, potential follow-on consequences of the fact that the National Research Council's Assessment of Research Doctorates typically used data based on departments (although a 2003 re-assessment recommended paying some attention to emerging and interdisciplinary fields): 'When emerging fields are not included in assessments, academic institutions tend to leave them out of the resource allocation as well' (National Academies 2005: 89). Feller identifies two of the factors influencing acceptance of interdisciplinarity, related to quality assessment: National Academies of Science rankings at the time (tending to give weight to conventional discipline-based units) and bibliometrics (the set of methods used to study the impact of texts) (Feller 2006).

Individual career advancement processes within an institution are often perceived to work against promotion of interdisciplinary researchers. The large-scale survey of institutions conducted by the National Academies revealed that one of the top three recommendations for departmental facilitation of interdisciplinary research was 'to recognize and reward faculty and other researchers for interdisciplinary work' (National Academies 2005: 92). Some institutions are conducting experiments along this line. For example, within the University of Wisconsin, the Nelson Institute for Environmental Studies has developed Guidelines for Merit Evaluation and Criteria for Excellence in Interdisciplinary Scholarship.[2] As another example, in 1994, the University of Southern California addressed interdisciplinary research specifically in its institutional guidelines for promotion review (including selection of referees) (National Academies 2005: 103). When a unit within a university is expressly dedicated to interdisciplinary work, it may be evaluated by the institution according to criteria specifically related to that mission (similar to programme evaluation for a funder). The National Academies cite as a 'toolkit' example the Beckman Institute at the University of Illinois, Urbana-Champaign where several cross-disciplinary themes were evaluated with external experts every few years, addressing questions such as: 'Is the work being done of the highest calibre? Is the research of individual faculty or groups of faculty taking advantage of the uniqueness of the institute? Is it interdisciplinary?' (National Academies 2005: 104–105).

Evaluation of interdisciplinary submissions for publication

The reviewing process for publications has implications for individuals' careers and for the overall embedding of interdisciplinary research results and outcomes into accepted knowledge. This can lead to a ripple effect of unintended consequences, for instance within the UK context of periodic centralized assessment of research quality (the Research Assessment Exercise, RAE) across institutions within each discipline:

> The outputs of interdisciplinary research are also harder to evaluate from the traditional academic perspectives. The contribution to knowledge is likely to involve bringing together insights from two normally unrelated academic areas. Finding an outlet for refereed interdisciplinary publications is not usually a problem, but the relevant journals are not highly regarded in the research assessment exercise and the size of the academic community likely to cite interdisciplinary publications is small. It is also difficult to do justice to an interdisciplinary project within the space limitations of most academic journals, so many researchers publish in book chapters or other publications with a lower RAE rating. (Tait 1999)

Life is not easy for those responsible for reviewing interdisciplinary publications. Lamont *et al.* cite the observation of the editor-in-chief of Duke University Press, who suggested that interdisciplinary work is harder to evaluate than it is to generate (Lamont *et al.* 2006). But because barriers to publication are barriers to career advancement, journal editors can encourage interdisciplinarity by, for example, adding individuals with interdisciplinary expertise to review panels and editorial boards and the establishment of special interdisciplinary issues or sections (National Academies 2005: 201).

Individual reviewers of interdisciplinary manuscripts would also benefit from explicit briefing as to issues involved in reviewing interdisciplinary articles, as summarized in Key Advice 7.7.

Self-evaluation

Interdisciplinarity is a challenge taken on by an individual, whether working alone or as part of a team. Interdisciplinary researchers may feel that they are groping their way through fog, with few if any signposts for guidance, but we would encourage such individuals to assess the quality and added value of their own interdisciplinary work. It will often be up to the individual to ensure that she or he is striving as hard as possible to conduct rigorous research. Developing empathetic colleagues can help to calibrate self-assessment of quality of effort and of products. This self-assessment may well be informal, but could include asking oneself questions such as:

- Have I framed my overall research goal clearly; have specific research objectives evolved (or need to evolve)?

Key Advice 7.7 Tips for evaluating interdisciplinary publications

Those *responsible for journals*, and related decision-making regarding interdisciplinary submissions, should consider:

- conspicuously 'opening up' the journal to demonstrate the credibility of interdisciplinary work (e.g. through special issues, overview articles, encouraging ready access based on topics);

- providing clear briefings for reviewers that alert them to issues arising in review of interdisciplinary manuscripts;

- providing journal-specific guidance to reviewers as to expectations of their approach to reviewing interdisciplinary manuscripts even, if appropriate, tailoring a review form to be used for such manuscripts;

- careful selection of reviewers, ensuring coverage of more than one of the component source disciplines as well as at least one reviewer with interdisciplinary empathy;

- gaining awareness of issues involved in integrating divergent reviews received on interdisciplinary submission and thus:

- developing the confidence to take on a senior decision-making role, despite possible diversity in reviews.

Those *acting as reviewers* for interdisciplinary submissions may wish to consider:

- the journal's apparent stance on interdisciplinarity, any guidelines given;

- how the manuscript could broaden coverage in/add new understanding to/provoke subsequent work in the field of the journal or its readers;

- what added value the manuscript derives from its interdisciplinarity;

- whether possible naïvety about some aspect of a component discipline is actually destructive, or not, to the value of the paper;

- the reviewer's own biases, so that the reviewing process is more 'self-aware' than usual within one discipline when many criteria are tacitly understood.

- Have I matched my choice of approaches or methods to the needs of the problem and am I using methods and related analyses correctly?

- Have I taken opportunities to get feedback on my work and subjected it to appropriate peer review?

- Have I found other interdisciplinary researchers with whom I have been able to discuss processes of deriving added value from interdisciplinary work?

- If I am working in a team, am I seeking and responding constructively to critical feedback?

Summary

In this chapter we have noted the critical role that evaluation can play in blocking or facilitating interdisciplinary research. We have stressed the need for ongoing development of two key dimensions: appropriate quality criteria for proposals or research outcomes and appropriate evaluation (review) processes. We maintain that, not only is good quality interdisciplinary research possible, it can also be subjected to rigorous evaluation. Development of appropriate criteria is necessary but not sufficient; processes too must be shaped carefully. This includes selection and briefing of appropriate reviewers. Appropriate evaluation processes are required for the evaluation of: interdisciplinary research proposals from individuals (particularly at early career stages) or small teams; interdisciplinary programmes, centres and funding schemes; interdisciplinary activity or careers within institutions; interdisciplinary submissions for publication; and self-evaluation. We have offered practical suggestions of points to be considered if interdisciplinary work is to be judged fairly, particularly when it is in competition with more conventional monodisciplinary work.

Questions

For researchers

1 When writing interdisciplinary research proposals, how could you best indicate both the quality of the research itself and the quality of your approach to integration of concepts, findings and people?

2 Could you recommend interdisciplinary reviewers for your work? Can you volunteer to be a reviewer yourself, for others' interdisciplinary proposals or manuscripts?

For research managers

1 What tactics would enhance the likelihood of publication in respected journals?

2 How would you go about positioning yourself and your team members as prospective reviewers (of proposals or manuscripts) to help spread interdisciplinary expertise throughout review processes?

For institutional leaders

1 Are there accidental or tacit assumptions embedded within your institution's internal assessment processes, including but not limited to promotion decisions, which could work against interdisciplinary researchers?

2 Could you establish formative evaluation of key interdisciplinary centres, institutes or programmes, so that you could capture learning for future efforts?

For research funders and evaluators

1 How can appropriate quality indicators be framed when developing interdisciplinary research competitions?

2 How would you select reviewers and panel members, and how will you brief them? Could you deliberately develop a panel culture that works for interdisciplinarity?

3 If you receive interdisciplinary proposals in competition with monodisciplinary proposals, how would you handle the review process to ensure that the interdisciplinary proposals are not disadvantaged?

4 If you were evaluating (formatively or retrospectively) an expressly interdisciplinary programme, centre or scheme, what criteria would you use? How might you compare the quality of outputs to the outputs of a monodisciplinary scheme?

8

Knowledge Travels

Getting interdisciplinary research into policy and practice

Introduction

Knowledge exchange can be defined as a two-way flow of communication between academic researchers and potential non-academic research users (for example in industry or policy) that may lead to impacts on the economy, the environment, well-being or society. Two converging trends point to the likely participation of interdisciplinary researchers in the knowledge exchange process (although it is worth emphasizing that knowledge exchange is not solely the domain of interdisciplinary research and can apply to any research effort).

Firstly, in this era of the 'knowledge economy', governments seek return on their investments in research. Even bodies that fund university research are responding to this driver with explicit expectations that, where possible, academic research should strive to have an influence beyond the ivory tower. While those public funding bodies that support research in the natural and physical sciences and engineering may find it difficult to point to tangible impacts beyond those of intellectual property generated or indeed to the economic contributions of spinout companies, the impacts that social science research (as well as the arts and humanities) may have on public policy or professional practice are often even harder to track (Meagher *et al.* 2008). Yet, basing public policy and practice upon sound research and evidence is frequently cited as a desirable social good – one towards which research funding bodies, researchers, policy-makers and practitioners should aspire (Davies *et al.* 2000); industry strategies may also benefit from input from a range of disciplines.

Secondly, there is a growing recognition that the challenges faced by society, as arenas where research has the potential to make a helpful impact, seldom if ever map neatly on to disciplinary divisions. Thus, there are growing calls for more interdisciplinary approaches to societal problems (for example, dealing with the impacts of climate change). Pressure to encourage interdisciplinary research often comes from the need to solve complex socio-scientific problems, where one discipline on its own cannot provide an answer. This chapter discusses the con-

̄ ̄ of interdisciplinary research to the process of knowledge exchange. It
how best to reach out beyond the boundaries of academia in order to

engage with prospective research users, and discusses some of the research design and research management issues that this may prompt. In many cases, knowledge exchange will involve industry in the classic case of technology transfer and the commercialization of research outputs. While acknowledging the importance of interdisciplinary research to industry, this chapter focuses primarily on what may be the particularly 'hard' case of interdisciplinarity aligned with knowledge exchange: the bridging of natural and social sciences in knowledge exchange processes involving the worlds of policy-making and professional practice. Processes taking place in these worlds are often subtle, complex and long term.

Finally, we would suggest that researchers comfortable with interdisciplinarity may be 'preconditioned' for effective participation in knowledge exchange. Very often, individuals are driven to do interdisciplinary research because they hope to help solve a complex socio-scientific problem. But even beyond choice of problems, the mindset and skill sets of researchers working in an interdisciplinary fashion may give them a head-start in tackling the challenges of knowledge exchange. In large-scale initiatives, research funding bodies tend to encourage increased levels of collaboration and networking among institutions, researchers and research users. Researchers who have developed a capacity to work with others from different disciplines can utilize this same capacity to develop effective working relationships with non-academics. A mindset willing to respect and learn from others who approach problems from different perspectives is a hugely valuable resource if a researcher is to participate in knowledge exchange. Skills vital to both successful interdisciplinary work and successful knowledge exchange include an ability to:

- learn others' language;
- take into account their priorities and premises;
- build up mutual trust and respect;
- explore new territory; and
- synthesize information in innovative ways.

Individuals who conduct interdisciplinary research may find that the latter part of this chapter resonates with what they already do, as it outlines issues of design, management and collaboration pertaining to knowledge exchange.

Knowledge goals

As we have discussed, effective interdisciplinary research often requires new types of thinking by researchers and cuts across the traditional discipline-based academic structures, and systems of reward and resource allocation, that are found in most universities. Gibbons *et al.* distinguish between Mode 1 and Mode 2 research (Gibbons *et al.* 1994). The former corresponds broadly to the traditional academic mode of knowledge production which is generally organized along homogeneous, single-discipline lines and is typically curiosity-driven research without a specific end goal in mind. The latter refers to a 'new production of knowledge' that cuts across disciplinary boundaries in order to create knowledge for a specific purpose. Nowotny *et al.* then extend this shift to integrated research beyond the research sector to encompass integration between producer and user organizations (Nowotny *et al.* 2001). As discussed in chapter 2, we have adapted this terminology to draw a further distinction between *academically oriented interdisciplinary research* (broadly equivalent to Mode 1) and *problem-focused interdisciplinary research* (broadly equivalent to Mode 2), which addresses issues of social, technical and/or policy relevance where the primary aim is problem-oriented and discipline-related outputs are less central to the project design.

Others have drawn distinctions between long-term, individual involvement in interdisciplinarity and the shorter term, situational interest (Lattuca 2001: 217) or the contrasts between the 'scholarship of discovery' versus the 'scholarship of integration' (Lattuca 2001: 263). In reality there is, of course, a broad spectrum of approaches to interdisciplinarity rather than a sharp polarization.

Knowledge exchange

Governments seek to make the most of all their investments and, since research is now seen very much as part of that investment portfolio, a 'return' to society is expected from publicly funded research. In the UK, for example, the Lambert Review of Business-University Collaboration made a series of recommendations aimed at enabling knowledge transfer between Britain's strong research base and the business community (Lambert Review of Business–University Collaboration 2003). Following the Lambert Review, the House of Commons Select Committee Inquiry into Knowledge Transfer and the External Challenge Report on Research Council Knowledge Transfer (the 'Warry Report') of 2006 exhorted the Research Councils to increase their economic impact (with 'economic' defined broadly enough to include policy, practice and other dimensions of importance to society) and improve public health and quality of life through the research that they fund. As a consequence, the UK's Research Councils are increasing their efforts to demonstrate how their support for research, training and knowledge exchange contributes to these goals (Research Councils UK 2006; Research Councils UK 2007; ESRC 2009a; ESRC 2009c).

It is generally recognized that the impact of academic research is long-term and often indirect and the current knowledge transfer literature emphasizes the non-linear nature of such research impacts. Indeed, the very term 'knowledge transfer' conjures up the image of a one-way flow of knowledge. In the light of this, the alternative term of 'knowledge exchange' is increasingly favoured. Figure 8.1 attempts to capture some of the complexity and non-linearity of this process.

A range of actors, including a variety of 'knowledge intermediaries', plays a critical role in the knowledge exchange process. Funding bodies themselves can

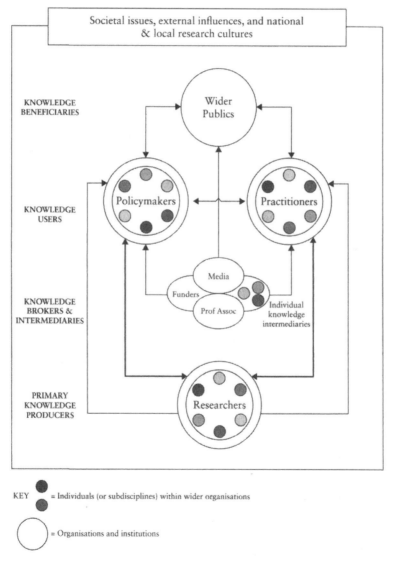

Figure 8.1 Flows of knowledge, expertise and influences
Source: First published in Meagher *et al.* 2008.

act as knowledge intermediaries, as can individual researchers, university units, dedicated staff hired by a research centre, advisory board members, learned society staff or indeed a wide variety of individuals who inhabit a professional space between academics and non-academics. Variously named and defined, these knowledge intermediaries, research brokers or boundary spanners can facilitate productive communication, dialogue, interactions and relationship-building, and act at the interface between researchers and non-academics who might take part in knowledge exchange.

The knowledge exchange process thus brings together researchers, potential users of research and wider community groups to exchange ideas, evidence and expertise which may in turn lead to new knowledge or understanding that might be used for academic, social, cultural and economic benefit (for example, see Case Study 8.1). The process is often prompted by a desire to address 'real life' issues that cut across disciplinary boundaries; the nuances of research design and research management, described in this chapter in the context of transforming knowledge into action, will be of particular interest to those undertaking problem-focused interdisciplinary research.

Policy analysis has traditionally been dominated by the linear, 'stages model' (e.g. Hill 1997) whereby policy-making is seen as a sequential process: identification of a policy problem, policy initiation and formulation, legislation, implementation, evaluation and iteration (Tait and Williams 1999). This often assumes that problems can be broken down into discrete elements mapping on to distinct disciplines whereas many policy issues transcend disciplines or indeed lie at the boundaries between them. While research can have a direct or 'instrumental' impact on policy and practice decisions – where a specific piece of research is used in making a specific decision or in defining the solution to a specific problem – far more common is the 'conceptual use' or enlightenment effect comprising the complex and often diffuse ways in which research can have an impact on the knowledge, understanding and attitudes of policymakers and practitioners (Nutley *et al.* 2007): while such uses of research may be less demonstrable, they are not less important.

Drivers for interdisciplinarity and impact

The availability of research funding has a critical influence on the directions and approaches taken by academic researchers. In the UK and Europe, for example, there are frequent calls from national and European Union funders for large-scale proposals based upon interdisciplinary collaboration between the social and natural sciences as a means to promote scientific and technological advance while also fostering its more effective acceptance and beneficial utilization in society. As one example, a study, conducted for the UK Rural Economy and Land Use (Relu) programme of other interdisciplinary, policy-oriented

Case Study 8.1   Cooperative Research on Environmental Problems in Europe (CRÊPE)

Cooperative research is currently viewed as a significant part of a European strategy which aims to achieve better knowledge as well as more effective science and technology governance. It is often defined as taking place when researchers and non-researchers participate together to produce new knowledge and where both parties gain from the process.

The CRÊPE project (Cooperative Research on Environmental Problems in Europe) brought together civil society organizations (CSOs) and academics to investigate agri-environmental issues. CSOs operate as leading partners in the project in the generation of environmental knowledge and bring a range of specific knowledge practices, research relationships and distributions of expertise. The project sought to empower and resource CSOs to participate in co-operative research and aimed to:

- strengthen CSOs' capacity to participate in research, while engaging with diverse perspectives and expertise – thus facilitating co-operation between researchers and non-researchers, as well as between academics and CSOs;

- design, implement, evaluate retrospectively and thus test the methods used for cooperative research in this project, as a basis to inform future efforts;

- analyse diverse accounts of 'the environment' in relation to agricultural methods, technologies, innovations and alternatives;

- relate research more closely to societal needs, as a means to inform policy debate and research priorities for Europe as a 'Knowledge-Based Society';

- suggest alternative solutions related to different understandings of societal problems, agri-environmental issues and sustainable development.

The CRÊPE project engaged with debates around interdisciplinarity, implementation and the involvement of users in the co-production of knowledge and is an example of transdisciplinarity in action. In multi-disciplinary research, different but distinct academic disciplinary knowledge is brought to bear on a particular issue, whereas in interdisciplinary research boundaries between disciplines are broken down as researchers from different disciplines work together in an integrated way. As

Case Study 8.1 *Continued*

noted in chapter 2, transdisciplinary projects take this one step further: researchers not only work together in an interdisciplinary way, but also work with and involve broader stakeholders and or publics. Thus, it is not only academic knowledge that is brought to bear on an issue, but also the knowledge of those who may have a stake in the practical applications of the research.

Working in this participatory way means that expert knowledge is complemented by the knowledge and experience of users, for example, citizens or policy actors (and vice versa). By involving different types of knowledge, uncertainty resulting from complex issues and imperfect scientific knowledge may be reduced and the research is more likely to be useful and used, because those affected by the issue are included. CRÊPE seeks to embrace diversity of knowledge/views in order to generate creativity, working in partnerships and drawing on networks to find ways forward.

The project is coordinated by the Open University, UK, and funded by the European Commission, Framework Programme 7, Science in Society programme.

Source: http://crepeweb.net [accessed 15 January 2011].

programmes and initiatives in the area of rural economy and land use, analysed some 15 programmes involving 24 countries (Raffaelli *et al.* 2005). One such initiative is MISTRA, the Swedish Foundation for Strategic Environmental Research (Case Study 8.2).

Funding priorities themselves are, of course, influenced in turn by political drivers. For example, as part of New Labour's 'modernising government' initiative in the UK in 2000, then Secretary for Education David Blunkett exhorted government and the research community to work together to address the lack of good research evidence, acknowledging that interdisciplinary research had a role to play (Blunkett 2000). A decade later, the UK's Research Councils have begun to publish regularly their accomplishments in terms of funded research that has led to impacts, on the economy, society, policy or practice. While maintaining commitment to research excellence, these funding bodies now encourage their award-holders to report wherever possible on the generation of non-academic impacts.

This development is exemplified in the empirical study by Barry *et al.*, which identified several rationales for conducting interdisciplinary research (Barry *et al.* 2008). These included breaking down barriers between science and society (the 'logic of accountability') and connecting businesses to customer

---

Case Study 8.2 MISTRA: Building bridges between the research community and the wider society

MISTRA, the Swedish Foundation for Strategic Environmental Research, states:

> Most problems in the environmental sphere are so complex that the knowledge generated within a single academic discipline is not sufficient to understand them or to help solve them.
>
> All Mistra programmes combine research in a number of different disciplines, with the aim of understanding and finding solutions to complex environmental problems. Often this requires a concerted effort across the boundary between natural sciences and engineering, on the one hand, and social sciences, economics and humanities on the other. For such an endeavour to succeed, programmes need to find productive arrangements for collaboration and for synthesis of the research undertaken.

Source: 'Running a research programme in support of sustainable development: What you need to think about. A guide for participants in MISTRA programmes.' http://www.mistra.org [accessed 15 January 2011].

---

demand (the 'logic of innovation'). There are also important internal, intellectual drivers where the appropriate goals of interdisciplinarity are seen to be reflections on the emergence of new disciplines (Barry *et al.*'s 'logic of ontology' or what we term 'academically oriented interdisciplinarity') where the focus is on learning and not expertise (Lattuca 2001: 164).

Nevertheless, many see interdisciplinary research as irrevocably consigned to a pragmatic, problem-solving mode (Petts *et al.* 2006) or in response to 'crisis' where complex socio-scientific problems cannot be addressed by one discipline on its own and methods and theories devised for other purposes may be called upon. Some regret that the 'persistent linking of the concepts of interdisciplinarity and "real world problems" has associated an interdisciplinary approach with instrumental, or applied research', and warn that uncritical advocacy of interdisciplinary research can over-simplify the different traditions and contributions made by different disciplines (Petts *et al.* 2006). For example, when a crisis with social dimensions arises, the social sciences may be required to act in a 'responsive mode' rather than as an outcome of the discipline's own theory-driven questions (Strathern, 2004: 2–4). A focus on stakeholder engagement may bring political pressures that challenge independent researchers' 'neutral competence': in these circumstances interdisciplinary researchers need to find a way to maintain balance and to focus on the quality of the evidence base used or generated by the knowledge exchange process.

A third wave of interdisciplinarity?

Despite the growing emphasis in academic research funding of interdisciplinarity, Frodeman and Mitcham assert that the 'knowledge society' is increasingly characterized by a disconnect between knowledge production and knowledge utilization (Frodeman and Mitcham 2007). To counter this they argue for 'a new, critical form of interdisciplinarity that moves beyond the academy into dialogue with the public and private sectors'. This 'third wave of interdisciplinarity' focuses on the problems of knowledge management and questions the nature and limits of expertise (whose knowledge 'counts'). These authors note that interdisciplinary efforts are often criticized for being 'shallow', but that this is true only in comparison with what they view as the 'stove-pipe narrowness' of monodisciplinary approaches, which may be deep in academic tradition but are often unable to see the broader context. Moreover, they claim that contemporary knowledge production should involve not only a horizontal axis stretching across academia, but also a vertical axis where academic research is integrated into society, 'moving beyond the academy into dialogue with the public sector, the private sector, and community and stakeholders'.

This approach to interdisciplinarity involves both integration and implementation and is characterized by some as 'transdisciplinarity'. Klein suggests that the most important difference between interdisciplinary and transdisciplinary research is that the latter includes the 'intentional involvement of stakeholders in the definition of problems and those criteria, objectives and resources used to analyse and resolve them' (Klein 2004). Transdisciplinarity is thus multidimensional, transcultural and transnational, and encompasses ethics, spirituality and creativity: it is not a new discipline or super-discipline but instead represents a unique set of problems 'that do not emanate from within science' (Klein 2004). Transdisciplinary projects usually involve stakeholders and access additional forms of knowledge. Transdisciplinarity is not a method or a discipline, it is a principle for how to treat problems between science and society which may involve research users: it therefore tends to be a question of who is involved in the collaborative project that distinguishes interdisciplinarity from transdisciplinarity (Wickson et al. 2006; Mobjörk 2009).

There is still no consensus on what transdisciplinarity is or how its quality can be evaluated (Wickson et al. 2006). There is also debate around whether or not distinct differences exist between interdisciplinarity and transdisciplinarity and the terms are often used interchangeably in funding and research practices (Hall et al. 2008). Pohl traces the origins of transdisciplinarity back to the 1972 Organisation for Economic Co-operation and Development report (Pohl 2008). Here transdisciplinarity represents the overall coordination of science, education and innovation towards a specific societal purpose. For Pohl, going a step further towards co-production with stakeholders is a core concept of transdisciplinary research, which Pohl defines as a collaborative process of knowledge production involving multiple disciplines and stakeholders from other sectors of society. While the French approach typically sees transdisciplinarity primarily as going 'beyond disciplines' (see chapter 2), transdisciplinary research seems to be understood in this much more specific knowledge exchange context in German-speaking countries (Pohl 2008) as illustrated in Case Study 8.3.

Although 'transdisciplinarity' is finding wider currency particularly in the United States, it is still one of many terms used to describe the process of getting cross-disciplinary knowledge in to practice. The British tend not to espouse the transdisciplinary taxonomy, instead retaining the interdisciplinary label but with an increasing, but often independent, focus on the non-academic impacts of publicly funded research (ESRC 2009c). This dual focus on interdisciplinarity and knowledge exchange is exemplified by the Research Councils UK Rural Economy and Land Use Programme (Relu) discussed in Case Study 8.4, which clearly demonstrates that relevance and quality should not be viewed as alternatives. In other English-speaking countries, such as Australia, there is both a combined focus on integration *and* implementation and even a drive to have this recognized as a discrete discipline in its own right (Case Study 8.5). In the United States, there is a long tradition of universities connecting to society, such that most institutions have an explicitly tripartite mission of 'education, research and outreach' (or 'service'). This is particularly true of the 'land-grant institutions', established in each state by the Morrill Act of 1862 as universities that would help people such as farmers and engineers by conducting research relevant to local development. Now these institutions incorporate a wide gamut of disciplines, with most of these displaying a spectrum of basic to applied research. This orientation toward usefulness continues as new subdisciplines and new problem areas arise.

Regardless of how the process is branded, there is a number of research design and research management issues that anyone planning, undertaking or leading research that is both cross-disciplinary and aimed at non-academic impacts should take into account. The remainder of the chapter deals with some of these practical considerations.

Design issues

Research oriented toward the world beyond academia can take a number of forms and this can affect the research design. This may depend, for example, upon the nature of the relationship with, or demand from, stakeholders. Some (not mutually exclusive) approaches include:

- researchers may design interdisciplinary work to achieve a rounded, in-depth understanding of what they perceive as a complex social problem. This might be done:

Case Study 8.3 td-net Network for Transdisciplinary Research

td-net was launched in 2000 to provide a platform for regular encounters between transdisciplinary researchers in Switzerland and elsewhere. td-net uses the term 'transdisciplinary' for research projects and programmes that deal with socially relevant problems that address knowledge of systems, of aims and of transformation and also take into consideration different social actors.

The annual Transdisciplinarity Conference (td-conference) is one of the Network's central means for promoting excellence in transdisciplinary research and teaching. Its main aim is to provide a platform for exchange between individuals and teams involved in transdisciplinary projects on a range of issues (including public health, migration, new technologies, climate change, globalization and cultural transformation processes) in order to share experiences and further develop integrative methods and approaches for knowledge-based solutions to pressing problems in the real world. The conference aims to develop and strengthen transdisciplinarity in Switzerland and act as a catalyst for transdisciplinary projects in Europe and beyond.

td-net maintains the Bibliography Transdisciplinarity database which is a comprehensive, structured source of literature in the field of transdisciplinary research. This database seeks to foster a common knowledge base within the community of transdisciplinary research and research on transdisciplinarity and is aimed at all those involved in the planning, realization and evaluation of transdisciplinary research projects.

The Swiss Academies offer a biannual award for transdisciplinary research (td-award), in recognition of excellence and innovation in transdisciplinary research. It provides an incentive to researchers from all fields to develop more integrative projects in order to better deal with the complexities of socio-cultural, technological, economic, environmental and health issues whose causes and effects are not well understood or uncertain. Based on the principles established by the td-net in dialogue with its national and international scientific community, the criteria by which a project may contribute to the enhancement and excellence of transdisciplinarity research are:

- a substantial contribution to knowledge production in the participating disciplines as well as to the building and transfer of solution-oriented research in the interest of a common good;

- a high level of awareness and a reflexive handling of the complexity of an issue, meaning the complex system of factors that together explain the issue's current state and its dynamic;

- integration of academic and non-academic perceptions and positions;

- participatory stakeholder and/or community engagement or policy development process;

- scientific and social contextualization.

td-net was launched by the Swiss Academic Society for Environmental Research and Ecology and taken over by the Swiss Academy of Sciences in 2003. Since 2008 the td-net for transdisciplinary research has been a project of the Swiss Academies of Arts and Sciences.

Source: This case study was prepared from material available from the td-net website, http://www.transdisciplinarity.ch [accessed 15 January 2011].

Case Study 8.4 Research Councils UK Rural Economy and Land Use Programme (Relu)

Launched in 2003 by coordinated support from multiple funding bodies to carry out strategic interdisciplinary research into the multiple challenges facing rural areas, involvement throughout the research process of a wide range of stakeholders is key to the Relu philosophy. The challenges range from restoring trust in food chains and tackling animal and plant disease in socially acceptable ways, to mitigating and adapting to climate change.

Working across disciplines, Relu brings together natural and social scientists to work on research projects that examine holistically the challenges facing rural areas today. Researchers from over 40 disciplines and more than 50 institutions are involved with Relu. The programme does not prescribe the specific form of interdisciplinary collaboration, only that each project must have well-integrated natural and social science components.

Relu consults widely among stakeholder organizations in the formulation and development of its research programme and all the projects produce plans for engaging stakeholders in their research. At programme level Relu's Strategic Advisory Committee, the Food Chain Forum, the People and Rural Environment Forum and Animal and Plant Disease Forum bring together key stakeholders from the public, private and voluntary sectors to act as sounding boards on programme and project development. At the project level researchers are working with a wide

Case Study 8.4 *Continued*

range of organizations and social groups, some in an advisory capacity, others as consultees, informants or research partners. Some projects are even sidestepping the conventional researcher/research subject divide to pursue an approach best described as the joint production of knowledge between researchers and practitioners.

The interdisciplinary approach adopted by Relu brings the knowledge of different disciplines into a positive dialogue, moving away from simplistic assumptions about 'technology push' or 'society pull'. The approach facilitates the involvement of stakeholders from the very early stages of formulating research questions and throughout the research process.

By involving stakeholders from an early stage, Relu's projects pave the way for genuine knowledge exchange. Recognizing that knowledge exchange is invariably people embodied, two schemes underline Relu's approach: work shadowing, where academics spend time in settings where their research may be used, and visiting fellowships, which provide an opportunity for staff from interested commercial, public or voluntary organizations to visit research teams.

The principles that underpin the approach within Relu are that stakeholder engagement:

- is a continuous and iterative process in which stakeholders are engaged as active partners in establishing the focus and priorities of the programme and not treated merely as passive recipients of the research when it is complete;

- is a two-way process of knowledge exchange between scientists and a wide range of policy-makers, practitioners, businesses and the public;

- embraces a pluralistic and inclusive stakeholder community;

- acknowledges that soft knowledge transfer through informal networks between research and practice can be more important than harder and more impersonal forms, such as the commercialization of knowledge or evidence-based policy-making;

- places emphasis on encouraging and enabling knowledge exchange among researchers and research users.

Many projects are also taking a reflective approach to their engagement with stakeholders, and thinking seriously about how the very processes they employ for identifying stakeholders influence how they define research problems.

Relu has also developed a range of methods for knowledge transfer at programme level, within the framework of a communication strategy and regularly updated communication plans. As well as the usual range of tools, including newsletters, media contacts, academic publications, conferences, a website and regular briefing papers, Relu's knowledge exchange activities also include:

- regular meetings of national stakeholder fora, where researchers present their work to a broad constituency of key national organizations from the public, private and voluntary sectors;

- a tailored communications plan produced by every project;

- workshops and other knowledge exchange events that bring together researchers and stakeholders from relevant sectors, with opportunities for open discussion and feedback;

- building up links with knowledge brokers as partners;

- production at the end of every project of a focused document to highlight key findings and their implications for future policy and practice.

As it approaches the end of its grant, Relu continues to account for its knowledge exchange activities (Phillipson *et al.* 2010) and reports that, of 21 projects (most in mid or end stages of their research) in the year 2008 alone, over 1,000 stakeholders were involved: 37 per cent public sector; 36 per cent private sector; 15 per cent members of the public (such as consumers); and 12 per cent third sector. Over 40 per cent were research subjects, but others were event participants, and still others (in smaller numbers) acted as steering/advisory group members, partners, consultees, customers, or visitors/work shadowees. By far, most Relu researchers saw knowledge exchange leading to positive impacts of stakeholders on the quality and relevance of their research.

Relu is a collaboration between the UK Economic and Social Research Council, the Natural Environment Research Council and the Biotechnology and Biological Sciences Research Council. Funded between 2004 and 2011, it has a budget of £24 million, with additional support from the Scottish Government and the Department for Environment, Food and Rural Affairs.

Source: This case study was prepared from material available from the Relu website http://www.relu.ac.uk [accessed 15 January 2011].

Case Study 8.5 Integration and Implementation Sciences (I2S)

Integration and Implementation Sciences (I2S) is an emerging field concerned with:

1 the synthesis of a range of knowledge, information and perspectives to improve understanding of complex issues;

2 using research knowledge to support decision-makers in various domains, including public policy, business, professional practice and community activism;

3 using research knowledge to underpin the implementation of decisions in effective social change.

Based at the Australian National University, it aims to provide an academic base for cross-cutting concepts and methods crucial for tackling complex issues. The network aims to bring together a 'college' of peers who can support and critically evaluate each other's work. I2S started in around 2001 and the ideas underpinning it are continuing to develop.

I2S covers four domains, namely concepts and methods to enhance:

1 fresh thinking on intractable problems;

2 integration of disciplinary and stakeholder knowledge;

3 understanding and management of ignorance and uncertainty;

4 the provision of research support for change in decision making and practice.

It asks how the contribution of university research and education to tackling complex social, environmental and technological problems could be boosted and believes that effectively tackling real-world problems requires a new type of researcher, who can enhance collaboration between discipline and practice experts. Although the necessity for cross-disciplinary research on complex real-world problems has long been recognized, it acknowledges that it has been difficult for such research to gain traction in universities and this has limited the contribution of university-based research to tackling important social challenges. It also supports the assertions that it is crucial that cross-disciplinary research is not regarded as a poor cousin to discipline-based research in terms of quality, so that mechanisms are required to enhance excellence as we have discussed in chapter 7.

I2S provides: (a) the hub around which research institutions can organize teams to investigate real-world problems; (b) a baseline level of quality for such work; (c) an avenue for transmitting new theory and methods between groups focusing on different real-world problems; and (d) a home for methodologies addressing recurrent concerns in tackling complex problems that are not the province of any discipline or practice area.

I2S underpins two major research programmes – the Drug Policy Modelling Program and the Australian Research Council Centre of Excellence in Policing and Security. I2S ideas are also being used in the Global Environmental Change and Food Systems (GECAFS) projects and in the National Cancer Institute.

The I2S network produces *Integration Insights*, a series of digests of concepts, techniques or real-world examples of integration in research; runs short courses for research leaders seeking an introduction to research integration; and provides a set of web-based resources for developing unified systems concepts and toolboxes to underpin Integration and Implementation Sciences.

The I2S website was established using funding from the Fulbright New Century Scholars program, awarded to Professor Gabriele Bammer, as well as funding from the National Centre for Epidemiology and Population Health, at the Australian National University.

Source: This case study was prepared from material available from the I2S website http://www.anu.edu.au/iisn [accessed 15 January 2011].

- by researchers alone;

- with input from policy-makers, perhaps through interviews, as a part of the research;

- with a partnership at some level between researchers and stakeholders (ranging from acting as a stakeholder advisory board to actual co-production of research);

• researchers may respond to a call for a broad research effort either from policy-makers directly or from research funding bodies representing them

• researchers may take on specific, short, timely highly targeted research commissioned (with most of the design done) by policy-makers.

While academic research usually generates its own research questions (even if directed at real-world issues), a study that has been commissioned is more likely to take its problems from government agendas or the research commissioner. They may be less interested in causal processes and the role of explanation, and more interested in description and prediction leading to social action. There may be a marked difference between the purposes of these types of studies, contrasting knowledge for understanding (e.g. whether there is an association between variables) with knowledge for action (e.g. whether this association matters).

Increasing the impact of research beyond academia demands more than just post-hoc dissemination. It requires careful planning as part of the design process and should aim to achieve dialogue with potential research users at the earliest possible stage, possibly even involving them in the design process itself. These issues are therefore highly relevant to the development of interdisciplinary research proposals as discussed in chapter 3. To have a practical influence, conclusions from research must be realistic and achievable. But it may take multiple approaches and change in understanding, attitudes or behaviour may only be incremental. As Case Study 8.6 illustrates, the central message is that researchers, stakeholders and funders all have roles to play at each stage (including design), and that clarity of communication is vital throughout.

From the design phase onward, it requires effort on the part of academic researchers in order to adjust to the world of policy and perhaps recognize their own limitations (Bulmer 1982). Policy-making is not a straightforward, linear process; policy development continues throughout implementation (John 1998) and the resulting knowledge is iterative rather than rational.[1] Policy is made by the pluralistic bargaining of interest groups; power and interests often have far more influence than research outputs. Researchers hoping to influence policy need to combine a realistic acceptance of this fact with a continuing drive to build relationships and pursue the dialogue that can lead to policy-making that is informed by research and evidence.

Research management issues

Research integration is often described as much more of a process than a product or an outcome and this shift from content integration to a focus on process can be helpful when considering how to link research into action, to generate impacts, just as it is when considering how to link disciplines.

We have noted in chapters 3 and 4 that interdisciplinary research may take longer, in part because the respective contribution of different groups may not be clearly understood at the outset and there may be a need to develop shared understanding/language. While this need is also present in knowledge-exchange

Case Study 8.6   SNIFFER and SEPA: Examples of integration

An evaluation of environmental research projects funded by the Scotland and Northern Ireland Forum for Environmental Research (SNIFFER) and the Scottish Environment Protection Agency (SEPA) analysed impacts and related processes, generated illustrative case studies of integration and captured lessons learned. The two organizations have taken the proactive step of embedding these lessons into guidance to improve integration in future research projects, providing reciprocal advice for researchers, stakeholders and funders. This guidance emphasizes key aspects of design and early development, including the importance of early dialogue, mutual clarity as to objectives, building of relationships and communication – all of which should resonate with individuals involved in interdisciplinary efforts.

One case study brought together diverse types of information to prepare *Guidelines for Practitioners on how to take account of air, water and soil* when preparing Strategic Environmental Assessments; the collaborative Steering Group for this project brought together people from different sections of government, with input from six experts in each of the three technical areas; in the long run, more soundly developed assessments should help responsible authorities consider the three dimensions as well.

Another project, *Differential Social Impacts of Climate Change in the UK*, addressed what was then a significant gap in understanding by conducting an analytical review of studies and information on how climate change, and adaptations to it, might affect different social groups in different ways, and how different social groups may be more or less able to respond. The project involved collaboration across multiple agencies and by raising awareness had the conceptual impact of legitimizing social aspects of climate change as a component of policy planning. The project was seen as influencing the UK Climate Change Risk Assessment being conducted by the UK, the Scottish Government's Climate Change Adaptation Framework and the Belfast Healthy Cities group. Illustrating how creativity of interdisciplinarity can spread to stakeholders, the project was seen as opening up cross-fertilization opportunities among policy stakeholders. As one governmental stakeholder noted, considering social inequities of climate change impacts:

> means that you are able to engage with practitioners from other settings, such as healthy cities, that you don't normally work with. As someone in a government agency, you get to work with different areas of research, different people in different agencies, which gives you a chance to talk about things and think about things that you wouldn't normally have thought of.

Source: Meagher *et al.* 2010; Meagher 2010.

oriented research, an immediate challenge to research management arises: policy-makers work with multiple and shifting political agendas, often with short timeframes for action, factors which have a significant influence on their engagement with research findings. It is also important to remember, from a research management point of view, that these and other factors that influence research impact, such as the nature and role of knowledge intermediaries and the heterogeneity of researchers and users, are not static but interact over time, giving a dynamic dimension to the process of knowledge exchange. We will discuss these issues in separate sections below but first two further research management issues are worth considering.

Academic research may only be concerned with very small groups but in policy and practice environments results may be required to be applicable and made general to much wider populations. This scaling-up may cause social researchers, in particular, concern. Another issue lies in the fact that, where research is sponsored by vested interests, there may be questions about independence and impartiality and the political aspects of such a study cannot be ignored or suppressed. This may lead to requirements for only restricted publication where the final report is confidential to the client. Even if the work is publicly available, a body of writing based on research reports and 'grey literature' may not enhance academic careers. One tactic in this case is to ensure an upfront agreement, wherever possible, that some element of such commissioned research will also be written up as a peer-reviewed, academic publication.

While policy research may not be methodologically distinctive in any systematic way from more theoretically focused academic research (Bechhofer and Paterson 2000), it may use distinctive combinations of methods and does require a different style of working and perhaps a different mindset. As noted above, it requires a willingness to engage with different audiences who may have quite different agendas and timescales from those of the academic researcher. It will require research outputs in a different format and language from traditional academic publications and an understanding – and acceptance – that research outputs are used selectively by policy-makers as dictated by political agendas and other external factors. Building relationships between researchers and prospective users who are policy-makers can take time and effort (especially when policy-makers often move posts fairly frequently, requiring constant tending of the network of contacts to keep it up to date). Not all of these approaches arise automatically when research is funded and may require an extra catalyst. The Scottish Funding Council, for example, set up a pilot scheme specifically to support attempts to trial innovative mechanisms for fostering knowledge exchange between researchers and policy-makers; this led to a briefing note (Meagher and Kettle 2009) on issues and approaches such as those captured here. For the reasons discussed above, research contributing to policy will often require an interdisciplinary or transdisciplinary approach.

Finally, there may be quite practical management requirements to ensure, for example, that the project outputs are written in a succinct, jargon-free style, comply with the research commissioner's specification and include a good Executive Summary (often all that will be read by decision-making stakeholders). This may also necessitate working to tighter timescales as set by the research commissioner and delivering promptly on project milestones throughout the contract. A good policy message which comes along after a decision has been taken will rarely have influence.

Working with non-academic partners

In countries such as the UK, where there is a governmental drive to increase knowledge exchange and the impact of research on both policy and practice, including commercial development, there is an increasing desire to engage potential users and other stakeholders in research projects. Including stakeholders in the research project is often regarded as both conducive to interdisciplinary research for its own sake but also, significantly, in terms of promoting research uptake. Such stakeholders may include policy-makers, local authorities, industry, professional groups (for example, educators or health professionals), civic society groups or citizens more generally.

Such stakeholders may, in theory, be incorporated at any or all stages of the research: from identifying and helping to frame the research question, to conducting the research and disseminating the results (e.g. Lowe and Phillipson 2006). Each of these constituencies will bring new aspects to be considered in managing the research team.

A key challenge may be how to maintain impartiality and avoid becoming completely immersed in stakeholder concerns. Where the research is intimately linked with stakeholder issues this may lead to conflicts (such as confidentiality issues) or impatience on the part of the research partner to achieve results. Hinrichs cites a project where 'stakeholder' engagement was delayed until the second year of the project (despite administrative advice) in order to avoid undue steering of the research by the public (Hinrichs 2008). This led to ongoing tensions between the engagement and ensuring the continuing progress in the project. Interactions with stakeholders/research users, while important, need to be handled carefully so that the project is not subject to too many competing demands. Also, it is important from an academic point of view to ensure that project results are not biased in a direction favoured by stakeholders.

Lingard *et al.* identified some insights into the complexity of relationships negotiated within and between scholarly communities in the context of an interdisciplinary project (Lingard *et al.* 2007). They identified, for example, the ambiguity of belonging to a profession and being willing to share the 'secrets' of that profession in order to inform the research, but at the same time wishing to protect that profession. This serves to highlight some of the potential difficulties that may arise when attempting to bring together different cultures in different types of institutions that are accustomed to different working rhythms and habits: this might be illustrated by the different tempo of research in industry and a university; different ambitions; and different expectations about the nature of results. Small and medium-sized enterprises (SMEs), in particular, may need to obtain results quickly in order to meet the strictures of start-up funding cycles, and the extended period of a research programme may be difficult for them. Working with industry partners may raise particular issues around commercial confidentiality and intellectual property issues.

When to involve stakeholders, especially those from policy communities, can be critical (McCulloch 2007); in order to maximize the likelihood of research uptake stakeholders may need to be involved in the initial framing of the research (Nutley *et al.* 2007). Involving partners from public administration, such as central or local government, in the project can be time-consuming. The hierarchical nature of such organizations may require support to be secured at higher levels and decision-making processes may be lengthy: local authorities may be pulled between realizing the need for new research and the lack of time and resources to work with researchers. This can be alleviated in some projects by the local authority becoming a partner in the research and thus gaining access to additional funding:

> Speaking from experience, I have to say that the absence of a user/stakeholder involvement in any research could lead [to] the results being ineffective or simply not practical enough in terms of the industry they are supposed to be enforced/ used [by]. Using only an academic approach to an industry problem could lead to single-sided results. After all, it is the end-user who is supposed to benefit from the research. (Interviewee in II-FP5 project, Tait *et al.* 2002)

But it is also worth noting that sometimes the most important insight an academic research focus can provide is that the stakeholders have an unhelpful, or even wrong, conceptualization of their problem.

Acknowledging the role of 'knowledge intermediaries'

'Knowledge intermediaries', who act at the interface between researchers and non-academics who might utilize research understanding, can play a critical role in the knowledge-exchange process by facilitating productive communication, dialogue, interactions and/or relationship-building. These individuals, units or organizations can have an impact far beyond technical management of intellectual property contracts, by bringing together academics and non-academics, helping them to find a common language, assisting them in distilling problems in ways that are meaningful to all involved, and facilitating a variety of interactive events and dialogue that, when sustained, enhance the likelihood that research findings will be utilized. Very often, an interdisciplinary mindset and experience can predispose an individual to be a very effective knowledge intermediary.

Considerable experience and tacit knowledge exists about the role of knowledge intermediaries yet this knowledge is latent and the role is not necessarily fully recognized by either funders or researchers – or indeed often by the knowledge intermediaries themselves.

We have often heard research centre directors speak about the importance of liaison staff, who facilitate connections among individuals, institutions, disciplines and sectors. In one study (Meagher and Lyall 2007b), we uncovered a surprising heterogeneity among knowledge intermediaries. Some of these we had anticipated (e.g. those in the media or in the relevant professional body) but we also demonstrated the existence of a wide diversity of individuals, often independently employed, who acted as 'go-betweens' distilling research information for use by particular non-academic bodies, such as groups of international CEOs, members of a criminal justice panel, teachers of the deaf or police educators. Such well-informed, highly motivated individuals who can translate research findings in targeted ways may be an under-utilized knowledge exchange resource. In another study (Meagher 2008) we again found that individuals played important knowledge intermediary roles and respondents identified many such facilitation roles including help in ongoing networking (with other academics, disciplines and/or non-academics) and help in providing credibility (with home institution, non-academics and/or funders).

We have found that non-academic impacts were more likely when genuine connectivity existed between researchers and stakeholders with some degree of proximity throughout the research. This required time, effort and resources to build long-term user-researcher relationships. Likely indicators of success include investment 'at the coalface' which allowed for flexibility and individuality and recognition of research brokerage as a specialized role, as well as specialist training (such as media training) and proactively facilitating the sharing of good practice among other knowledge intermediaries.

Thus, recognizing the essence of the knowledge intermediary role (and the many forms it can take), providing incentives for the involvement of knowledge intermediaries and making explicit (and sharing widely) the tacit understanding of how best to use such knowledge intermediaries may help to ensure the wider uptake of research findings beyond the boundaries of academia.

Contrasts with 'traditional' academic research

With the foregoing factors in mind, Table 8.1 summarizes some of the design and management considerations for interdisciplinary research for policy and practice and contrasts them with some traditional aspects of more theoretically

Illustration 8.1 Involving research users can help you see the whole picture

focused, academic research. Various checklists have been developed to assist research-policy interactions and to help these two 'communities' appreciate how they differ from each other. Bammer (Bammer 2008) summarizes six such checklists covering some of the barriers to cooperation between policy-makers and researchers (Gregrich 2003); their different emphases in relation to establishing evidence, making decisions and achieving change (Heymann 2000); the 'irrefutability' of evidence versus the 'immutability' of policy (Gibson 2003a); indicators of policy-maker responsiveness to research (Gibson 2003b); and a series of questions for researchers to think strategically about their interactions with policy-makers and practitioners (Jones and Seelig 2004; Court and Young 2006).

Table 8.1 Some contrasting characteristics of basic academic and policy/
practice-oriented research

	Basic academic research	Research for policy and practice
Purpose	Knowledge for understanding *Whether* there is an association between variables	Knowledge for action Whether this association *matters*
Agenda setting	Generates its own research questions	Takes its problems from government or the research commissioner
Role of explanation	Interested in causal processes e.g. the causes of poverty	Less interested in explanations, more interested in description and prediction – primarily concerned with social action
Political position	Not overtly political	Political aspects cannot be ignored or suppressed
Applicability	May only be concerned with very small groups	Results must be generalizable to wider population
Independence	Research sponsored by independent funders	Research sponsored by vested interests
Discipline	Often single discipline	Often interdisciplinary
Validity	Judged on the basis of research *process*	Judged on the basis of research *outcomes*
Primary audience	Other social scientists	Politicians, civil servants, lobbyists, practitioners, etc., also public and advocacy groups
Research informants	Participate as individuals	Participate as holders of roles

(continued)

Table 8.1 Continued

	Basic academic research	Research for policy and practice
External judgement of evidence	Validity of evidence is prime consideration	Impartiality of evidence is very important
Role of knowledge intermediaries	Less evident during research process but may facilitate dissemination	May provide an important brokerage function during research
Role of research users	Less evident during research process but may facilitate dissemination	May be significant actors throughout the research process
Publication	Papers in peer reviewed journals, books	Research reports and 'grey literature'; sometimes confidential
Language	Academic language	Requires succinct, jargon free style and a good Executive Summary
Timetable	Usually longer and more flexible timescales	Strict timetable set by research commissioner

It has also been suggested (Bammer 2005) that researchers skilled in integration and implementation studies can complement, rather than replace, traditional disciplinary and specialist perspectives. They should be able to offer a range of collaborative skills across a broad framework of knowledge, encompassing a range of skills set out in Key Advice 8.1.

Summary

This chapter has discussed an extension of the journey that many individuals involved in interdisciplinary research may wish to make: exchange of knowledge with potential research users so that interdisciplinary research may lead to impacts on the world beyond academia. We have described briefly some

---

Key Advice 8.1 Core skills for integration and implementation specialists

- An ability to see 'the bigger picture' and alternative conceptualizations of possible research approaches.

- An appreciation of the potential linkages between disciplines and stakeholders, while maintaining the ability to set boundaries around a problem and be clear of the resultant implications in terms of who/what is then included/excluded.

- An understanding of the complexities of collaborative processes involving academic and non-academic researchers and other stakeholders.

- Appropriate understanding of policy development (or product development) and how these can be influenced by research.

- Performing a knowledge brokerage or boundary spanning role in order to link research and practice.

- Expertise in knowledge management.

- An ability to deal with uncertainty and change.

(See also Bammer 2005)

---

of the drivers for knowledge exchange and how they might affect different knowledge goals of interdisciplinary research. We have offered a number of different approaches, practical design points and management considerations for interdisciplinary research that seeks to have impacts beyond academia. In so doing, we have highlighted the natural resonance in problem choice, mindset, skills and research style that can exist between interdisciplinary research and knowledge exchange processes.

Questions

For researchers

1 If there is a problem that motivates you to conduct interdisciplinary research, how might you translate your results into action?

2 What stakeholders might you be able to engage?

For research managers

1 In managing your team, how could you engage stakeholders at an early stage and keep them engaged throughout the research process?

2 What 'pathways to impact' could you envision for your work, so that your results might inform or otherwise influence people beyond academia?

For institutional leaders

1 If you want to increase the impact of your institution's research on the outside world, are there ways in which you could invest in current or prospective interdisciplinary initiatives (projects or centres) to extend their reach?

2 How could you/your staff facilitate early and continuing interaction between interdisciplinary researchers and stakeholders who might someday make use of research findings?

For research funders

1 How could you support the extra efforts that interdisciplinary individuals or teams would have to make to engage with non-academic stakeholders?

2 How would you evaluate proposals to engage stakeholders? During or after interdisciplinary programmes with a knowledge exchange component, how would you evaluate the processes employed and the impacts (or steps toward impacts) achieved?

9

Navigating the Interdisciplinary Landscape

How to shape interdisciplinary futures

Introduction

In this concluding chapter, we draw together key points and threads from earlier chapters to weave a 'big picture' of how the promotion, facilitation, implementation and utilization of interdisciplinary research might take place in the future. If the ultimate 'destination' is excellent interdisciplinary research that generates innovative outcomes or societal impact, then various sorts of individuals will need to play different roles affecting the journey. We will recap useful navigational aids for individuals pursuing interdisciplinary research or leading interdisciplinary teams. We will also pose challenges for individuals who have the potential to influence the context within which interdisciplinarity is pursued – those who could contribute to 'terraforming' which could make the landscape, itself, more amenable to interdisciplinary journeys. In other words, when we look to the future, we see a research landscape shaped by the interacting, aggregate effects of:

- actions of individual researchers and team (programme, centre) leaders, and the early career and established researchers whom they influence, as they pursue interdisciplinary excellence – these individuals have the potential to create productive local habitats around them;

- university research leaders/managers who create the local context within which interdisciplinarity flourishes (or not) – these individuals have the potential to smooth obstacles and make the terrain much more navigable for those undertaking interdisciplinary journeys;

- research funders, policy-makers or stakeholders who support (or not) the broader context such that high quality interdisciplinarity thrives (or not) – these individuals have the potential to make significant changes to the actual landscape through which interdisciplinary researchers travel, as they can influence the dynamics of the overarching ecosystem within which research occurs.

Therefore in this final chapter we seek to do three things, recognizing that each of these elements interacts with the others. First, we offer some guidance to leaders of interdisciplinary research groups, including centres and programmes, and senior managers of research institutions in order to help in the development of sustainable interdisciplinary research strategies. This chapter therefore deals with issues such as:

- building a shared research vision and joint sense of identity across disciplines;

- helping individuals develop their expertise and a long-term research strategy;

- accessing resources and sharing the credit across institutional structures;

- rewarding, engaging and balancing the needs of multiple stakeholders (e.g. students, researchers, parent institution(s), external funders, research users);[1]

- establishing networks to develop professional communities.

Our second goal is to offer suggestions to institutional leaders. Institutions aspiring to benefit from interdisciplinarity (and, when appropriate, related knowledge exchange) need to proactively create an environment that fosters genuine, excellent and productive interdisciplinary work. We will note the importance of issues such as:

- the fit with institutional strategies and opportunities to seize niches;

- top-down fostering of bottom-up interdisciplinarity;

- facilitation of the extra administrative burdens posed by interdisciplinary (and often inter-institutional and/or inter-sectoral) work;

- reward structures, credit-sharing;

- protection of next-generation researchers and recognition of non-conventional career tracks.

Context is clearly important for interdisciplinary success so our third goal is to locate this discussion within the context of current policies for interdisciplinary research and consider how this might have an impact on the future landscape for interdisciplinarity. Speaking particularly to funders and policymakers, we will therefore touch on such issues as:

- conceptualization and implementation of funding schemes promoting high quality interdisciplinarity;

- managing the tensions inherent in evaluation of innovative research that falls outside of disciplinary conventions for excellence;

- capacity-building along with inclusion of interdisciplinarity within recognized career tracks.

A dynamic is beginning to emerge in research, between discipline-based research and interdisciplinary research. Discipline-based research provides an essential set of standards, an established way of framing problems, key theories and methods, but the model of the lone scholar working in one narrow discipline is now much less common. There is a typical view that the interdisciplinary drivers are political, commercial or other 'external' forces, and do not arise from the science itself. Many would link the growing emphasis on interdisciplinarity, not just with issues that cross disciplinary boundaries, but with the increasing focus on 'impact' and the needs of potential research users. The world of policy and practice transcends disciplinary divides: as we discussed in chapter 8, tackling research challenges which address complex problems necessitates a change to traditional discipline-based research strategies.

For others, interdisciplinary research is more epistemologically oriented: there is often a sense of excitement that motivates researchers to seek the creativity often found at the edges, analogous to the phenomenon seen within biological evolution, that 'hybrid zones' at the interfaces of species are known to generate novel variation.

Disciplines place boundaries around bodies of knowledge. As we established in chapter 2, this confers many advantages: it facilitates efficient teaching and provides guidance on research norms. Quality can often be more readily tested against disciplinary criteria, which means that the evaluation of interdisciplinary research can pose particular challenges, as discussed in chapter 7. Set against this, there is, of course, an increasing and widening recognition of the advantages of interdisciplinary approaches.

But effective interdisciplinary working does not simply happen. As well as the obvious barriers to communication between different specialisms, we have discussed some of the institutional barriers that university-based interdisciplinary researchers may encounter – departmental structures, management systems and career pathways that are most often based around disciplines. Early chapters (3 and 4) signposted some of the approaches needed to tackle individual interdisciplinary studies and lead interdisciplinary project teams. Chapters 5 and 6 considered some of the issues around growing the necessary talent to populate these teams with experienced interdisciplinary researchers who can, in turn, nurture future interdisciplinary research capacity. But these challenges also need to be addressed at higher institutional and policy levels if individual researchers and centres are to build effective and successful programmes of interdisciplinary research.

Illustration 9.1 Institutional leaders play a key role in conducting harmonious and effective interdisciplinary research

Research leaders

Building strategic visions

As we hope we have already demonstrated, different kinds of interdisciplinarity require different approaches and there is no single model for success: this is often simply a case of 'learning by doing'. However, in developing and delivering a shared research vision, a leader of an interdisciplinary unit should consider the paramount importance of team-building and leadership, and the need to develop, and communicate, this joint vision and research goals.

In broad terms, we have said that interdisciplinary research can be geared towards advancing the academic knowledge base, or more towards tackling practical problems. But this does not have to be antithetical: when developing an overarching strategy for an interdisciplinary research group or unit within an academic setting, consideration should be given to where the main thrust of the effort lies on the spectrum between these two approaches. Depending on the motivations of individuals within the group, it can be helpful to reflect on this in order to maximize the opportunities for advancing knowledge by building longer term synergies with other academic units and/or external stakeholders.

If interdisciplinary encounters remain narrowly pragmatic and short-term (for example, responding to numerous stakeholder commissions), there is a risk that constant shifts in focus between practical interdisciplinary enquiries will reduce the scope for expertise to accumulate (although the researcher will gain expertise in managing interdisciplinary projects per se). The learning costs will be high if the unit's strategy is based solely on a series of short, interdisciplinary projects in different topic areas. It is therefore important to make sure that new knowledge and techniques are acquired in a cumulative manner, allowing individuals and centres to develop and demonstrate their core capabilities within an academic setting.

As already suggested in chapter 4, interdisciplinary collaborations fail when there is a lack of understanding of the roles that the contributing disciplines can play. This can lead either to unrealistic over-expectations or to a trivialized view, for example, of the role of the social sciences within, say, an engineering-led project. The problems of collaboration are amplified where different research cultures (embodied in individuals) have incompatible approaches to research collaboration, funding and management.

We discussed the role of communication in chapter 4 and its importance obviously increases as complexity grows. Very often, interdisciplinary initiatives, which by definition include multiple individuals from multiple disciplines, may also sit within multiple institutional contexts and networks. To succeed, an interdisciplinary strategy may need to be based less upon the integration of disciplines (which are often rather broad) but rather on sub-disciplines or schools of analysis with their specific analytical strategies and narrative structures. Some subjects, such as medicine or architecture, are already extremely heterogeneous; others may represent the more recent coalition of knowledge around a problem area (e.g. transport studies). Significantly, some disciplines may be more open than others to external knowledge contributions: an appreciation of the nature and status of the intellectual components being woven together may help to solidify a research strategy.

Research leaders need to be clear about their multiple goals and play a multilevel game in order to satisfy a number of stakeholders including the sponsor, the parent institution, the research unit's objectives and the personal goals of the researchers involved. Research leaders embarking upon interdisciplinary trajectories need to consider how their expertise will evolve and be recognized. This might be achieved by:

1 sustaining links with the original disciplines (in which case consider how to retain links with developing specialized knowledge in the original disciplinary domain and how to ensure these are recognized by the host domain, for example through institutional promotion systems);

2 aligning with an emerging discipline: (in which case consider retaining control/leadership over an emerging interdisciplinary arena or niche and

generating/sustaining centrality to such an emerging school of analysis – or proto-discipline – by, for example, creating new journals and conferences).

Persistent (and well-rehearsed) institutional factors can discourage interdisciplinary research, for example a lack of opportunities to publish in high-ranking, refereed journals and discrimination by referees against interdisciplinary proposals and publications. A research unit (or individual researcher) risks being reduced to a service role where staff provide specific, well-defined inputs (e.g. data sets, tools) to another domain without the need for significant interdisciplinary interaction or contribution to advance their own core knowledge. Active researchers may migrate away from such collaborations if they are not seen to benefit their own research.

Engaging partners in the strategy

While bringing disciplines together under one organizational umbrella may help to establish interdisciplinary exchange and learning, more needs to be done to ensure that it fulfils its potential to become a successful interdisciplinary research unit, sustained long enough for expertise and synergies to accumulate over time. Interdisciplinary research leaders should consider how best to define and create the unit's identity while at the same time maintaining individuals' intellectual flexibility. They should probably resist the temptation to encompass 'everything' but will need to negotiate multiple identities and roles in order to establish a common purpose. A research leader's ability to address these challenges will be strengthened by careful attention to the diverse sorts of rewards that may engage all necessary stakeholders. This requires:

- a shared vision;
- an agreed focus on a suite of research problems;
- networking/community-building processes;
- systems to develop relationships and trust within the centre and with other partners (a theme we pick up in the following section);
- a reward structure that acknowledges individual motivations and expertise;
- organizational structures that promote effective management and encourage innovation;
- self-reflection and continuous evolution.

In seeking to achieve this, it is worth considering that the different stakeholders in the interdisciplinary research unit may be motivated by different rewards which will need to be factored in to the strategy development and sustainability of that unit. Involvement in such a 'pioneering' research unit may bring individual academics greater recognition and enable them to engage more widely with other researchers and potential research users with consonant interests. But there may be issues to resolve regarding institutional governance structures to ensure that they are not disadvantaged, for example, by promotion criteria.

The interdisciplinary unit itself may be able to achieve a greater profile both internally within the parent institution and externally with research funders and research users (academic and non-academic). This can increase credibility with partners, particularly if the unit can achieve a degree of financial independence which will both enhance its intellectual flexibility and improve its chances of long-term influence and impact. Relationships with others – including potential sponsors and research users – may be enhanced if it is possible to support core staff who are independent of project work and therefore more able to undertake relationship-building, acting as liaison across disciplines (and institutions) or as knowledge intermediaries with stakeholders, for example.

Get the balance right and interdisciplinary research centres provide opportunities for knowledge-led collaborations which result in a 'win-win' situation: advancing knowledge *and* solving societal problems through sustained engagement, which in turn develops into new interdisciplinary domains. The benefits can be both intellectually rewarding (for the individuals involved) and financially remunerative (for their parent institutions).

Networking for success?

There is considerable demand from a large and growing population of interdisciplinary researchers worldwide for both capacity- and community-building resources. The Masterclass model, described in chapter 5, worked extremely well as a way of conveying codified knowledge but also, crucially, tacit knowledge of how interdisciplinary research can be conducted. Yet, as useful and stimulating as such interactive learning occasions can be, interdisciplinary collaborations and capacity-building are continuous processes that need more than one-off events to promote and sustain them. In order to ensure a motivated and mobilised research community able to address future interdisciplinary research and policy challenges, research leaders might, in addition, envision new forms of professional networks of interdisciplinary researchers.

A number of projects are already investigating the use and utility of online tools, now being termed 'Academia 2.0'. Could an existing online tool foster networking among this community and complement the currently small international membership of associations such as, for example, the Association for Integrative Studies?[2] Such an online community-building initiative could support the work of interdisciplinary researchers and provide opportunities for collaboration, collective development of interdisciplinarity, mutual support, a mentoring network, opportunities for face-to-face interaction and a forum, where issues that confront interdisciplinary research could be addressed by drawing on the tacit knowledge and experience of people working in this field. Research leaders should consider whether their own interdisciplinary community is sufficiently supported by such networks of practice, both internally within their own institutions, and externally in terms of professional representation through membership organizations, journals, learned academies or events.

This sort of networking could complement the natural process of evolution of a particular interdisciplinary area. As an area evolves, people will naturally find ways to cluster around common interests, so that early, informal workshops can turn into regular annual events which can grow into full-scale professional conferences. This confers respectability upon a medley of individuals, whose common interests have, over time, coalesced into a recognized area of research.

Institutional managers

Making strategic use of interdisciplinarity

Of necessity, institutional managers such as research vice-principals/vice-presidents need to consider overall institutional strategy when deciding how to allocate precious money, time or administrative effort. Some universities will aim for a full spectrum of research excellence; some will make tough decisions as to particular research niches in which they want to position themselves as world leaders. Some universities will pursue pioneer status in emerging academic research areas that draw from more than one conventional discipline; others will seek stakeholder engagement through addressing multifaceted problems. The particular strategic aims of the institution will inevitably colour perceived contributions of interdisciplinary work to institutional success. Some lines of interdisciplinary research may fit together more naturally than others. (For example, a centre dedicated to interdisciplinary assessments of the efficacy and acceptability of particular foods with supposed health benefits might fit very well in an institution encompassing agriculture, business and medical research, but less well in an institution seeking a high profile in the humanities.) In any event, interdisciplinary research will not form the totality of work championed by university managers; the strategic question is rather the extent and form of its contribution to the institutional research portfolio as a whole.

The host university and – importantly – various parent departments will have a stake and may be more inclined to be supportive if they perceive that return on investment in interdisciplinary work may include:

- access to new revenue streams;
- greater potential for innovative thinking (with accompanying academic prestige and possible leadership in a new area);

- wider engagement (which may lead to important non-academic impacts and may broaden the host institution's public profile).

Despite the benefits that interdisciplinary work can offer, tactics for strengthening institutional support can be problematic and raise challenging questions that institutional research managers will need to address as appropriate for their university (Key Advice 9.1).

Facilitating interdisciplinarity

Where institutions want to promote interdisciplinarity there are practical steps they can take to facilitate this, to support individuals involved in their future careers and to encourage others to take up interdisciplinary careers. Top-down fostering of bottom-up growth of interdisciplinarity may be a powerful approach here (Key Advice 9.2).

Steps such as these may seem straightforward, but are often not taken. Each institution will need to decide on the extent to which it pursues any or all of them, either in relation to one or two prioritised interdisciplinary ventures or for the creation of an institution-wide culture more accepting of interdisciplinarity. Facilitation of high-quality interdisciplinarity is likely to be most effective if multiple approaches are coordinated to develop a new culture as an institutional priority.

In Table 9.1 we: (i) identify the potential gatekeeping roles played by institutional research managers, research funders, and interdisciplinary researchers and research leaders; and (ii) suggest how, instead, these same individuals and groups can become agents for change, promoting actions that might be taken if the terrain and overall landscape are to change in the future.

Key Advice 9.1 Strengthening institutional support: Questions for institutional research managers

- How is interdisciplinarity accommodated within the discipline-based governance structures in your institution?

- How feasible are matrix structures where, for example, social scientists within other faculties are encouraged to retain links with social science?

- Will interdisciplinary researchers be disadvantaged with regard to promotion and quality assessment exercises?

- Will attempts to link cognate groups paradoxically inhibit interactions between more distal groups (resulting in fewer but bigger 'silos')?

Key Advice 9.2 A proactive approach to creating an interdisciplinary culture

- Afford opportunities for researchers from multiple departments to come together and explore an emerging area, societal problem or novel theme (perhaps, for example, through externally facilitated retreats or workshops).

- Make even small seed money grants available, to support the intangible but critical stage of early dialogue and distillation of common research goals for an interdisciplinary venture.

- Offer support to staff (e.g. from research or knowledge exchange offices, administrative support); when possible also dedicating time of a professional to play a liaison role.

- Ease the path toward institutional status for an interdisciplinary venture (e.g. as a formal Centre) and troubleshoot concerns of involved department chairs (for example, sharing of incoming funds and kudos). Take a constructive approach if more than one institution is involved.

- Show flexibility as to space requirements (e.g. for creative spaces or shared postgraduate/postdoctoral space mixing disciplines).

- Support key tactical staff appointments to complete a required interdisciplinary spectrum or add boundary-spanners.

As interdisciplinary initiatives become more multifaceted, university research managers may themselves need to model good interactive behaviours as they are drawn into partnership-building between their institution and other institutions, or between their institution and stakeholders. University research managers may also need to become better informed about interdisciplinary ventures so that they recognize the potentially protracted development stage and are sufficiently engaged to help the leaders of such ventures procure sufficient, diversified funding to sustain them until their research bears fruit.

Protecting and rewarding interdisciplinary researchers

Cumulatively, even relatively minor deterrents, the nature of which we have discussed in preceding chapters in terms of career milestones such as raising funds, publishing the results of research or sustaining a long-term research programme, can substantially disadvantage interdisciplinary research. As chapter 6 illustrates, interdisciplinary researchers therefore need to plan their personal development more carefully than academic colleagues with more traditional career paths. They may consequently need better mentoring both from immediate supervisors and line managers but also at an institutional level so that they both respond to sponsors' requirements but also think strategically about their own personal research and publication strategy. Addressing some of these issues might require institutions to address a lack of research leadership and/or systemic implementation throughout academic management structures.

To achieve a 'virtuous spiral' through which a culture conducive to interdisciplinarity is created (of the sort illustrated in Figure 2.1), an institution needs to ensure first that interdisciplinarity does no harm to those pursuing it. Beyond this, explicit recognition of the value of interdisciplinary work done by institutional pioneers can encourage subsequent researchers and middle managers such as department chairs to adopt interdisciplinary approaches when appropriate. When the word spreads, and individuals from postgraduate stages onward are seen to do well through interdisciplinary work, relatively easy pathways will begin to form, removing some of the obstacles from future interdisciplinary research journeys. Ensuring that interdisciplinary researchers have full access to reward structures is key. This may entail the streamlining of 'credit-sharing' across departmental lines, for example if a large-scale grant is won by a mixed team. It will be critical to protect those pursuing non-conventional career tracks, particularly those who are in vulnerable early stages of their careers. Some steps that can be taken by institutional research managers are summarized in Key Advice 9.3.

Ideally, interdisciplinarity will be facilitated by steps taken at both the highest level of the institution and the leadership of a department (or other such intellectual 'home'). While commitment at the top is crucial, it is the latter context that can contribute most directly to an environment that fosters creativity and that is most directly responsible for the presence or removal of career obstacles. The case study (Case Study 9.1) on the School of Human Evolution and Social Change, Arizona State University, illustrates a deliberate, two-level approach to development of interdisciplinarity.

Funders and policy-makers

The evolution of the future academic landscape

Throughout our work, we have developed a strong interest in the evolution of the future academic landscape and how funders might help pave the way to interdisciplinarity. We have witnessed a significant increase in planned funding

---

Key Advice 9.3 Tips for institutional research managers when promoting interdisciplinarity

- Through word and deed, send a message to researchers, department chairs and deans that high-quality interdisciplinary research is valued as a legitimate component of the institution's portfolio.

- Provide coaching or mentoring and high-level strategic advice (e.g. as to how to encourage two or more funding bodies to provide joint support, or how to engage key stakeholder partners).

- Include explicit acknowledgement of interdisciplinary work as a legitimate element of an individual's promotion package; provide explicit criteria and ensure that fair judgement takes place within what may normally be opaque committee promotion procedures.

- Develop a policy/process within the graduate school that is fair to interdisciplinary postgraduates, ensuring that they receive high-quality (if unconventional) training and that selection of external or internal examiners does not disadvantage them.

- Celebrate or formally recognize interdisciplinary successes (e.g. through intra-institutional awards, whether monetary or not).

- Cite interdisciplinary successes in inward or outward-facing high-level institutional presentations, annual reports, alumni publications, etc.; direct press offices to promote the visibility of interdisciplinary ventures as a compelling facet of the institution's profile.

---

for strategic interdisciplinary programmes in the UK where public funding for basic research is channelled through the Research Councils that develop programmes to support interdisciplinary research. This requires active collaboration between Research Councils but the experiential knowledge arising from such initiatives can be hard to codify. Crucially, where knowledge remains primarily embedded in individuals, it may be unexploited and indeed lost if these players move to different areas of work (for example, when academic programme coordinators are 'bought out' for finite periods of time to lead particular programmes and then return to their previous role). While it is evident that the relationship between disciplines is strongly influenced by national funding agencies, lack of organizational memory in these bodies can be an issue when the staff involved in championing cross-council or cross-disciplinary initiatives

Case Study 9.1 Interdisciplinary commitment: A two-level approach

The current President of Arizona State University took office in 2002 and included promotion of interdisciplinary thinking in the vision he laid out in his inaugural address. The President changed the custom of having rotating chairs of departments and, within a couple of years, appointed a majority of chairs and deans who shared his vision. Some departments were dismantled and transformed, and schools created as new structures; some of these schools became interdisciplinary and a great many interdisciplinary research centres were created. Thus, there was endorsement of interdisciplinarity at the very top of the institution.

But, to make it work, university research managers closer to the researchers had to be involved. For example, the School of Human Evolution & Social Change was envisioned from its start as interdisciplinary in nature. As described on its website, 'the school integrates advanced tools and knowledge from across the sciences and the social sciences to discover not only who we were but where we are going and how we may alter our destiny'; the school includes anthropologists, but also geographers, sociologists, economists, mathematicians and natural scientists. The school grew significantly between 2004 and 2010, recruiting some 30 academics, many of whom have an interdisciplinary cast to their work. The school's Director, Professor Sander van der Leeuw, came to the institution about a year after the President, and found that his own interdisciplinary research track record made him very much in synch with the President's way of working.

In reflecting on his role, van der Leeuw (who is now taking on the challenge of promoting interdisciplinarity at a higher level, in the university's new post of Dean of Sustainability) offers some suggestions for institutional managers creating an institutional context that facilitates interdisciplinarity. The importance of leadership that genuinely values individuals and that removes obstacles from their path is clear:

> You cannot create the atmosphere that truly fosters ID from the top. You need to lead as a person and let it grow bottom up. To do that, you have to be yourself at all times; deal with everyone as an individual, with respect and without prejudice about what they're doing; value what their different contributions can be. You also have to be able to translate between different conceptualizations, approaches, disciplines ... so that everyone feels respected and stimulated in what they do. A really important element is choice of people. Be a good judge of people and their potential ... You need intuition and empathy, which

Case Study 9.1 *Continued*

lets you see if people within themselves have potential for empathy. Judge their openness and willingness to change ... This is really difficult but important. You need to see yourself as the person who takes away difficulties and the one who can inspire new interests. To some extent, you have to be a social architect, trying to secure space in which you can create a viable environment.

Source: Interview with Professor Sander van der Leeuw, August 2010, and http://shesc.asu.edu/about [accessed 15 January 2011].

Key Advice 9.4 Tips for research funding bodies when promoting interdisciplinarity

- Be sufficiently bold to conceptualize and define novel funding schemes that promote interdisciplinary approaches, whether to build a new research area or to solve a complex issue confronting society.

- Work flexibly with other funding bodies to implement joint funding schemes.

- Develop and support approaches necessary for success in interdisciplinary research, such as providing seed-corn funding for interdisciplinary groups to explore and develop together, or allowing budget items such as retreats, travel for face-to-face meetings, liaison staff, etc.

- Recognize the tensions inherent in evaluation of innovative research that falls outside disciplinary criteria for excellence; work with informed individuals to develop and share explicitly appropriate criteria for interdisciplinary work; draw on established interdisciplinary researchers for review processes.

- Build interdisciplinary capacity in next-generation researchers (and their supervisors) while at the same time ensuring their access to networks and career tracks through useful career steps (such as availability of interdisciplinary postdoctoral fellowships, first small grants, larger grants, and so on).

move on to new areas. Research Councils have developed effective systems to run research programmes within their core areas but may require additional assistance to capture occasional 'idiosyncratic' experiences – such as running interdisciplinary initiatives. Moreover, at either a funding body level, or the level of an institution, such initiatives can be vulnerable and regarded as dispensable when money is tight.

Despite these challenges, there are ways of turning gatekeepers into agents for change (Table 9.1) and positive steps that can be taken by individuals in research funding bodies who aim to align reality with rhetoric (Key Advice 9.4).

In some sense, funders of innovative interdisciplinary programmes, centres or initiatives are themselves travellers in only roughly charted territory. They too, like research leaders, can learn by doing. Sensitive evaluation of interdisciplinary funding schemes, of the type discussed in chapter 7, can inform future tactics for support by, for example, gathering lessons learned by research leaders, researchers, next-generation researchers, external stakeholders and funders themselves. Without the development, spread and acceptance of appropriate evaluation, capacity-building in interdisciplinarity will falter and the research landscape of the future will suffer.

Concluding remarks

When we pick up our rose-coloured binoculars and look to the academic landscape we would like to see in the future, we do not see one vast blur of interdisciplinarity. There will be new hybrid zones of genuine interdisciplinarity, with some of these stabilizing into new disciplines themselves. But there will always be a rich patchwork of disciplines – areas of research that are bounded by conventional questions, epistemologies, approaches and standards. Disciplines will persist within academic structures and for good reason. At the same time, many initiatives deemed fashionably interdisciplinary will, in fact, simply be relabelled traditional modes of research rather than reconceptualizations of new ways of working. We are emphatically not arguing for an either/or model but a productive and mutually supportive coexistence of discipline-based and interdisciplinary research where the skills and the knowledge required to make interdisciplinarity successful may be transferable between different research contexts.

While we have identified some of the barriers and disincentives to interdisciplinarity throughout this book, we have also tried to focus on strategies to make this a rewarding and successful research experience. We have suggested in this chapter actions that can be taken by institutional research managers to smooth the terrain, and we have suggested approaches that can be taken by policy-makers and research funding bodies to actually reshape the landscape.

Such changes could hearten and fortify even the hardiest of interdisciplinary adventurers. The landscape we would like to see in the future will be a dynamic one, with easily negotiated pathways between areas, suddenly emerging short-cuts and new springs of creativity.

Our goal throughout this book has been to equip fellow travellers with a portmanteau of research and management skills to take with them on their interdisciplinary journey. Whether trespassing for a short time or setting out on a longer voyage that may last a whole career, we hope this book has given readers a few tips on how to plan and execute the route: even if the maps are a bit unclear, there are new worlds still waiting to be discovered by well-equipped, enthusiastic explorers.

Table 9.1a Turning gatekeepers into agents for change

Institutional research managers		
	Gatekeeping actions	Facilitating changes
Organizational structures and administration	Departmental divisions, reporting and record-keeping	Top-level encouragement of middle managers to act flexibly and support interdisciplinary work
Procedures and policies	Procedures for channelling funds (e.g. indirect cost return) or credit are usually located within discipline-based units	Top-level imprimatur and advocacy policies explicitly stating value of interdisciplinarity Institutional research managers deliberately facilitating and creating conducive culture Streamlined procedures for sharing funds, credit, time across departments
Culture	Activities such as seminars and retreats tend to be discipline-based and discipline-reinforcing Physical space distribution underscores disciplines as distinct 'territories' Interactions among PhD students primarily in discipline	Provision of funding for non-traditional seminar series on interdisciplinary topics, including interdisciplinary visitors; seed funding for retreats or workshops on interdisciplinary topics Provision of 'creative interactive spaces' between disciplines' territories, such as cafeterias, coffee rooms, hallway alcoves, conducive to informal conversations; show flexibility in grouping or regrouping individuals by area or theme of research, as interests evolve Fund/create informal opportunities for PhD students to interact across disciplines; support interdisciplinary journal clubs or PhD student-run seminar series
Resources and infrastructure	Usually provided to discipline-oriented work	Seed monies, support staff, release time
Recognition, reward and incentives	Usually based on discipline	Highest level and proximate level recognition of legitimacy of interdisciplinary work Celebration and dissemination of successes Seed money/resources Inclusion of interdisciplinarity in promotion system

Table 9.1b Turning gatekeepers into agents for change

Research funders		
	Gatekeeping actions	Facilitating changes
Organizational structures and administration	Often divided into different 'territories' or research areas	Acting as role-models by collaborating across funding bodies, divisions
Procedures and policies	Established banks of reviewers unlikely to approve non-conventional proposals Post-programme evaluation may be challenged by disciplinary orientation	Top-level articulation of value, feeding into policies and procedures Establishment of clear criteria and procedures for fair review of interdisciplinary bids (and post-programme reviews) Straightforward procedures for joint funding across bodies or divisions
Culture	Funding tends to support discipline-based activities Capital investments may often be directed to 'safe' discipline homes Many PhD support schemes tied to disciplines	Provide funds for explicitly interdisciplinary seminar series, exchange visits etc. If funding development of research spaces, be open to aligning them with interdisciplinary research when appropriate; respond positively to inclusion of informal meeting and interacting spaces Consider developing interdisciplinary PhD schemes; review interdisciplinary proposals for PhD support appropriately; convene (or fund events which convene) PhD students from across disciplines; give interdisciplinary students the opportunity to reflect and learn about interdisciplinarity through masterclasses etc; help interdisciplinary PhD students form professional communities and networks, including online
Resources and infrastructure	Usually provided to discipline-oriented work	Seed grants, inclusion of funding for liaison staff, etc.
Recognition, reward and incentives	Usually based on discipline	Funding for interdisciplinary work Celebration and dissemination of successes (including in the media)

Table 9.1c Turning gatekeepers into agents for change

Interdisciplinary researchers and research leaders		
	Gatekeeping actions	Facilitating changes
Organizational structures and administration	Aligning with disciplines, accepting status quo	Cultivating high-level champions within management who are aware of obstacles and how they can be removed; articulating advantages and offering media-friendly examples of interdisciplinary work
Procedures and policies	Aligning with disciplines, accepting status quo	Cultivating high-level champions within management who are aware of obstacles and how they can be removed; articulating advantages and offering media-friendly examples of interdisciplinary work
Culture	Aligning with disciplines, accepting status quo	Seek funding for and creatively develop events such as seminars, retreats, exchange visits, journal clubs that promote interdisciplinary understanding
		When possible, finding or protecting informal space for interactions
		Carefully choosing PhD supervisors, mentors; provide opportunities for PhD students to learn about processes of interdisciplinarity, encourage them to lead on interdisciplinary journal clubs or seminars; encourage academics to serve as lively role models
Resources and infrastructure	Aligning with disciplines, accepting status quo	Articulating why seed monies or support staff or extra time are necessary for interdisciplinary work. Developing one or more 'champions' in higher level management
Recognition, reward and incentives	Aligning with disciplines, accepting status quo	Seek funding for interdisciplinary work, ensuring that high quality work ensues. Publish appropriately Make a practice of letting highest level university leaders know about successes
		Create rewards and celebrational events (and invite highest level leaders)
		Work with media so that the interdisciplinary work and the institution(s) involved are shown to advantage
		Carefully watch out for careers of young researchers, mentoring them and fighting for them to be reviewed appropriately

Appendix 1

The Authors' Own Interdisciplinary Research Journeys

As we noted in chapter 1, this book has been written by a team of authors with experience of interdisciplinary research in a wide variety of contexts. Catherine Lyall, Ann Bruce, Joyce Tait and Laura Meagher have had a professional association for over ten years, working together as collaborators on a range of research and consultancy projects. In this final section, we say a little about our own personal interdisciplinary research journeys in order to describe how we have reached a point where we feel ready to share some of the things that we have learned along the way.

Catherine Lyall started her working life with a BSc in Chemistry from the University of Aberdeen. Having worked in various laboratory settings as a student, on graduation she decided to pursue a career in scientific publishing. She followed this path for five years before returning to academia to complete a Masters in Science and Technology Policy at the University of Sussex. This then took her on to a number of policy-related roles including a few years as a civil servant in London. Following her return to Scotland, she took the opportunity to join Joyce Tait who was then leading the recently established Scottish Universities Policy Research and Advice (SUPRA) network. This was probably the first time that she had heard the word 'interdisciplinarity' and it soon became a focus for her research at the University of Edinburgh alongside other research interests in science policy and, more recently, the governance of the life sciences.

In parallel with these part-time, university roles, Catherine maintained a portfolio of consultancies through her company, Information Browser Ltd. This enabled her to develop a strong working partnership with Laura Meagher, often focusing on the evaluation of interdisciplinary research programmes and, increasingly, on the assessment of impacts beyond academia of the results of such research. This experience contributed to her being appointed Director of Knowledge Exchange within the University of Edinburgh's School of Social and Political Science, a position that she holds concurrently with the post of Deputy Director of the ESRC Innogen Centre.

Somewhere along the way, Catherine managed to complete a part-time PhD at the University of Edinburgh, which enabled her to add the word 'governance' to her lexicon when she studied the operation and evolution of the new system of governance for science, technology and innovation in Scotland following

THE AUTHORS' OWN INTERDISCIPLINARY RESEARCH JOURNEYS 211

devolution. Her interdisciplinary thesis integrated two analytical systems concepts – 'the political system' and the 'innovation system' – forging a nexus between the innovation studies literature and the political studies literature on governance and the role of policy networks in the policy-making process.

When Catherine is not making interdisciplinary connections and juggling professional commitments, she can be found in her garden, tending her poultry and her bees.

Ann Bruce originally trained with a BSc in Agriculture. This was already an interdisciplinary degree with business management, tractor mechanics and understanding the historical role of agriculture in human development included alongside basic sciences. After a further degree in natural sciences (MSc in animal breeding), Ann spent over a decade working in the animal-breeding industry, which took her to a number of countries in Europe and Asia. A family move meant relocating to Scotland and an opportunity to broaden out her thinking in the ethical and social aspects of genetics in which she had increasingly become interested. This in turn led to a number of posts in the University of Edinburgh's School of Social and Political Science, the most recent of which is as a Senior Research Fellow in the ESRC Innogen Centre.

Here Ann has developed a portfolio of research with two main strands. One involves innovation and regulation of life science industries, focusing on what might be loosely termed 'agricultural biosciences'. The second involves the wider context of research, particularly the conduct of interdisciplinary research and the way in which stakeholders are engaged in that research and the use of information in research.

Ann has very practical experience of working in interdisciplinary environments having been a Scientific Administrator in a publicly funded biological research centre. She has recently undertaken a research placement with the UK Department for Environment, Food and Rural Affairs where she completed a science and technology study on newly emerging diagnostic technologies in agriculture, exploring attitudes, behaviours and wider social impacts so she is well-placed to understand the wider policy and industrial applications of interdisciplinary research.

Joyce Tait graduated with a BSc in Pharmaceutical Chemistry and then became distracted for about ten years by the demands of a young family. By a rather serendipitous route, she got the chance to do a PhD degree in Land Economy at the University of Cambridge, with complete freedom to choose the topic. At that time, the UK was in the process of developing its first formal regulatory system for controlling the production and use of pesticides, and this seemed to provide an ideal opportunity to do a PhD that linked pharmaceutical chemistry with land economy. This was in the 1970s and there was very little guidance on how to do interdisciplinary research. The PhD was completed by a process of reading widely in disciplines that seemed relevant to the topic and linking contributions from applied biology, economics, decision analysis and pesticide chemistry.

Talking to farmers about their use of pesticides generated an interest in their attitudes to risk – they were clearly making trade-offs between financial risk (if they did not use pesticides), personal health risk (if they used organophosphate insecticides) and environmental risk (if they used organochlorine insecticides), and this became the subject of her postdoctoral research on farmers' attitudes to the risks of using pesticides.

By this time Joyce was so interdisciplinary that it was proving difficult to find employment as an academic, but serendipity intervened again and she joined the staff of what was then the Systems Group in the Open University and spent the next 12 years writing courses on systems approaches to analysis and decision-making for complex problems, in effect teaching interdisciplinary research techniques.

Joyce's research over this period continued on the pesticide-related path and then, when the agrochemical industry became interested in genetically modified (GM) crops, it moved into that area with a focus on: (i) company strategies in developing the technology; (ii) policy and regulatory developments; and (iii) public and farmer attitudes to the new technology. Linking detailed insights from these three different perspectives (in 1990) enabled her to predict fairly accurately the European crisis in public confidence in GM technology that took place in 1998. This 'triangulation' approach has formed the basis of her subsequent research in health-related applications in life sciences most recently at the University of Edinburgh where she has developed an extremely influential programme of research on the Appropriate Governance of the Life Sciences.

Laura Meagher's career has been characterized by her unwillingness to be characterized. In her final year of high school, she wrote an essay on C.P. Snow's 'Two Cultures' theory. This need to bridge the cultures of arts and sciences defined her university studies where she combined English literature with biology, becoming the first of Middlebury College's 'Independent Scholars' and the sole student on the Carnegie Commission-funded Committee on the College, which considered how to foster intellectual growth through exposure to different disciplines.

Laura had warned Duke University's Zoology Department that she wanted to study evolutionary biology, but then act in some role between science and society. Sure enough, Laura's PhD developed an unexpected focus: teasing apart the dynamics of change in the field of biology due to Darwin's theory of evolution, in what could be seen as a Kuhnian scientific revolution. Her approach sat well with the biologists and sociologist on her committee, but less so with the historians; she had to keep her own equilibrium while teetering on the brink of Snow's chasm.

A Pre-doctoral Fellowship with the Duke Roundtable on Science and Public Affairs introduced Laura to the world of science policy, where she later had her first job, working with the Governor's Science Advisor. Soon after, she helped to plan and was then co-founder and first Vice President of the North Carolina Biotechnology Center, the first state-wide biotech centre for economic development. As a not-for-profit entrepreneur, she relished the creativity of being a change agent and boundary spanner, catalysing knowledge exchange, institutional alliances and explorations of numerous future interdisciplinary niche areas.

After some time as an independent consultant, Laura became associate dean for research at Rutgers University, with the enjoyably creative remit of building interdisciplinary, inter-sector, inter-institutional and sometimes international initiatives. She spent a year at the University of Edinburgh as a Fulbright Fellow in institutional change, helping to generate new research policy alliances across the Scottish universities. Something about Scotland grabbed Laura and her family; they moved back in 1999 and have been there ever since. Laura re-established her independent company, Technology Development Group, with a special focus on strategic change in research, knowledge exchange and higher education. Her work includes: advising on strategic planning and facilitating development of new initiatives and alliances; designing interdisciplinary future-oriented workshops; and evaluating research programmes (both formatively and retrospectively), impacts of research and knowledge-exchange processes, and experimental schemes to promote changes such as interdisciplinary capacity-building. Complexities and dynamics of change continue to fascinate her.

Our personal journeys to date have brought us together under the aegis of the ESRC Innogen Centre which has provided a focus for our collaborations over the past eight years. We conclude this book with a final case study – that of Innogen itself – which draws together many of the strands that we have been seeking to illustrate throughout this book.

Case Study A.1 ESRC Innogen Centre (Centre for Social and Economic Research on Innovation in Genomics)

Life science and related technologies are an area of rapid change in the application of knowledge to new products and processes. The ESRC Innogen Centre, a partnership between the University of Edinburgh and the Open University in the UK, looks at 'the cutting edge' – where this science is taking us and how technology is being shaped – in order to deliver a sound evidence base for decision-making. Innogen has grown into the foremost European centre in the analysis of innovation and translation processes in the life sciences, in the contexts of regulation, governance and stakeholder perspectives.

Case Study A.1 *Continued*

Innogen was established in 2002 to bring together leading researchers from a wide range of backgrounds including the social sciences, law, business, international development and the life sciences. Innogen's interdisciplinary research programme focuses on two interacting themes. First, the study of how and why the life sciences evolve – what new science is possible, and how that may improve the ways health and agriculture are practised. Second, the study of the regulation and governance of the life sciences, not only because these sectors are highly regulated but also because citizens have serious concerns about new biological and chemical products and processes. The Centre's focus is not just confined to the United States and Europe: Innogen also studies developments all over the world at regional, national and international levels.

Innogen's aims are therefore to:

- build an innovative research programme on the themes: 'Evolution of the new life-science economy' and 'Governance of Innovation in the life sciences';

- build on our strengths in interdisciplinary, collaborative research, including the development of methodology;

- build on our expertise in: economics and business studies, law, risk analysis, policy and regulation;

- engage with innovation and policy communities in the UK, Europe and internationally.

Innogen's origins

Innogen grew out of a number of long-term, interdisciplinary collaborations on a range of projects, small and large, national and international, among a consistent group of people with a clear, evolving interdisciplinary theme. Total funding for these initiatives since 1996 has amounted to over £12 million, including funding for the Innogen Centre itself. Many of the underpinning themes for this research were issues related to pesticide development, GM crops, agriculture and environment. Most members of these original collaborations were themselves interdisciplinary, offering expertise in both natural and social sciences. We had already demonstrated an ability to deliver on major interdisciplinary projects and the ability to influence decision-makers in industry and government. We also had a good publication track record in a variety of types of publications.

This interdisciplinary collaborative expertise had built up over a period of 15–20 years so that when the UK Economic and Social Research Council (ESRC) announced its intention to develop a centre for genomics research covering all aspects of the social sciences, we knew that we were well-placed to deliver. However, because of the team's strong science and technology as well as social science-based interdisciplinary background, we also knew that we were unlikely to be the favoured candidates. In order to strengthen our chances of success in this competition for funding we had to develop a strategy with the following components:

- we needed to engage with the funding agency to make sure that they realized the importance of having an interdisciplinary approach that could bridge the relevant science/social science elements;

- we also needed to ensure that the funders understood the potential benefits of a new social science approach that brought solutions rather than problems to scientists, industry and stakeholders;

- up until that point we had not consciously thought about our interdisciplinary research processes – so we developed an explanation of how we did interdisciplinary research and why our approach was so powerful;

- we developed a research programme for the proposed Centre that built on existing strengths and took our research into new areas (e.g. health-related applications of genomics).

We encountered a number of problems including:

- scepticism that we could deliver across the wide range of disciplines proposed;

- questions about whether we needed particular partners, particularly involving two academic institutions in the one Centre;

- disciplinary challenges, e.g. from economists, who wanted to see a particular interpretation of economics followed in our research;

- lack of appreciation among some reviewers and evaluators of the science involved and the importance of a good understanding of the science, but strong appreciation from others;

- the usual challenges from single discipline evaluators when faced with an interdisciplinary proposal.

Case Study A.1 *Continued*

Innogen's future

Ultimately, after a rigorous mid-term review, we were successful in extending Innogen's funding to 2012. A regular theme in evaluators' comments throughout this review process was the 'need to focus', the direction of this focus depending on the individual evaluator's own discipline. We always managed to negotiate a compromise in response to these comments, but the issue of the breadth of the research programme has remained a source of debate between the Innogen Centre and its main funders, although this has also been a major factor in enabling us to respond creatively to opportunities to bring in additional funding from other sources.

Innogen's staff are now research leaders in health, agricultural and environmental applications of life sciences, working closely with scientists and medical professionals. We have worked on pharmaceuticals, stem cells and regenerative medicine, genetic databases, pharmacogenetics, translational medicine, GM crops, biofuels, nanotechnology and synthetic biology. Our policy analyses have influenced decision-makers in industry, government and public bodies in the UK, European Union and internationally.

We plan to build on this success, to extend our analysis to new areas of scientific discovery, to build on existing insights and to engage more widely with key actors in the life sciences. Our uniqueness continues to lie in our creative, interactive, interdisciplinary approach to research and policy development.

Appendix 2

Shaping Interdisciplinary Research Futures – Questions for Readers

We have provided a set of questions at the end of chapters 2–8. For ease of reference, these questions are collated here and ordered by category of respondent (researchers, research managers, institutional leaders and research funders).

Questions for researchers

Approaches to interdisciplinarity

1 Why do interdisciplinary research?

2 How can you improve your chances of being funded to do interdisciplinary research?

3 How can you ensure that it produces outcomes of high quality?

Designing interdisciplinary research projects

1 How might you ensure that you are networked with the disciplines that you may wish to work with in the future?

2 How would you reassure a prospective funder that your interdisciplinary research design will actually work?

3 How would you reassure a prospective funder that your interdisciplinary research design will deliver added value?

4 How would you balance thoughtful planning with opportunistic seizing of new, creative lines of enquiry?

Managing interdisciplinary projects and teams

1 Interdisciplinary collaborations are often put together under a great deal of time pressure and may be conducted by people who do not know each other (or each others' disciplines) well. What are the key management issues that you need to address when working in these less than ideal circumstances?

Supporting the next generation of interdisciplinary researchers

1 Where do you want to make your contribution? (Publish within one or across several fields; create new interdisciplinary fields; lead in the development of creative solutions to a critical problem?)

2 What support and training do you need in order to achieve this?

Establishing and sustaining interdisciplinary careers in and beyond universities

1 How can you tell if interdisciplinary work is for you?

2 What tactics can you imagine employing to make sure that interdisciplinarity adds value to your career rather than making you vulnerable?

3 If you were to pursue your ideal interdisciplinary career, how in five words or less would you describe yourself to: a prospective employer? a student?

Evaluating interdisciplinarity

1 When writing interdisciplinary research proposals, how could you best indicate both the quality of the research itself and the quality of your approach to integration of concepts, findings and people?

2 Could you recommend interdisciplinary reviewers for your work? Can you volunteer to be a reviewer yourself, for others' interdisciplinary proposals or manuscripts?

Getting interdisciplinary research into policy and practice

1 If there is a problem that motivates you to conduct interdisciplinary research, how might you translate your results into action?

2 What stakeholders might you be able to engage?

Questions for research managers

Approaches to interdisciplinarity

1 How could you improve the research environment to support interdisciplinary research in your institution?

2 How could your institution benefit from providing an improved environment for interdisciplinary research?

Managing interdisciplinary projects and teams

1 What steps (and in what order) need to be taken to proactively build and manage a team so that it makes the most of the potential value of interdisciplinarity?

2 What roles do you see yourself playing? How will you manage wearing multiple hats? Can you get support to help with any of your roles?

3 What role models do you have for successful interdisciplinary research? Can you find other managers of interdisciplinary initiatives with whom you can discuss issues?

4 In what way does the labelling of research team members in a collaboration (e.g. Principal Investigator, Co-investigator, etc.) influence their role in the team and their responsibilities and benefits institutionally and how might that affect specifically interdisciplinary projects?

Supporting the next generation of interdisciplinary researchers

1 Would you say that you and your colleagues (team members, co-supervisors/mentors) have had the opportunity to step back and think through issues and processes related to the generation of high quality interdisciplinary research?

2 Are there opportunities to attend masterclasses or other focused events to learn more?

3 How might it help you and your team members to participate in a dispersed community or network across which practical learning about interdisciplinarity could be shared and extended?

Establishing and sustaining interdisciplinary careers in and beyond universities

1 What steps could you take to ensure that less-established individuals who participate in your interdisciplinary teams rack up achievements that will 'count' in academic promotion currency?

2 Can you develop a strategy for a portfolio of outputs, so that everyone in the team benefits?

Evaluating interdisciplinarity

1 What tactics would enhance the likelihood of publication in respected journals?

2 How would you go about positioning yourself and your team members as prospective reviewers (of proposals or manuscripts) to help spread interdisciplinary expertise throughout review processes?

Getting interdisciplinary research into policy and practice

1 In managing your team, how could you engage stakeholders at an early stage and keep them engaged throughout the research process?

2 What 'pathways to impact' could you envision for your work, so that your results might inform or otherwise influence people beyond academia?

Questions for institutional leaders

Designing interdisciplinary research projects

1 How might you provide stimulating events to assist your researchers and their collaborators in developing ideas, designs and proposals for interdisciplinary projects?

2 Do you have a system for 'early alerts' as to interdisciplinary funding opportunities?

3 Do you have qualified and enthusiastic academic-related support staff who can help with the hard work of the early design stage?

Managing interdisciplinary projects and teams

1 What kind of job security do interdisciplinary researchers have in your organization? How does that compare with disciplinary experts?

2 How are 'teams' rewarded for research – or is all the reward on the basis of individuals?

3 How might this policy impact on interdisciplinary research?

4 Has your organization established any 'environments' conducive to interdisciplinarity?

Supporting the next generation of interdisciplinary researchers

1 How could you go about creating an environment conducive to interdisciplinarity among early career researchers?

2 In what ways could you support researchers and research managers through continuous professional development, so that they have the freedom to be creative combined with a supportive infrastructure?

3 How could you celebrate interdisciplinary successes and otherwise send positive messages throughout your institution?

Establishing and sustaining interdisciplinary careers in and beyond universities

1 What could you do to support promotion, community-building or other ways of treating interdisciplinary researchers at your institution?

Evaluating interdisciplinarity

1 Are there accidental or tacit assumptions embedded within your institution's internal assessment processes, including but not limited to promotion decisions which could work against interdisciplinary researchers?

2 Could you establish formative evaluation of key interdisciplinary centres, institutes or programmes, so that you could capture learning for future efforts?

Getting interdisciplinary research into policy and practice

1 If you want to increase the impact of your institution's research on the outside world, are there ways in which you could invest in current or prospective interdisciplinary initiatives (projects or centres) to extend their reach?

2 How could you/your staff facilitate early and continuing interaction between interdisciplinary researchers and stakeholders who might someday make use of research findings?

Questions for research funders

Approaches to interdisciplinarity

1 How could you stimulate effective interdisciplinary research as part of a research portfolio?

2 How could you institute criteria and evaluation processes suitable for interdisciplinarity that will select for good quality interdisciplinary work?

3 How could you contribute to improved quality in the interdisciplinary research that is funded?

4 How can greater academic, public and commercial added-value be generated from the increased levels of investment in interdisciplinary research?

Designing interdisciplinary research projects

1 Given the extra effort and resources needed to run interdisciplinary projects, it is only worthwhile doing them if there is a realistic expectation of some sort of pay-off. By what criteria would you make this decision?

2 How would you judge the degree to which the proposed team either has become integrated or is on track to become integrated so as to lead to synergistic results?

Managing interdisciplinary projects and teams

1 How would you evaluate the quality of a research team and the Principal Investigator's proposed management approach for an interdisciplinary research project?

2 Would you consider offering seed-corn funding to launch projects in new interdisciplinary directions?

3 Have you considered how self-evaluation or critical friend formative evaluations could help complex interdisciplinary projects evolve?

4 Would you consider bringing together interdisciplinary researchers to share experiences, approaches, issues and good practice regarding the management of interdisciplinary projects?

Supporting the next generation of interdisciplinary researchers

1 What steps could you take to catalyse or support long term capacity-building? Through formal degree training? Through short courses or other events focused on the processes of interdisciplinarity?

2 Are there ways in which you could help interdisciplinary researchers develop networks and communities?

Establishing and sustaining interdisciplinary careers in and beyond universities

1 If you believe that the future academic landscape should include (though not be limited to) interdisciplinary research, what sorts of funding

opportunities could you make available so that interdisciplinary careers are viable?

2 What role(s) might you play in ensuring that researchers who do excellent interdisciplinary work progress in their careers?

Evaluating interdisciplinarity

1 How can appropriate quality indicators be framed when developing interdisciplinary research competitions?

2 How would you select reviewers and panel members, and how will you brief them? Could you deliberately develop a panel culture that works for interdisciplinarity?

3 If you receive interdisciplinary proposals in competition with monodisciplinary proposals, how would you handle the review process to ensure that the interdisciplinary proposals are not disadvantaged?

4 If you were evaluating (formatively or retrospectively) an expressly interdisciplinary programme, centre or scheme, what criteria would you use? How might you compare the quality of outputs to the outputs of a monodisciplinary scheme?

Getting interdisciplinary research into policy and practice

1 How could you support the extra efforts that interdisciplinary individuals or teams would have to make to engage with non-academic stakeholders?

2 How would you evaluate proposals to engage stakeholders? During or after interdisciplinary programmes with a knowledge exchange component, how would you evaluate the processes employed and the impacts (or steps toward impacts) achieved?

Notes

Chapter 3 Planning the expedition

1 http://webarchive.nationalarchives.gov.uk/+/www.dh.gov.uk/en/
Publicationsandstatistics/Pressreleases/DH_4013031 [archived website, accessed
29 July 2010].
2 Research Councils are the government agencies charged with investing public
money in research in the UK, providing grants on a competitive basis to UK higher
education institutions for specific research projects and programmes.

Chapter 4 Making the expedition a success

1 Personal communication and http://www.sage.wisc.edu/igert/index.html
[15 January 2011].

Chapter 5 Permit to travel

1 http://www.esrcsocietytoday.ac.uk [15 January 2011].
2 http://www.Relu.ac.uk/funding/WorkShadowsVisitingFellows/workshadowing.htm
[15 January 2011].
3 The Masterclasses were funded by a grant from the UK Economic and Social
Research Council RES-035-25-0001.
4 http://www.tinyurl.com/idwiki [15 January 2011].
5 http://www.tinyurl.com/idwiki [15 January 2011].

Chapter 6 Charting a course for an interdisciplinary career

1 http://www.middlebury.edu/academics/#story256693 [accessed 15 January 2011].
2 http://www.archanth.cam.ac.uk/ProspectiveStudents/arch-anth-at-cam.html
[accessed 15 January 2011].
3 http://www.rcuk.ac.uk/aboutrcuk/publications/policy/20060727acfellow.htm
[accessed 15 January 2011].
4 http://cstsp.aaas.org/opportunity.html?Type=JP [accessed 15 January 2011].
5 http://artsci.wustl.edu/~szwicker/mellonpostdoc/introduction.htm [accessed
15 January 2011].

Chapter 7 Assessing the route

1 http://www.chi-med.ac.uk [accessed 15 January 2011].
2 http://www.nelson.wisc.edu/docs/criteria.pdf [accessed 15 January 2011].

Chapter 8 Knowledge travels

1 In contrast to incremental models of policy-making.

Chapter 9 Navigating the interdisciplinary landscape

1 Leaders of interdisciplinary groups also need to consider many of the other management issues, including the development of collaborative, interdisciplinary research proposals, mentoring early career researchers, and supervising interdisciplinary PhD students, described in earlier chapters.

2 http://www.units.muohio.edu/aisorg [accessed 15 January 2011].

Bibliography

Abbott, A. (2001), *Chaos of Disciplines*. Chicago, IL, and London: University of Chicago Press.

Abt Associates Inc. (2006), *Evaluation of the Initial Impacts of the National Science Foundation's Integrative Graduate Education and Research Traineeship Program*, Final Report, prepared for National Science Foundation, Arlington, VI.

Anon (2009), 'News of the Week. National Science Foundation: the money to meet the President's priorities', *Science*, 324, 29 May.

Armsworth, P.R., Gaston, K.J., Hanley, N.D. and Ruffel, R.J. (2009), 'Contrasting approaches to statistical regression in ecology and economics', *Journal of Applied Ecology*, 46: 265–8.

Ashby, W.R. (1956), *An Introduction to Cybernetics*, London: Chapman and Hall.

Atherton, J.S. (2010), 'Learning and Teaching; Convergent and Divergent Learning [On-line] UK', http://www.learningandteaching.info/learning/converge.htm [accessed 12 September 2010].

Badham, J. (2010), 'A Compendium of Modelling Techniques', *Integration Insights*, 12, May. Available at http://i2s.anu.edu.au [accessed 25 June 2010].

Bammer, G. (2005), 'Integration and Implementation Sciences: building a new specialization', *Ecology and Society*, 10/1: 6, http://www.ecologyandsociety.org/vol10/iss2/art6/ [accessed 16 December 2009]

Bammer, G. (2008), 'Checklists for assessing research-policy interactions', *Integration Insights*, 11, July. Available at http://www.anu.edu.au/iisn [accessed 16 December 2009].

Barry, A. (2007), 'The meeting of disciplines. Why interdisciplinarity is a central strategy', *Britain Today 2007*, available from ESRC.

Barry, A., Born, G. and Weszkalnys, G. (2008), 'Logics of interdisciplinarity', *Economy and Society*, 37/1: 20–49.

Becher, T. (1989), *Academic Tribes and Territories: Intellectual Inquiry and the Cultures of Disciplines*, Buckingham: Open University Press.

Bechhofer, F. and Paterson, L. (2000), *Principles of Research Design in the Social Sciences*, London: Routledge.

Beer, S. (1966), *Decision and Control: the Meaning of Operational Research and Management Cybernetics*, Chichester: Wiley.

Blackwell, Alan F., Wilson, Lee, Street, Alice, Boulton, Charles, Knell, John (2009), *Radical Innovation: crossing boundaries with interdisciplinary teams*, University of Cambridge Computer Laboratory Technical Report Number 760, UCAM-CL-TR-760. ISSN 1476-2986, http://www.cl.cam.ac.uk/techreports/UCAM-CL-TR-760.pdf [accessed 7 October 2010].

Blunkett, D. (2000), 'Influence or irrelevance: Can social science improve government?', London, Speech to the Economic and Social Research Council.

Boix Mansilla, V. (2006), 'Assessing expert interdisciplinary work at the frontier: an empirical exploration', *Research Evaluation*, 15/1: 17–29.

Boix Mansilla, V., Feller, I. and Gardner, H. (2006), 'Quality assessment in interdisciplinary research and education', *Research Evaluation*, 15/1: 69–74.

Bolles, R.N. (2010), *What Color is Your Parachute? 2010: A Practical Manual for Job-Hunters and Career-Changers*, Berkeley, CA: Ten Speed Press.

Bracken, L.J. and Oughton, E.A. (2006), '"What Do You Mean?" The Importance of Language in Interdisciplinary Research', *Transactions of the Institute of British Geographers*, NS 31: 371–82.

Braun, A., Bruce, A., Gertz, R., Oram, C., Suk, J., Tait, J., Warkup, C. and Whitelaw, B. (2005), *Animal Cloning and genetic modification: a prospective study*, Series of confidential reports to the Institute for Prospective Technology Studies (European Commission Joint Research Centre).

Brown, V.A., Harris, J.A. and Russell, J.Y. (eds) (2010), *Tackling Wicked Problems*, London: Earthscan.

Bruce, A., Lyall, C., Tait, J. and Williams, R. (2004), 'Interdisciplinary Integration in the Fifth Framework Programme', *Futures*, 36/4: 457–70.

Bruun, H., Hukkinen, J., Huutoniemi, K. and Klein, J.T. (2005), *Promoting Interdisciplinary Research: The Case of the Academy of Finland*, Helsinki: Academy of Finland.

Bulmer, M. (1982), *The Uses of Social Research. Social Investigation in Public Policy-Making*, London: Allen & Unwin.

Calvert, J. (2010), 'Systems biology, interdisciplinarity and disciplinary identity', in J.N. Parker, N. Vermeulen and B. Penders (eds), *Collaboration in the New Life Sciences*, Aldershot: Ashgate.

Calvert, J. and Martin, P. (2009), 'The role of social scientists in synthetic biology', *EMBO reports*, 10/3: 201–204.

Checkland, P. and Scholes, J. (1990), *Soft Systems Methodology in Action*, Chichester: Wiley.

Chettiparamb, A. (2007), *Interdisciplinarity: a literature review*, Southampton: Interdisciplinary Teaching and Learning Group, University of Southampton, http://www.heacademy.ac.uk/assets/York/documents/ourwork/tla/sustainability/interdisciplinarity_literature_review.pdf [accessed 17 December 2009].

Chubin, D.E., Rossini, F.A. and Porter, A.L. (1986), *Interdisciplinary Analysis and Research Design: Theory and Practice of Problem-focused Research and Development*, Mount Airy, MD: Lomond Publications.

Chuck, E. (2008), 'Successful collaboration and mentoring', *Analytical and Bioanalytical Chemistry*, 390/7: 1677–9.

Corbyn, Z. (2009), '"Sandpits" bring out worst in "infantilised" researchers', *Times Higher Education*, 2 July.

COSEPUP (Committee on Science, Engineering, and Public Policy) (1995), *Reshaping the Graduate Education of Scientists and Engineers*, Washington, DC: National Academy Press.

Council of Environmental Deans and Directors (n.d.), *Interdisciplinary Hiring, Tenure and Promotion: Guidance for Individuals and Institutions*, http://www.ncseonline.org/00/Batch/CEDD/ITCDC/Interdisc_Hiring_and_Career_Dev.pdf [accessed 17 March 2010].

Court, J. and Young, J. (2006), 'Bridging research and policy in international development: an analytical and practical framework', *Development in Practice*, 16/1: 85–90.

Crick, F. (1989), *What Mad Pursuit: a personal view of scientific discovery*, London: Penguin.

Crossland, L. (2010), 'Research in the Real World', *EGN Newsletter*, March, http://www.genomicsnetwork.ac.uk/media/genmarch2010.pdf [accessed 2 June 2010].

Cummings, J.N. and Kiesler, S. (2005), 'Collaborative Research Across Disciplinary and Organizational Boundaries', *Social Studies of Science*, 35/5: 703–22.

Davies, H.T.O., Nutley, S.M. and Smith P.C. (2000), *What Works? Evidence-based policy and practice in public services*, Bristol: Policy Press.

Defila, R. and Di Giulio, A. (1999), 'Evaluation Criteria for Inter and Transdisciplinary Research', *Panorama*, Special Issue 1/99, Swiss National Science Foundation Newsletter, http://www.ikaoe.unibe.ch/forschung/ip/Specialissue.Pano.1.99.pdf [accessed 10 August 2010].

Defra (2010), *Defra's Evidence Investment Strategy 2010–2013 and beyond* http://www.defra.gov.uk/evidence/science/how/strategy.htm [accessed 2 June 2010].

ESRC (2009a), *Delivering Impact through Social Science ESRC Strategic Plan 2009–2014*, Swindon: ESRC.

ESRC (2009b), *ESRC Postgraduate Training and Development Guidelines 2009*, Swindon: ESRC.

ESRC (2009c), *Taking Stock. A Summary of ESRC's Work to Evaluate the Impact of Research on Policy & Practice*, February, Swindon: ESRC, http://www.esrcsocietytoday.ac.uk/ESRCInfoCentre/Support/Evaluation/publications [accessed 15 January 2011].

European Commission (2007), *FP7 Taking European Research to the Forefront*, http://ec.europa.eu/research/fp7/pdf/fp7-brochure_en.pdf [accessed 18 December 2009].

Feller, I. (2006), 'Multiple actors, multiple settings, multiple criteria: issues in assessing interdisciplinary research', *Research Evaluation*, 15/1: 5–15.

Flood, R.L. and Jackson, M. (1991), *Creative Problem Solving*, Chichester: Wiley.

Frodeman, R. and Mitcham, C. (2007), 'New Directions in Interdisciplinarity: Broad, Deep, and Critical', *Bulletin of Science, Technology & Society*, 27/6: 506–14.

Frodeman, R., Klein, J.T. and Mitcham, C. (eds) (2010), *The Oxford Handbook of Interdisciplinarity*, Oxford: Oxford University Press.

Gibbons, M., Limoges, C., Nowotny, H., Schwartzman, S., Scott, P. and Trow, M. (1994), *The New Production of Knowledge*, London: Sage.

Gibson, B. (2003a), 'From Transfer to Transformation: rethinking the relationship between research and policy', PhD, Canberra: Australian National University.

Gibson, B. (2003b) 'Beyond "two communities"', in V. Lin and B. Gibson (eds), *Evidence-based Health Policy. Problems and Possibilities*, Oxford: Oxford University Press, 18–30.

Golde, C.M. and Gallagher, H.A. (1999), 'The Challenges of Conducting Interdisciplinary Research in Traditional Doctoral Programs', *Ecosystems*, 2/4: 281–5.

Gray, B. (2008), 'Enhancing Transdisciplinary Research through Collaborative Leadership', *American Journal of Preventive Medicine*, 35/2 (Supplement 1, August): S124–32.

Graybill, J.K., Dooling, S., Shandas, V., Withey, J., Greve, A. and Simon, G.L. (2006), 'A Rough Guide to Interdisciplinarity: Graduate Student Perspectives', *Bioscience*, 56/9: 757–63.

Greaves, J. and Grant, W. (2010), 'Crossing the Interdisciplinary Divide: Political Science and Biological Science', *Political Studies*, 58: 320–39.

Gregrich, R.J. (2003), 'A note to researchers: communicating science to policy-makers and practitioners', *Journal of Substance Abuse Treatment*, 25/3: 233–7.

Hall, K.L., Feng, A.X., Moser, R.P., Stokols, D. and Taylor, B.K. (2008), 'Moving the Science of Team Science Forward: Collaboration and Creativity', *American Journal of Preventive Medicine*, 35/2 (Supplement 1, August): S243–9.

Hargreaves, T. and Burgess, J. (2009), *Transition Pathways to a Low Carbon Economy Pathways to Interdisciplinarity: A technical report exploring collaborative interdisciplinary working in the Transition Pathways consortium*, http://www.

lowcarbonpathways.org.uk/lowcarbon/publications/Interdisciplinary_Working_
Technical_Report_FINAL.pdf [accessed 6 October 2010].

Haynes, C. (ed.) (2002), *Innovations in Interdisciplinary Teaching*, American Council on
Education, Series on Higher Education, Westport, CT: Oryx Press/Greenwood Press.

HEFCE (2009), *Research Excellence Framework. Second consultation on the
assessment and funding of research*, September, London: Higher Education Funding
Council for England.

Heymann, S.J. (2000), 'Health and social policy', in L.F. Berkman and I. Kawachi
(eds), *Social Epidemiology*, New York, NY: Oxford University Press, 368–82.

Hill, M. (1997), *The Policy Process in the Modern State*, Harlow: Prentice Hall.

Hinrichs, C. (2008), 'Interdisciplinarity and boundary work: challenges and
opportunities for agrifood studies', *Agriculture and Human Values*, 25: 209–13.

Inns, T. (2007), *Designing for the 21st Century: Interdisciplinary Questions and
Insights*, Farnham: Gower.

Inns, T. (2010), *Designing for the 21st Century: Interdisciplinary Methods and
Findings*, Farnham: Gower.

IRGC (2009), *Risk Governance Deficits: an analysis and illustration of the most
common deficits in risk governance*, Geneva: IRGC, http://www.irgc.org/IMG/pdf/
IRGC_rgd_web_final.pdf [accessed 6 October 2010].

Jeffrey, P. (2003), 'Smoothing the Waters: Observations on the Process of Cross-
Disciplinary Research Collaboration', *Social Studies of Science*, 33: 539–62.

John, P. (1998), *Analysing Public Policy*, London: Pinter.

Jones, A. and Seelig, T. (2004), 'Understanding and Enhancing Research-Policy
Linkages', in *Australian Housing: A Discussion Paper*, Brisbane: Australian
Housing and Urban Research Institute, http://www.ahuri.edu.au/publications/
download.asp?ContentID=20216_pp [accessed 16 December 2009]

Klein, Julie Thompson (1990), *Interdisciplinarity – History, Theory and Practice*,
Detroit, MI: Wayne State University Press.

Klein, Julie Thompson (2004), 'Prospects for transdisciplinarity', *Futures* 36: 515–26.

Klein, Julie Thompson (2010), *Creating Interdisciplinary Campus Cultures*, San
Francisco, CA: Jossey Bass with AACU.

Kwa, C. (2006), 'Speaking to Science. The programming of interdisciplinary research
through informal science-policy interactions', *Science and Public Policy*, 33/6: 457–67.

Lambert Review of Business-University Collaboration (2003), http://www.hm-
treasury.gov.uk/d/lambert_review_final_450.pdf [accessed 17 December 2009]

Lamont, M. (2009), *How Professors Think: Inside the Curious World of Academic
Judgment*, Cambridge, MA: Harvard University Press.

Lamont, M., Mallard, G. and Guetzkow, J. (2006), 'Beyond blind faith: overcoming
the obstacles to interdisciplinary evaluation', *Research Evaluation*, 15/1: 43–55.

Langfeldt, L. (2006), 'The policy challenges of peer review: managing bias, conflicts of
interests and interdisciplinary assessments', *Research Evaluation*, 15/1: 31–41.

Lattuca, L. (2001), *Creating Interdisciplinarity: Interdisciplinary Research and Teaching
among College and University Faculty*, Nashville, TN: Vanderbilt University Press.

Lau, L. and Pasquini, M. (2008), '"Jack of all trades"? The negotiation of
interdisciplinarity within geography', *Geoforum*, 39: 552–60.

Ledford, H. (2008), 'With all good intentions', *Nature*, 452, 10 April.

Lélé, S. and Norgaard, R.B. (2005), 'Practicing Interdisciplinarity', *BioScience*, 55/11:
967–75.

Lingard, L., Schryer, C.F., Spafford, M.M. and Campbell, S.L. (2007), 'Negotiating the
politics of identity in an interdisciplinary team', *Qualitative Research*, 7: 501–19.

Lowe, P. and Phillipson, J. (2006), 'Reflexive Interdisciplinary Research: The Making of a Research Programme on the Rural Economy and Land Use', *Journal of Agricultural Economics*, 57/2: 165–84.

Lowe, P. and Phillipson, J. (2009), 'Barriers to Research Collaboration across Disciplines: Scientific Paradigms and Institutional Practices', *Environment and Planning A*, 41: 1171–84.

Lowe, P., Whitman, G. and Phillipson, J. (2009), 'Ecology and the social sciences', *Journal of Applied Ecology*, 46: 297–305.

Lyall C., Bruce A., Firn J., Firn M. and Tait J. (2004), 'Assessing end-use relevance of public sector research organisations', *Research Policy*, 33/1: 73–87.

Marzano, M., Carss, D.N. and Bell, S. (2006), 'Working to Make Interdisciplinarity Work: Investing in Communication and Interpersonal Relationships', *Journal of Agricultural Economics*, 57/2: 185–97.

McCarthy, J. (2004), 'Tackling the challenges of interdisciplinary biosciences', *Nature Reviews Molecular Cell Biology*, 5/11: 933–7.

McCulloch, C.S. (2007), 'Integrating Research for Water Management: Synergy or Dystopia?', *Water Resources Management*, 21/12: 2075–82.

Meagher, L. (2008), *Impact Evaluation of People at the Centre of Communication and Information Technologies (PACCIT)*, Report to ESRC, December

Meagher, L. (2010), *A Review of the Impact of SNIFFER Projects*, Report to SNIFFER/SEPA, http://www.sniffer.org.uk/news/4118/SNIFFER-and-SEPA-Review-the-Impact-of-our-Research.aspx [accessed 7 October 2010].

Meagher, L.M. and Kettle, A. (2009), *Knowledge Exchange in Public Policy & Practice*, SFC Briefing Note, 30 October, http://www.sfc.ac.uk/web/FILES/Our_Priorities_Knowledge_Exchange/KE_Public_Policy_Practice_-_Briefing_Note.pdf [accessed 6 October 2010].

Meagher L. and Lyall C. (2005a), *Evaluation of the ESRC/NERC Interdisciplinary Research Studentship Scheme*, Report to ESRC, October, http://www.esrcsocietytoday.ac.uk/ESRCInfoCentre/Images/ESRC-NERC%20Scheme%20Review%20Final%20Report_tcm6-17593.pdf [accessed 6 October 2010].

Meagher L. and Lyall C. (2005b), *Phase Two Evaluation of Research Development Grant. Volume 1: Returns on Investment*, Report to SHEFC.

Meagher L. and Lyall C. (2005c), *Phase Two Evaluation of Research Development Grant. Volume 2: Capturing Views from RDGs*, Report to SHEFC.

Meagher, L. and Lyall, C. (2007a), *Review of the RELU Programme's Seed-Corn Funding Mechanisms*, http://www.relu.ac.uk/news/Evaluation.htm [accessed 6 October 2010].

Meagher, L. and Lyall, C. (2007b), *Policy and Practice Impact Case Study of ESRC Grants and Fellowships in Psychology*, Report to ESRC, June, http://www.esrc.ac.uk/ESRCInfoCentre/Support/Evaluation/evaluatingimpact/Impact_Case_Studies.aspx [accessed 6 October 2010].

Meagher L. and Lyall C. (2009), *Evaluation of ESRC/MRC Interdisciplinary Research Studentship and Post-Doctoral Fellowship Scheme*, Report to ESRC.

Meagher, L., Lyall, C. and Nutley, S. (2008), 'Flows of knowledge, expertise and influence: a method for assessing policy and practice impacts from social science research', *Research Evaluation*, 17/3: 163–73.

Meagher, L., Jarron, S., Kind, V., Staines, A., Lyall, C. (2010), *A Review of the Impact of SNIFFER and SEPA Projects, Summary Report*, Report to SNIFFER/SEPA, http://www.sniffer.org.uk/news/4118/SNIFFER-and-SEPA-Review-the-Impact-of-our-Research.aspx [accessed 7 October 2010].

Mervis, J. (2009), 'Digging for Fresh Ideas in the Sandpit', *Science*, 324/5931: 1128–9.

Mitrany, M. and Stokols, D. (2005), 'Gauging the Transdisciplinary Qualities and Outcomes of Doctoral Training Programs', *Journal of Planning Education and Research*, 24: 437–40.

Mobjörk, M. (2009), *Crossing Boundaries. The Framing of Transdisciplinarity*, Örebro University and Mälardalen University, Sweden: Centre for Housing and Urban Research Series Report 64.

Nash, Justin M. (2008), 'Transdisciplinary Training: Key Components and Prerequisites for Success', *American Journal of Preventive Medicine*, 35 (2S): S133–140.

National Academies (2005), *Facilitating Interdisciplinary Research*, National Academy of Sciences, National Academy of Engineering, and Institute of Medicine, Washington: National Academy Press.

Newell, Barry, Crumley, Carole L., Hassan, Nordin, Lambin, Eric F., Pahl-Wostl, Claudia, Underdal, Arild and Wasson, Robert (2005), 'A conceptual template for integrative human-environment research', *Global Environmental Change*, 15: 299–307.

Nowotny, H., Scott, P. and Gibbons, M. (2001), *Re-Thinking Science: Knowledge and the Public in an Age of Uncertainty*, Cambridge: Polity Press.

Nutley, S., Walter, I. and Davies, H. (2007), *Using Evidence. How Research can Inform Public Services*, Bristol: Policy Press.

Öberg, G. (2009), 'Facilitating interdisciplinary work: using quality assessment to create common ground', *Higher Education*, 57: 405–15.

Öberg, G. (2010), *Interdisciplinary Work in the Environmental Field: A Primer*, Oxford and New York, NY: Wiley-Blackwell.

OECD/CERI (1972), *Interdisciplinarity: Problems of Teaching and Research in University*, Paris: OECD.

Papaioannou, T., Wield, D. and Chataway, J. (2009), 'Knowledge ecologies and ecosystems? An empirically grounded reflection on recent developments in innovation systems theory', *Environment and Planning C: Government and Policy*, 27/2: 319–39.

Pennington, D.D. (2008), 'Cross-disciplinary collaboration and learning', *Ecology and Society*, 13/1: 8, http://www.ecologyandsociety.org/vol13/iss2/art8/ [accessed 6 October 2010].

Petts, J., Owens, S. and Bulkeley, H. (2006), 'Crossing boundaries: Interdisciplinarity in the context of urban environments', *Geoforum*, 39/2: 593–601.

Phillipson, J., Lowe, P. and Bullock, J. (2009), 'Navigating the social sciences: interdisciplinarity and ecology', *Journal of Applied Ecology*, 46: 261–4.

Phillipson, J., Liddon, A., Proctor, A. and Lowe, P. (2010), *Telling Stories: Accounting for Knowledge Exchange*, Newcastle-upon-Tyne: Rural Economy and Land Use Programme Briefing Paper 10.

Pohl, C. (2008), 'From science to policy through transdisciplinary research', *Environmental Science and Policy*, 11: 46–53.

Punch, K. (2005), *Introduction to Social Research*, London: Sage.

Raffaelli, D., White, P. and Seivwright, L. (2005), 'International Interdisciplinary research: a review of programmes and the implications for RELU', Workshop presentation http://www.relu.ac.uk/events/WorkshopMay05/1BWhite.pdf [accessed 6 October 2010].

Randle, B. (2009), 'Rules of engagement', Letter to *Times Higher Education*, 23 July.

Repko, A.F. (2008), *Interdisciplinary Research. Process and Theory*, Thousand Oaks, CA: Sage.

Research Councils UK (2006), Research Councils' Economic Impact Group, *Increasing the Economic Impact of Research Councils* ('the Warry Report'), July, Swindon: RCUK.

Research Councils UK (2007), *Excellence with Impact: Progress in implementing the recommendations of the Warry Report on the economic impact of the Research Councils*, Swindon: RCUK.

Rhoten, D. (2004), 'Interdisciplinary Research: Trend or Transition', *Items and Issues*, 5/1–2: 6–12.

Rossini, F.A. and Porter A.L. (1979), 'Frameworks for Integrating Interdisciplinary Research', *Research Policy*, 8/1: 70–79.

Schön, D. (1983), *The Reflective Practitioner: How Professionals Think in Action*, London: Temple Smith.

Scottish Universities Policy Research Consortium (1997), 'Interdisciplinary Research: Process, Structures and Evaluation', SHEFC-Funded Regional Strategic Initiative.

Shearer M.C. (2007), 'Implementing a new interdisciplinary module: the challenges and the benefits of working across disciplines', *Practice and Evidence of the Scholarship of Teaching and Learning in Higher Education*, 2/1: 2–20.

Simons, H., with Squires, G., Becher, T. and Parlett, M. (1975), *Interdisciplinarity: A General Report*, Group for Research and Innovation in Higher Education, London: Nuffield Foundation.

Smith, Richard D., Keogh-Brown, Marcus R., Barnett, Tony and Tait, Joyce (2009), 'The economy-wide impact of pandemic influenza on the UK: a computable general equilibrium modelling experiment', *British Medical Journal*, 339: b4571.

Snow, C.P. (1959, 1963) *The Two Cultures: and a Second Look*, Cambridge: Cambridge University Press.

Stokols, D., Harvey, R., Gress, J., Fuqua, J., and Phillips, K. (2005), 'In Vivo studies of transdisciplinary scientific collaboration: Lessons learned and implications for active living research', *American Journal of Preventive Medicine*, 28/2S2: 202–13.

Stokols, D., Misra, S., Moser, R.P., Hall, K.L. and Taylor, B.K. (2008a), 'The Ecology of Team Science: Understanding Contextual Influences on Transdisciplinary Collaboration', *American Journal of Preventive Medicine*, 35/2S: S96–115.

Stokols, D., Hall, K.L., Taylor, B.K., Moser, R.P. (2008b), 'The Science of Team Science: Overview of the Field and Introduction to the Supplement', *American Journal of Preventive Medicine*, 35/2S: S77.

Strathern, M. (2004), *Commons and Borderlands. Working Papers on Interdisciplinarity, Accountability and the Flow of Knowledge*, Wantage: Sean Kingston Publishing.

Strathern. M. (2005), 'Experiments in interdisciplinarity', *Social Anthropology*, 13/1: 75–90.

Suk, J., Lyall, C. and Tait, J. (2008), 'Mapping the future dynamics of disease transmission: risk analysis in the United Kingdom Foresight Programme on the detection and identification of infectious diseases', *Eurosurveillance*, 13/44: Article 7.

Sutherland Olsen, D. (2009), 'Connecting Different Disciplines to Develop New Technology: nanomaterials to combat bird-flu', Paper prepared for the international conference on Organizational Learning, Knowledge & Capabilities (OLKC) Amsterdam, 26–8 April.

Szostak, R. (2007), 'How and why to teach interdisciplinary research practice', *Journal of Research Practice*, 3(2): Article M17, http://jrp.icaap.org/index.php/jrp/article/view/92/89 [accessed 12 July 2009].

Tait, J. (1987), 'Research policy and review 14. Environmental issues and the social sciences', *Environment and Planning A*, 19: 437–45.

Tait, J. (1999), 'Help for the academic nomads in search of their own sympathetic tribe', *Times Higher Education Supplement*, 5 March, http://www.timeshighereducation.co.uk/story.asp?sectioncode=26&storycode=145362 [accessed 6 October 2010].

Tait, J. (2009), 'Governing Synthetic Biology: Processes and Outcomes', in M. Schmidt, A. Kelle, A. Ganguli-Mitra and H. de Vriend (eds), *Synthetic Biology: The Technoscience and its Consequences*, Dordrecht, Netherlands: Springer, 141–54.

Tait, J. and Williams, R. (1999), 'Policy Approaches to Research and Development: Foresight, Framework and Competitiveness', *Science and Public Policy*, 26/2: 101–112.

Tait, J. *et al.* (2006a), *Consequences, Opportunities and Challenges of Modern Biotechnology for Europe (Bio4EU)*, European Techno-Economic Policy Support Network report for IPTS/European Commission Joint Research Centre.

Tait, J., Meagher, L., Lyall, C., and Suk, J. (2006b), *Foresight. Infectious Diseases: Preparing for the Future. T2: Risk Analysis*, Report to Office of Science and Innovation, London.

Tait, J., Williams, R., Bruce, A., Lyall, C., with Grávalos, E., Rodriquez, P., Jolivet, E., Jorgensen, U., Læssøe, J. (2002), *Interdisciplinary Integration in the Fifth Framework Programme (II-FP5)*, Final Report to European Commission, project SEAC-1999-00034.

Tyndall Centre (ed.) (2006), *Truly Useful ... doing climate change research that is useful for both theory and practice*, May, Norwich: Tyndall Centre, http://www.tyndall.ac.uk/sites/default/files/TrulyUsefulTyndall.pdf [accessed 6 October 2010].

US News & World Report (2010), 'Liberal Arts Rankings', http://colleges.usnews.rankingsandreviews.com/best-colleges/liberal-arts-rankings [accessed 24/5/10].

Vickers, J. (1997), '"[U]framed in open, unmapped fields": Teaching and the Practice of Interdisciplinarity', *Arachne: An Interdisciplinary Journal of the Humanities*, 4/2: 11–42.

Watrall, E. (2010), 'Building an Interdisciplinary Identity in a (Mostly) Non-Interdisciplinary Academic World', blog, April, http://www.ProfHacker.com (Tips and Tutorials for Higher Ed), now available from http://chronicle.com/blogPost/Building-an-Interdisciplinary/23080/ [accessed 6 October 2010]

Watson, J.D. (1970), *The Double Helix: A personal account of the discovery of the structure of DNA*, London: Penguin.

Watson, J.D. and Crick F.H.C. (1953), 'A Structure for Deoxyribose Nucleic Acid', *Nature*, 171: 737–8.

Weingart, P. and Stehr, N. (eds) (2000), *Practising Interdisciplinarity*, Toronto: University of Toronto Press.

Wickson, F., Carew, A.L. and Russell, A.W. (2006), 'Transdisciplinary research: characteristics, quandaries and quality', *Futures*, 38: 1046–59.

Wiles, R., Durrant, G., De Broe, S. and Powell, J. (2005), *Assessment of Needs for Training in Research Methods in the UK Social Science Community*, Discussion Paper, http://eprints.ncrm.ac.uk/91/ [accessed 17 December 2009].

Interdisciplinary short guides available to download from http://www.tinyurl.com/idwiki

1 *Short Guide to Developing Interdisciplinary Research Proposals* (Tait and Lyall).

2 *Short Guide to Reviewing Interdisciplinary Research Proposals* (Lyall, Bruce, Tait and Meagher).

3 *Short Guide to Building and Managing Interdisciplinary Research Teams* (Lyall and Meagher).

4 *Short Guide to Supervising Interdisciplinary PhDs* (Lyall, Meagher and Tait).

5 *Short Guide to Troubleshooting Common Interdisciplinary Research Management Challenges* (Lyall and Meagher).

6 *Short Guide to Designing Interdisciplinary Research for Policy and Practice* (Lyall).

7 *Short Guide to Developing Interdisciplinary Strategies for Research Groups* (Lyall, Williams and Meagher).

8 *Short Guide for Funders of Interdisciplinary Research* (Marsden, Lyall, Bruce and Meagher).

9 *Short Guide to Evaluating Interdisciplinary Research* (Lyall, Tait, Meagher, Bruce and Marsden).

10 *Short Guide to Leading Interdisciplinary Initiatives* (Meagher, Lyall, Bruce and Marsden).

Index